Loneliness

for dummies®
A Wiley Brand

Loneliness

by Andrea Wigfield

Loneliness For Dummies®

Published by: **John Wiley & Sons, Inc.,** 111 River Street, Hoboken, NJ 07030-5774, www.wiley.com

Copyright ©2024 by John Wiley & Sons, Inc., Hoboken, New Jersey

Published simultaneously in Canada

For general information on our other products and services, please contact our Customer Care Department within the U.S. at 877-762-2974, outside the U.S. at 317-572-3993, or fax 317-572-4002. For technical support, please visit https://hub.wiley.com/community/support/dummies.

Wiley publishes in a variety of print and electronic formats and by print-on-demand. Some material included with standard print versions of this book may not be included in e-books or in print-on-demand. If this book refers to media such as a CD or DVD that is not included in the version you purchased, you may download this material at http://booksupport.wiley.com. For more information about Wiley products, visit www.wiley.com.

Library of Congress Control Number: 2024932607

ISBN: 978-1-394-22932-1 (pbk); ISBN 978-1-394-22934-5 (ePDF); ISBN 978-1-394-22933-8 (ePub)

SKY10067993_022224

Contents at a Glance

Table of Contents

Introduction

Loneliness affects millions of people across the globe and is something that everyone experiences from time to time. It's just a natural part of being human. When you feel lonely, it's your body's way of sending you a message to make more or different connections. It's like your body's way of getting you to drink water by making you thirsty.

Although loneliness is unpleasant and unwanted, it doesn't usually last for long. Once you start making connections with other people or with places you feel a sense of belonging to, the loneliness often disappears. However, if you don't take action when you feel lonely, the feeling can linger for some time. And the longer it remains, the more likely it is to lead to other health implications. Long-term loneliness can affect your physical health and mental well-being.

It's important, then, to understand why you're feeling lonely, what you can do to avoid that, and how you can tackle loneliness when it emerges. You can take measures to make yourself more resilient to loneliness and to stop yourself from feeling lonely in different aspects of your life — at home, at school, at work, and in your community. You can also take action to combat loneliness when you're more susceptible to it, such as when you go away to college, move, experience bereavement, become a caregiver, or retire.

By being aware of loneliness, understanding why it surfaces, accepting it, and taking appropriate action, you can improve your health and well-being and lead a happy life.

About This Book

As *Loneliness For Dummies* demonstrates, you can prevent and reduce any feelings of loneliness by following a range of techniques and strategies in different aspects of your life. You can easily incorporate these into your daily life, whether you're a young person who's in school or working at your first job, an older person who has retired, a high-flying executive working long hours, or a full-time caregiver looking after a child or adult.

In this book, I explain that you don't have to be afraid of being lonely. I help you understand what loneliness is, if you're at risk, and why you might feel lonely. I explain the health and well-being implications of feeling lonely and provide you with the signs to look out for and tools to assess whether you or your loved ones are lonely.

I help you examine if you're lonely in different parts of your life so that you can judge whether those parts are a source of loneliness or a haven of connection. These include your home, your place of education or employment, your neighborhood or community, and your interactions with technology (such as social media or gaming). For each, I explain the pitfalls that can lead to loneliness and offer ways out of loneliness to make your home, your school, your workplace, your community, and your interaction with technology places where you feel connected and experience a sense of belonging.

I also demonstrate how to deal with loneliness at different transition times, such as when you lose someone you love, when you experience changes in your school or employment environment, when you encounter a physical or mental health problem, and when you either become a caregiver or cease becoming one.

Finally, I give you some key strategies and techniques to improve your connections so that you can beat loneliness. I focus on improving your meaningful connections with other people, enhancing your sense of connection and belonging to different places, and developing a positive relationship with yourself so that you feel comfortable being yourself.

Importantly, I assist you in becoming more resilient to loneliness so that if it does strike at a particular time in your life, in a particular place, or due to a life change, you're better equipped to deal with it and move on.

Foolish Assumptions

I wrote this book for everyone and anyone. You don't have to have any knowledge or understanding of loneliness to read it. You can be of any age, position in society, gender, sexual orientation, or health condition. This book is designed for all of you. Likewise, even if you already know a lot about loneliness, you'll find this book useful.

Who might want to read this book? I assume, perhaps foolishly, that you or someone you love is feeling lonely. I also assume that you want to eliminate those feelings of loneliness from your life. And you're most likely interested in helpful strategies that can fit your lifestyle and personality. If these descriptions strike a chord, this book is for you.

On the other hand, you may be a health professional, social worker, employer, or teacher who's looking for a comprehensive, easy to-understand resource for your patients, customers, employees, or students who are feeling lonely or are at risk of loneliness. Readers over the years have said that the *For Dummies* books on mental health issues have been helpful in both their recovery and their understanding of what they're dealing with in therapy.

Icons Used in This Book

Throughout this book, I use icons in the margins to quickly point out different types of information. Here are the icons you'll see and a few words about what they mean.

REMEMBER

As the name of this icon implies, I don't want you to forget the information that accompanies it.

TIP

This icon emphasizes pieces of practical information or bits of insight that you can put to work.

WARNING

This icon appears when you need to be careful or seek professional help.

**REAL WORLD
EXAMPLE**

This icon appears when I provide an example of a real person's experience with loneliness.

Beyond the Book

You can find a free Cheat Sheet online. Go to www.dummies.com and type "Loneliness for Dummies Cheat Sheet" in the Search box. The cheat sheet informs you of the signs that you may feel lonely, offers some loneliness dos and don'ts, as provides resources for additional help.

Where to Go from Here

Most books are written so that you have to start on page 1 and read straight through. But I've written *Loneliness For Dummies* so that you can use the detailed Table of Contents to pick and choose what you want to read based on your individual interests. Don't worry too much about reading chapters and parts in any particular order. Read whatever chapters apply to your situation.

However, I suggest that you at least skim Part 1 because it contains a variety of fascinating facts as well as important ideas for getting started. In addition, if you're feeling particularly lonely and have been for some time, I suggest you start with Chapter 5 and continue with Part 4. These chapters cover a variety of ways to become more resilient to loneliness and overcome it. They guide you to making connections with other people, gaining a sense of belonging, and developing a positive relationship with yourself so that you can beat loneliness. After you read those chapters, feel free to continue picking and choosing other topics you want to explore.

Help Us Assess How the Book Helps You

I'm eager to find out how this book helps you feel less lonely, so would encourage you to complete a short survey found here: https://shusls.eu.qualtrics.com/jfe/form/SV_a2WvrHIYq2tVvLM or by clicking the QR code.

1

Understanding Loneliness

Look at what loneliness really is.

Identify who is at risk of loneliness.

Consider the various costs of loneliness.

Chapter **1**

Loneliness and Why You Feel It

M illions of people worldwide experience loneliness. It's so widespread that governments across the globe are implementing national strategies and action plans to tackle it.

It's common to feel lonely at some point in your life. Although loneliness is a natural part of being human, when it strikes it can be particularly unpleasant. If you're persistently lonely it can affect your mental health and well-being, and it can make you feel depressed, anxious, and insecure. It can also cause you to be more susceptible to physical health conditions such as heart disease and dementia.

But the good news is that loneliness doesn't usually last for a long time, and even if it does, you can use several tactics to combat it and start to live a positive and happy life again. If you know someone you suspect is lonely and want to help them, or if you're currently feeling lonely yourself, this book can offer perspective and strategies for overcoming loneliness.

For better or worse, as this chapter explores, you're not alone in experiencing loneliness. Unfortunately, it's a common issue worldwide. This chapter looks at what loneliness is and what it isn't — in particular by clarifying the difference between loneliness and social isolation, which, contrary to popular belief, aren't the same. It defines loneliness and examines the reasons behind those feelings.

What Is Loneliness?

Loneliness is an unwelcome and generally unpleasant emotional feeling that you get when you have a lack or loss of companionship. It happens when there is a discrepancy between the quantity and quality of the social relationships that you have, and those that you want.

Loneliness is categorized into two types: transient, and chronic.

Transient loneliness

In the short term, psychologists and neuroscientists don't see loneliness as a problem but more of an indicator that a change is required. This kind of short-term loneliness, which often arises as a signal to make a change, is called *transient loneliness*.

Transient loneliness is temporary and can be the result of a life change. A number of life changes can cause you to experience transient loneliness. These can include changing schools, going away to college, starting a new job, moving to a new neighborhood, experiencing an empty nest when your children grow up and leave home, separating or divorcing, being recently unemployed or retired, or becoming a care-giver. Chapter 2 explains more about life transitions.

Although transient loneliness can be unpleasant, psychologists see it as an inherent part of human nature. It's not necessarily problematic because it may prompt you to take action to connect with others and invest time and effort toward relationship building.

If you're experiencing transient loneliness, it's a good idea to work on it as soon as possible so that it doesn't become chronic loneliness.

Chronic loneliness

Unaddressed transient loneliness can lead to chronic loneliness. Chronic loneliness can be more difficult to escape from, which means it can also be more damaging for your long-term health.

With chronic loneliness you start to develop negative perceptions of yourself and think that other people are negative toward you too. This can make you feel lonelier because you might be less likely to reach out to connect with others. This kind of chronic loneliness can lead to mental and physical health conditions, as I explain in Chapters 9 and 10.

Is It Loneliness Or Something Else?

It's easy to mix up feeling lonely with being socially isolated, but they're different. Assessing whether you're feeling lonely or are socially isolated will help you decide which solutions are the most appropriate for you. You might be both socially isolated and lonely. If you are, there are ways to address that, too.

Experiencing social isolation

With social isolation, you don't have any, or many, social ties with other people. This isolation is strongly connected to the quantity of contacts that you have. If you're socially isolated, it means that you have a lack of social interaction. In any given week of the year, you don't see, hear from, or talk to many, or any, other people.

REMEMBER

Social isolation can be both voluntary and involuntary. You might choose to be socially isolated and actually enjoy it. If this is you, it's fine. It's okay to like being alone and to enjoy solitude, which I discuss later.

Because you can enjoy social isolation, it's not necessarily something negative. But not everyone enjoys being alone, and you might find yourself socially isolated and unhappy about it. If that's the case, the good news is that you can alleviate social isolation quite quickly. You just need to have more contact with other people. I provide some tips on how to connect with other people quickly in Chapters 5 and 14.

ARE YOU SOCIALLY ISOLATED?

For a quick way to measure whether you're socially isolated, ask yourself the following question:

- In a typical week how often do you have contact with family and friends?

    ❑ Every day or almost every day

    ❑ Several times a week

    ❑ About once a week

    ❑ Less than once a week

    ❑ Never

If your answer is once a week or less often, you're probably socially isolated. If you enjoy being alone and are perfectly happy, then carry on as you are. But if you'd prefer more social contact, Chapters 5 and 14 have some helpful tips.

REMEMBER

Loneliness is subtly different from social isolation. I mentioned earlier that social isolation is an objective count of your social contacts. Well, loneliness is more subjective. It's a personal, unpleasant condition that arises when you have fewer, or different kinds of, social relationships than you'd like. Loneliness can emerge because the quality of your relationships is poorer than you'd like or because you feel that your relationships are subpar to those of your peers. Because loneliness is an unpleasant feeling, it's always a negative condition, and it's always involuntary. No one chooses to feel lonely.

Loneliness can take a little longer to resolve than social isolation because it's based more on the formation of a bond with other people. But you'll be pleased to know that you can create bonds to help you feel less lonely by following some simple steps in Chapter 5. And while you're waiting for those bonds to form, you can rekindle your sense of belonging to places that you enjoy visiting. (See Chapter 15 for some quick tips.) You can also build your resilience to feeling lonely and stop that negative cycle of loneliness by improving the way you feel about yourself. I help you with techniques for accomplishing this in Chapters 13 and 16.

REMEMBER

The measures of social isolation and loneliness that I provide here are designed to be a basic and quick assessment only. For a full assessment of your levels of loneliness, see Chapter 2.

HOW OFTEN DO YOU FEEL LONELY?

A quick way to measure if you're lonely is to answer the following question:

How often do you feel lonely?

- ❏ Often/always
- ❏ Some of the time
- ❏ Occasionally
- ❏ Hardly ever
- ❏ Never

If you've ticked often/always, some of the time, or occasionally, you're probably feeling lonely. Loneliness is a common emotion. Recognizing that you're lonely is the first step to reducing your feelings of loneliness. There are tips and techniques to help you throughout the book. For a quick snapshot of top tips turn to Chapter 17.

Feeling lonely in a crowd

Although social isolation and loneliness are quite different, they're also closely related. You can be both socially isolated and lonely. Or you can be socially isolated and not feel lonely. Likewise, you can feel lonely and not be socially isolated. This is where the phrase "feeling lonely in a crowd" comes from.

You might be surrounded by people, so not socially isolated, yet still feel lonely. When this happens it's often because you don't have meaningful relationships with the people you're in contact with. (For more on meaningful relationships, see Chapter 14.) This could be for a whole range of reasons. You might not get along with the people you're in contact with or not have anything in common with them. Or you might only have fleeting encounters with them, which makes meaningful connections difficult.

A classic example of people feeling lonely in a crowd is older people living in residential care. Just because all the residents are old and unable to live alone in their community anymore doesn't mean they share common ground.

REAL WORLD EXAMPLE

Here's another example. Lydia is an 18-year-old tennis player who finds the world of tennis lonely. Her training partners are also competitors, so she finds it difficult to get close and make real friends with them. She decides to enroll in an art course at her college so she can find other young people to interact and socialize with. Unfortunately, she feels even more lonely there because the other students aren't anything like her. Lydia pays a lot of attention to eating healthily and keeping fit and active, but the other students go out partying and can't understand Lydia's lifestyle. So even though Lydia has surrounded herself with other people, she still feels lonely; in fact, she feels lonelier than she had previously.

TIP

Sometimes you might feel lonelier if you're surrounded by people you don't connect with because it reminds you that you're alone. If you feel lonely in a crowd, go to Chapter 14, which offers some tips on how to create meaningful relationships.

Suffering alone or enjoying solitude

As I mentioned earlier, loneliness is a negative feeling about being alone, one of feeling lonely. But that doesn't mean that everyone who's alone feels lonely. Maybe you enjoy spending time alone. When you do, it's normally referred to as *solitude*. Solitude is commonly referred to as a neutral or positive experience of being intentionally and physically alone. You can also experience solitude when other people are around, perhaps because you're in a world of your own enjoying your own thoughts and mental space and not interacting.

REAL WORLD
EXAMPLE

Brandon has lived alone ever since moving out of his parents' home to study at college. He's 46 and has only ever had one romantic partner. He has a few work colleagues and friends, but he doesn't really spend much time with them. Because Brandon spends a lot of time alone, his work colleagues and others who know of him perceive him to be lonely. But Brandon is far from lonely. He enjoys his own company and his own thoughts.

TIP

Although loneliness can be damaging for your health and well-being, solitude is generally believed to be a positive experience. However, the way in which people perceive solitude varies in different cultures. In the western world, people who enjoy solitude are sometimes classified as "loners," which can have a negative connotation and a stigma attached to it.

It's fine and natural to enjoy alone time. Don't feel pressured to interact with others. You're not lonely unless your time alone gives you an unpleasant feeling. If it does, you're not alone in feeling like this, and you can take some steps to curb your loneliness.

Why Do You Feel Lonely?

Researchers from all different academic disciplines study loneliness, from psychologists and sociologists to social workers, geographers, and health scientists. As a result, there are various explanations for why you feel lonely.

An evolutionary perspective

Many explanations for why humans feel lonely come from psychologists and neuroscientists. They often view loneliness from an evolutionary perspective, viewing it as a neurological reaction. So, like hunger is a signal that you need to eat, loneliness is a signal that you need to improve your social situation and seek out people to connect with. This view suggests that some people are more likely to experience loneliness than others, with a combination of genes and the environment playing a role in this.

TIP

Given that psychologists see loneliness as a signal for you to reach out to connect with other people, you need to understand what circumstances can cause this feeling and trigger the signal in the first place. If you're more aware of this, you can recognize the feeling, acknowledge why it's there and reach out to others.

Absence of meaningful relationships

Sociologists explain that the feelings of loneliness come about because you have insufficient meaningful social relationships. This might mean that you have less meaningful relationships than you'd like. For others it might mean that you have less meaningful relationships than you think other people have. Or perhaps the quality of your relationships is inadequate. This can mean that your relationships are superficial and don't provide the depth that you want or need.

TIP

I discuss more about the importance of meaningful relationships and how you can maintain and expand yours in Chapter 14. But for now, it's useful to know that you can have meaningful relationships with a whole range of different people — friends, romantic partners, relatives, work colleagues, health practitioners, therapists, and hair and beauty personnel. It's also helpful to think about what a meaningful relationship means for you. A meaningful relationship has one or more of these factors present:

>> You feel valued by the person.

>> You share a common goal or interest.

>> You have a positive relationship.

>> The relationship has depth and isn't superficial.

>> The relationship is sustainable in the long term.

REMEMBER

You can also have a meaningful relationship with yourself when you accept yourself (see Chapter 13). And you can have a meaningful relationship with places and spaces when you feel a sense of belonging (see Chapter 15).

Lack of belonging

Alongside a lack of meaningful relationships to other people, sociologists have identified an absence of belonging as a reason for feeling lonely. This could be belonging to a place or belonging to an experience.

The places and experiences that create a sense of belonging vary according to each individual but can be places such as sporting venues, workplaces, educational establishments, or open spaces such as lakes, beaches, and local parks. They can also be experiences such as dancing, singing, skiing, and climbing.

Humans have a universal need to feel like they belong. However, everyone has different levels of need in relation to belonging, so some people need to feel a greater sense of belonging than others. If your need for belonging is unmet, you can feel lonely.

If you have a meaningful relationship with a certain place, a sense of belonging to that place, it can act as a kind of buffer against loneliness even if you don't have a meaningful relationship with other people. So if you're feeling lonely, try visiting that special place to give yourself a belonging boost.

Poor self-perception

You might also experience a loneliness signal, or trigger, based on your perception of yourself. If you don't feel very good about yourself, or you think that other people don't like you, you might feel lonely. You can start to feel uncomfortable in your own skin. Maybe this came about because you experienced a trauma, such as being bullied at school, or you were the victim of a crime and were abused. Or perhaps you have a mental or physical health condition that has created a distorted and negative self-perception. You might be struggling to accept your gender or sexuality. If left unchecked, negative self-perceptions can deteriorate over time and lead you to disconnect from yourself, other people, and your physical surroundings.

TIP

If you find yourself being overly self-critical or often struggle to understand why other people would like to know you, the first step to work on is your relationship with yourself. By improving this, you can feel a greater desire to engage with other people and places where you have a sense of belonging. Both will help you feel less lonely. Chapter 13 offers some key tips on how to improve your relationship with yourself.

Symptom of society

The common factor that shapes your relationships with other people, your sense of belonging to places and spaces, and your relationship with yourself is the role of society. Wider societal factors influence everything you see, feel, and do. These factors vary by culture, and everyone interprets them differently. Multiple societal influences play a role in your relationships and therefore affect how lonely you feel.

These include the safety of your neighborhood, the diversity of your community, and the availability of facilities and resources where you live. They can include the design of your neighborhood, home, workplace, or school. They might also include the influence of social media or other forms of technology or the dominant culture in your workplace or educational establishment.

REMEMBER

You can't always make immediate or major alterations to the way these wider societal factors affect you. However, understanding their role in your behavior and feelings of loneliness can help you identify the things in your life that are within your control and that you can change.

The Prevalence of Loneliness

Loneliness has existed for time immemorial. People have always felt lonely. As I explained earlier, loneliness is a basic human response to having a lack of desired social connections, which psychologists view as a signal to change your behavior or take action. Just like being thirsty is a signal to get a drink. When you're lonely, it's a signal to improve your social situation and to seek out people to connect with.

When you think about loneliness in this way, you can see that it's a normal part of being human. And you can see why loneliness is so widespread and commonplace. In some countries, around half the population say they experience loneliness. So, if you're lonely, remember that you're definitely not the only person feeling that way. Many others, worldwide, are experiencing similar feelings.

Although loneliness is prevalent in many countries, there isn't really evidence at the moment of a long-term trend toward increased loneliness. Evidence on this provides mixed results. As I explain in Chapter 2, adolescents and seniors are most likely to experience loneliness, but we're not sure yet if today's young adults and older people are more likely to feel lonely than their counterparts did in the past.

REMEMBER

A number of events have occurred recently that have given loneliness more prominence and publicity. Loneliness has started to enter public discussion much more. It's been triggered by awareness-raising campaigns such as the Campaign to End Loneliness in the UK, the Coalition to End Social Isolation & Loneliness in the US, and Ending Loneliness Together in Australia. These campaigns have helped get loneliness into the public consciousness.

There's also been a lot of publicity about the health threats of loneliness (see Chapters 9 and 10), which has contributed to the impetus behind these campaigns and led various governments to take action. This action has taken the form of government-led strategies designed to understand and combat loneliness. The UK Government's national loneliness strategy and the US Surgeon General's advisory called The Healing Effects of Social Connection are two of note.

The Covid-19 pandemic also raised awareness of loneliness. The pandemic itself was responsible for forcing people to isolate themselves to prevent the virus from spreading. This triggered more loneliness among certain people, at least in the short term. Covid-19 suddenly cut people off from their social lives and from their friends and family. Although most people are now back to socializing as they were prior to the pandemic, certain general societal changes have become more pronounced following the pandemic. Some of these changes have exacerbated loneliness. For example, more people are working at home, or remotely, than previously, thus reducing their opportunities for face-to-face contact.

There may well be a long-term trend toward an increase in loneliness, but at the moment it's too early to tell.

International trends

Loneliness is being experienced by large chunks of the population, in many countries across the globe. Reports suggest that loneliness affects about a third of the world's population. But evidence of the prevalence of loneliness worldwide is patchy and inconsistent because the data on loneliness are collected in different ways, and with different degrees of robustness, around the world. In particular, high-income countries generally have good data availability, whilst low- and middle-income countries often have scant data availability.

Around half of US, UK, and Australian adults report experiencing loneliness. Data from Canada suggest that loneliness may be slightly less prevalent there. Other countries where loneliness is reported to be high include Brazil, Turkey, India, and Saudi Arabia. In some other countries, loneliness is said to be less prevalent. These countries include the Netherlands, Japan, Germany, and Russia. But because of the difficulties with the data, it's important to view these reports with an open mind.

TIP

The important thing to note is that wherever you live in the world, loneliness is a normal human response. If you feel lonely, just realize that you need to make a change of some kind. I give you numerous suggestions in this book to help you with that.

Cross-country variations

REMEMBER

In addition to the inconsistencies in data collection that can make it hard to compare levels of loneliness across countries, general cultural factors can influence levels of loneliness across nations. Some of these include:

>> **Socioeconomic status:** Low socioeconomic status as measured by education and income or large inequalities in socioeconomic status generally mean higher rates of loneliness.

>> **Welfare state:** More generous welfare states are linked with lower levels of loneliness, especially in older adults.

>> **Health:** Vast inequalities in health and poor health can be associated with higher levels of loneliness.

>> **Cultural adverse health behaviors:** Behaviors such as alcohol use can lead to a great propensity for loneliness.

>> **Family and community ties:** The expectation of strong family and community ties in some cultures can have a dual effect. People can feel less lonely because they have a large family and community around them. But others can feel lonelier because they don't necessarily get along with those around them. Sometimes high expectations of strong ties can increase feelings of loneliness if these expectations aren't met.

>> **Climate:** A mild Mediterranean-style climate is likely to facilitate greater social interaction because people can spend more time outdoors.

>> **Stigmatization of loneliness:** In cultures where loneliness is highly stigmatized, people are less likely to talk about feeling lonely or report feeling lonely. In these countries, reported loneliness figures are likely to be substantially lower than they really are.

Thinking about Ways to Overcome Loneliness

Although loneliness can seem quite complex, if you start to identify why you feel lonely, the issues involved will start to unravel. One of the first steps is being aware that you're lonely and accepting it. Once you do that, you're on route to finding a way forward.

Snubbing the stigma

Sometimes there's a stigma attached to loneliness. Those who feel lonely might be perceived as loners, odd, strange, sad, socially inept, and a whole range of other negative terms. This stigma, like all stigmas, is created and perpetuated by a societal lack of understanding. The stigma around loneliness often deters people from accepting that they're lonely, admitting they're lonely to other people, and seeking out support for their loneliness. This can make them feel even more lonely and isolated and feel as though there's something wrong with them.

Some societies and population groups stigmatize loneliness more than others. For example, more stigma is often attached to being a young, lonely adult than a senior, lonely adult. That's because young people are expected to have an active social life; if they don't, people perceive that something is wrong with them.

TIP

Whoever you are, whatever your age or circumstance, wherever you live, it's important to remember that feeling lonely is a natural part of being human, and everyone at some point in their lives will feel lonely.

Awareness and acceptance

Loneliness is a natural human emotion that you encounter when you don't have sufficient meaningful relationships. Most people will feel lonely at some point, yet it's not often spoken about. People don't like to admit their loneliness to themselves or to others, but the first step to overcoming loneliness is awareness and acceptance. Once you accept that you feel lonely, you can start finding solutions.

REMEMBER

Numerous campaigns and strategies in different countries are designed to raise awareness of loneliness and encourage people to start talking about their experiences. The UK Government national loneliness strategy, for example, emphasizes the importance of building a national conversation about loneliness so that people feel okay talking about loneliness and reaching out for help. Similarly, the US Surgeon General's advisory called The Healing Effects of Social Connection emphasizes the importance of public awareness and education as the drivers and solutions to loneliness. The various national loneliness campaigns in the UK, US, and Australia emphasize having public conversations about loneliness. Every June in the UK is a national loneliness awareness week dedicated to raising awareness of loneliness. It's all about creating supportive communities by encouraging conversations among family, friends, and colleagues about loneliness.

Keep a look out for any national or local campaigns to raise awareness about loneliness where you live and get involved.

Knowing where to begin

Once you acknowledge that you're lonely, think a bit more about your feelings of loneliness, why they've arisen, and what might help to alleviate your feelings so that you can start to gain control and take positive action. This book is full of useful tips and strategies to help you. But first you need to create a simple mind map of your experiences of loneliness.

TIP

Try this activity to help you identify which areas of your life you might want to start working on to reduce your feelings of loneliness. You can then focus on those areas as you read through the rest of the book.

1. Get a blank piece of paper and create a mind map of your experience of loneliness.

2. Draw three interlinked circles, as shown in Figure 1-1. In circle one, write the names of those who you have your main meaningful relationships with. In circle two, write some key words that describe how you view your relationship with yourself. In circle three, write any places and spaces you have a relationship with — where you feel a sense of belonging. Then put a score in each circle from 1 to 5. One means that you feel your meaningful relationships are poor, and 5 means that your meaningful relationships are very good.

3. Think about any transitory life events you're currently experiencing or that you've experienced in the past that have triggered you to feel lonely, and circle those that are appropriate to you. Some examples are shown in Figure 1-1, but they're explained more in Chapter 2. If you've experienced additional life changes that are relevant, add those here.

4. Think about any potential barriers that prevent you from having meaningful relationships with yourself, with other people, and with places and spaces. Insert those in the mind map in the relevant box. To make it easier for you, I've grouped these into personal characteristics, personal circumstances, health, and geographical factors.

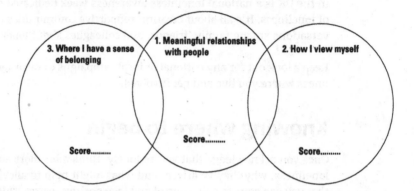

Transitory life events

Bereavement   children leaving home   changed caring role   divorce/separation   moving home

diagnosis of health condition/s   redundancy   retirement   unemployment

3. Where I have a sense of belonging

Score..........

1. Meaningful relationships with people

Score..........

2. How I view myself

Score..........

Personal Characteristics	Personal Circumstances	Health Conditions	Geographical Area
Young adult/older person	No car	Alcoholism and substance misuse	Layout of streets
Introvert	No internet/don't know how to use	Cognitive impairment	Lack of local amenities
Have a disability	internet	Long-term health condition (s)	Fear of crime
Ethnic minority	A carer	Mental health condition	Feeling unsafe
Gender identity	Lack of money	Physical immobility	Lack of places to meet
Have a different first language	Live alone	Sensory impairment	Lack of public transport
Gay/Lesbian	Single/no partner	Urinary incontinence	Live in an isolated community
Transgender	Unemployed	Weight-related issues	Live in apartment/flat or remote house

FIGURE 1-1:
Mind map of your experience of loneliness.

5. Once you've completed your mind map, leave it for 30 minutes or so. Get a drink or go for a short walk before looking at the completed mind map again.

6. When you return to looking at your mind map, use a red pen to underline the main area of your life that's currently causing you to feel lonely or acting as a barrier to you feeling less lonely. Don't worry if several areas are making you feel lonely. If this is the case, use the red pen to number the areas in order of priority to work on. So put a 1 for the area that you want to work on first, followed by 2, 3, 4, and more.

7. Pay particular attention to the chapters in this book that coincide with your results in Step 6. They'll give you more information and tips on how to beat loneliness in these parts of your life.

8. Choose a different colored pen (green is ideal) to identify the areas of your life that are positive or where you feel you have good, meaningful relationships. Once you've identified those, spend more time on these areas. You can use the tips provided in the relevant chapters.

Figure 1-2 shows how George completed the mind map exercise. He identified his age, health conditions, and retirement as the main influences on his experiences of loneliness. These factors are affecting his meaningful relationships with other people. George should then turn to Chapters 9 and 12 in this book to look for tips on working through these factors.

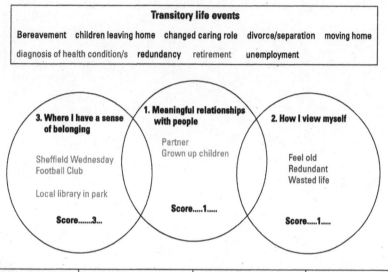

FIGURE 1-2: George's experience of loneliness.

Furthermore, George identified that his health conditions are affecting his relationship with himself, so he would benefit from reading Chapter 13. On a positive note, George feels that he has a strong and meaningful sense of belonging to the football club he supports, Sheffield Wednesday, and to a library in his local park. That's why he's encouraged to think about spending more time in these places and is directed to read Chapter 15 for some useful tips.

IN THIS CHAPTER

» Identifying groups of people
vulnerable to loneliness

» Looking at the circumstances that
can lead to loneliness

» Understanding the trigger points that
can make people feel lonely

» Assessing the scale and frequency of
loneliness

Chapter **2**

Who's at Risk of Loneliness and How It's Measured

Loneliness can strike at any time, but some population groups are more prone to feeling lonely than others. It's helpful to understand if you're more at risk of experiencing loneliness so that you can take action to avoid it or deal with it.

Groups that are typically more vulnerable to experiencing loneliness are those with certain demographic characteristics based on age, gender, disability, ethnicity, and sexual orientation. Your personal circumstances also play a role in the likelihood of your falling foul of loneliness. These can include factors such as marital status, being a caregiver, having access to a car, social class or wealth, and the presence of health conditions.

In addition to these, certain triggers can increase your likelihood of feeling lonely. These occur when major changes are taking place, such as moving away from home, having a baby, going away to college, retiring, or facing unemployment or layoffs. Sometimes a major global event occurs, such as a war or a pandemic. These events can trigger loneliness for millions of people at once.

TIP

Maybe you're reading this and realize that you're more prone to feeling lonely. Perhaps you appear to be facing multiple risks of loneliness. The first step to combatting loneliness is to realize that you're at risk. Then you can start working on strategies to avoid feeling lonely and to combat loneliness if it rears its ugly head.

Remember that you're not alone. At some time in your life, you're likely to face a heightened risk of loneliness. You might even face multiple risks at specific points in your life.

In this chapter I help you identify whether you're more at risk of loneliness than average. I explain the demographic groups more likely to be lonely and the kinds of personal circumstances that can lead to loneliness. I then go through the different life trigger points that can promote loneliness. At the end of the chapter, I offer some ways you can assess whether you're lonely and, if so, to what degree. Once you've measured just how lonely you are, you can use the useful tips throughout this book to kick those feelings of loneliness to the curb.

Demographic Characteristics That Can Lead to Loneliness

Demographic characteristics are the features or attributes that define you. They include factors such as your age, gender, sexual orientation, ethnicity, and disability. Your demographic characteristics influence your everyday life experiences, including loneliness. Although everyone is suspectable to feeling lonely, people with certain demographic characteristics are more likely to experience it.

REMEMBER

Societal factors such as cultural norms and values, economies, and inequalities shape your experiences of loneliness. The way in which these factors interact with your demographic characteristics affect if you feel lonely and, if so, to what degree. This is why different societies and cultures have different experiences of loneliness.

Age as a factor

Age is arguably the demographic characteristic that has the most significant influence on loneliness. People are most likely to feel lonely within two age groups: young adults aged 16–24, and those 65 and older.

The age factor of loneliness is a U-shaped curve on a graph, with loneliness rising at ages 16–24, decreasing in middle age, and then increasing again as people get older. Young adults or older persons are more likely to feel lonely for a variety of reasons.

Loneliness in young adulthood

Loneliness is actually one of the main fears that young people have in today's society. If you're young, it's often assumed that you'll have lots of friends and an active social life. There's a general expectation that it's easy for you to make friends, and you'll be out partying whenever you get the chance. But that isn't necessarily true.

REMEMBER

In fact, many young people find it difficult to connect with others in a meaningful way. They have a hard time forming friendships. (I explain more about meaningful relationships in Chapters 5 and 14).

As a young person, you don't always realize that other young people are experiencing the same loneliness that you are. You might believe that other young people have more friends than you and are happier than you, which can make you feel even lonelier. This is sometimes made worse by the images you see on TV, on ads and posters, in magazines, and on the internet where young people appear happy and surrounded by lots of friends.

Social media can exacerbate this. When you look through your social media feeds, you might see your peers posting photos of what appears to be an active social life. But it's important to remember that these are just images; the reality behind the images can be distorted. People post on social media what they want you to see and believe about their lives. What you think you see isn't always the reality.

Young adulthood is also a time when various life transitions can take place and trigger loneliness. These transitions can include going to a new school, college or university, starting your first job, leaving home, getting married, and becoming a parent. If you're encountering any of these changes, you may also be more susceptible to feeling lonely.

TIP

If you're a young adult and are feeling lonely, remember that loneliness is common among people of your age. It's particularly important not to believe all you see or to compare yourself to others. This book has tips to help you feel less lonely, but a good place to start is by reducing your social media usage (see Chapter 7).

There are some useful helplines and links to valuable resources for young people who feel lonely in the Appendix.

Loneliness in older adults

Older people are also especially vulnerable to loneliness and can feel cut off from society. The older you are, the more likely this is to be the case. Many older people can go for weeks at a time without speaking to a friend, neighbor, or family member. Sometimes older people say that they only have their TV for company. If you're an older person, you might feel lonely for a whole range of reasons.

You might be living alone following the death of a spouse or partner. Maybe you're getting frailer or have health conditions that affect what you can do. You might be homebound, unable to get outside like you used to. Perhaps you've retired from work and miss social contact with your ex-work colleagues or feel you don't have a sense of purpose. Or you might miss no longer being the hub of your family because your children have grown up and created their own lives elsewhere.

TIP

Loneliness in later life has been commonplace for many years. The key is to find other like-minded people with whom you can make meaningful connections and to spend time doing meaningful activities that you enjoy (see Chapter 14 for some helpful advice). It's also a good idea to visit places where you feel a sense of belonging (see Chapter 15). If you can't physically get there, you might be able to use technology to help you (see Chapter 7).

The role of gender

Regardless of their age, women are more likely than men to feel lonely. Women are more likely to experience both transient (temporary) and chronic (longer term) loneliness (see Chapter 1 for more details about the different types of loneliness). This due to a number of factors, such as having higher risks for widowhood, living alone, chronic illness, and disabilities.

These gender differences also vary according to your marital status. Indeed, single men tend to be lonelier than single women, and married women tend to be lonelier than married men. This suggests that marriage can act as a kind of buffer to men feeling lonely, whereas it's more of a trigger to loneliness for women. If marriage is making you feel lonely, you can find more information and some helpful advice in Chapter 4.

Loneliness is also more likely for transgender and nonbinary individuals, whose gender identity doesn't align with their sex at birth. If this sounds like you, a combination of factors is likely making you feel lonelier. You might be having difficulties accepting yourself (see Chapter 13). Or you might be having challenges expressing who you are to others or being accepted by others for who you are. All this can make it difficult to create and retain meaningful social connections (see Chapters 5 and 14).

CONQUER LONELINESS BY FINDING OTHER LONELY PEOPLE

David was an older man I came across in Leeds, a city in the North of England. His wife had recently died, and he was living alone for the first time and feeling lonely. He retired just before his wife passed; they were planning to travel together but didn't get the chance. Since his wife's death, David struggled with his purpose in life. He had a hard time getting through each day. David knew he was lonely but didn't want to admit it, even to himself. He saw a leaflet about a project in Leeds called the Time to Shine, which was designed to help older people in the city become less lonely and isolated. Because David didn't acknowledge that he was lonely, at first he didn't get involved in the project.

But when David saw that the Time to Shine project also had opportunities for volunteers, he decided to get involved. He thought that, as a volunteer, he could help other lonely people. The volunteering helped David regain a sense of purpose. It also helped him feel less lonely. By being involved in the project, he started to admit to himself that he was lonely, which gave him the impetus to seek out further support.

REMEMBER

If you're a man and feel lonely, don't be alarmed, and know that there's nothing unusual about how you feel. Although women are more likely to be lonely, men are less likely to admit their loneliness. So it's likely that loneliness among men is higher and more common than the statistics show.

TIP

If you're a man and feel as if you might be lonely but you're not sure you want to admit it, even to yourself, know that you're not alone. Try completing the exercise at the end of this chapter to assess whether you're lonely. If the results show you are, it's okay. Help is at hand. You might want to try volunteering like David did so that you can help others and in turn help yourself. (See Chapter 14 for ideas on how to get involved in volunteering in your community, and see Chapter 6 for tips on volunteering through work.) There are also other useful techniques you can try throughout the book.

Whether you're a lonely man or women there are some useful resources and hotlines for you in the Appendix.

Sexual orientation as a factor

Another factor that plays a role in determining risk of loneliness is sexual orientation. People who fall into the LGBTQIA+ (lesbian, gay, bisexual, transgender, questioning, intersex, asexual, and others) category are generally more at risk of loneliness than heterosexual individuals.

REMEMBER

If you fall into the broad LGBTQIA+ category, you're more likely to feel lonely for a whole variety of complex and interrelated factors. You might have difficulties accepting your sexuality or your body image, which may lead to both low self-esteem and poor confidence. You might be experiencing rejection from family and friends. Or perhaps you're facing negative attitudes from others, which could constitute homophobia (and might lead to hate crimes against you) or discrimination.

You might experience these negative factors in your home, in school, in your workplace, in your neighborhood, or in your community, and this can make it challenging for you to visit places and spaces. In fact, you may feel unsafe in doing so. Coming out and disclosing your sexuality can sometimes help, but it can also make you feel lonelier and more isolated, at least initially, because it can take you, and others around you, time to come to terms with it. You might experience stig-matization, which can affect your ability to form or maintain meaningful rela-tionships with people sometimes long after you've come out. All this is likely to lead you to feel lonely and isolated at some point in your life.

If you're gay, lesbian, transgender, bisexual, or questioning your sexuality, regardless of whether you've come out or not, it's important to accept yourself for who you are. Your relationship with yourself is critical in your experiences of loneliness. This isn't always easy or quick, but you can get some helpful advice on techniques to help with this in Chapter 13. There are also other tips throughout the book on how to create and maintain meaningful relationships with others.

Numerous support groups for the LGBTQAI+ community can help you overcome these challenges and connect to like-minded people. A list of useful hotlines and links to resources is available in the Appendix.

Ethnicity's role

Research on the links between ethnicity and loneliness appears to produce incon-sistent results. There aren't any specific ethnic groups which are lonelier than others. But minoritized ethnic groups are more likely to be at risk of loneliness. People from Black, Asian, and minority ethnic backgrounds living in predomi-nantly white communities, for example, can be more vulnerable to loneliness and may also face more barriers in accessing help to overcome loneliness.

REMEMBER

Racism can exacerbate experiences for minorities. Unfortunately, racism can be experienced everywhere, from schools to workplaces, in the local community, on public transportation, in public places, and even in health care settings. Language can also create a barrier. If your first language isn't the dominant language where you live, you can feel excluded from society and unable to interact.

You might have trouble riding public transportation, finding your way around towns and cities, and engaging with people you meet. All these factors can combine to make it difficult for you to form meaningful relationships with others and form a sense of belonging to places. You might also start feeling as though you don't fit in, don't belong, and feel uncomfortable just being yourself.

Some ethnic cultures and norms can have a direct impact on how lonely you feel. In South Asian culture, for example, the extended family is an important feature of society. Some South Asian people feel less lonely because they're surrounded by family all the time. Yet other South Asians actually feel lonelier because they don't necessarily get along with their extended family and don't have meaningful relationships with them.

TIP

If you're feeling lonely because of your ethnicity, seek out help and support so that you feel safe and comfortable being yourself in public places and can interact and form meaningful relationships with others. It's also important to report racism wherever and whenever you can. You'll find lot of help throughout this book but also additional resources and hotlines, including for discrimination, in the Appendix.

Disabilities and loneliness

Millions of people worldwide are living with a disability. Disability is another demographic factor that can lead to a greater incidence of loneliness. Indeed, 40 percent of US adults with a debilitating disability or chronic condition report feeling lonely or being socially isolated, while in the UK disabled people are a staggering four times more likely to feel lonely than those without a disability. What's more, many lonely disabled people are chronically lonely, which means they've been lonely for some time. Both physical and learning disabilities can lead to greater risk of loneliness.

If you have a disability, you're more likely to feel lonely than someone who isn't disabled. You might have mobility difficulties that restrict your ability to participate in everyday life, which can reduce your opportunities for social interaction. You might have difficulties using public transportation, getting into and around public buildings and shops, and just being out and about.

You may also be suffering from chronic pain, prohibiting you from spending long periods of time out of the house and limiting your ability to interact socially. You might have a learning disability that affects your ability to interact socially with others. Your capacity and skills may be affected by your disability, which can lead to difficulties engaging in education and employment opportunities. And, like the other demographic groups who are more prone to loneliness, your disability can be stigmatized. You might be subject to negative stereotypes, hate crimes, and discrimination.

If you have a disability, many of these challenges can come together to make you more at risk of loneliness. These can lead to a lack of self-confidence, difficulties accepting yourself, and trouble forming meaningful relationships with others. You may lack a sense of belonging to places, and if you do form a bond somewhere, it might be hard for you to get there.

If you have a disability, whether it's a physical disability or a learning one, whether it's obvious or hidden, it's common to feel lonely. But loneliness isn't an inevitable outcome of disability, and help is at hand. This book offers many tips that may work for you.

If you're having mobility difficulties, some of the technological-based approaches in Chapter 7 might help. If you feel like you need some assistance in accepting yourself for who you are, Chapter 13 has useful techniques. You can also find some useful hotlines and resources listed in the Appendix.

How Personal Circumstances Influence Loneliness

Alongside your demographic characteristics, your personal circumstances play a role in determining the extent to which you're at risk of loneliness. Personal circumstances are the conditions or settings you find yourself in. These can, and often are, influenced by your demographic characteristics, as well as the wider societal norms and cultures.

Many personal circumstances can increase your likelihood of feeling lonely. In this section, I discuss some of the key ones.

Marital status

Marital, or relationship, status is a key indicator of loneliness risk. If you live with a partner (married, in a civil partnership, or cohabiting), you're less likely to be lonely than if you live alone, without a partner. You're more likely to feel chronically lonely if you've been married or cohabited in the past and are no longer doing so because you're widowed, separated, or divorced. You're also more likely to be chronically lonely if you've never been married. It's important to remember, though, that the precise impacts of marital status vary by factors such as the societal norms of the country in which you live, your gender, and your ethnic cultures and beliefs.

REMEMBER

In general, living with a partner offers opportunities for emotional connectedness with a soulmate, which can protect you from loneliness. Men seem to gain from this emotional protection from loneliness in marriage more than women do. This is because men tend to center their lives around their partners more than women do. Also, women sometimes have expectations about marriage that aren't met. They can feel lonelier in a marriage that isn't offering the kind of emotional support they desire. Cultural issues and the way in which marriages or relationships emerge and develop can also play a role in how lonely you're likely to feel in a partnership.

Women in arranged marriages can initially feel quite lonely. One woman I spoke to had moved across the country to live with her husband and her in-laws. Even though she was living with a large family, she felt very lonely. She hadn't yet formed an emotional bond with her husband or his family and felt completely isolated and depressed.

TIP

If you feel lonely because you're living alone without a partner or are living with a partner but aren't getting the emotional connectedness you desire or expect, see Chapter 4, where I include some advice about dealing with loneliness in the home.

You can also find some useful hotlines and resources in the Appendix.

Health conditions

REAL WORLD EXAMPLE

I've suffered from migraines for more than 30 years. When I get a migraine attack, I'm often confined to a dark room for up to three days. I can't eat, move, or speak because the pain is so excruciating. If I have plans with friends or family at the time I experience an attack, I have to cancel. I used to feel guilty about that, but I've started alerting people to the fact that if I have an attack I'll have to cancel or postpone. This takes the pressure off me and helps my family and friends understand that I'm genuinely ill, not just being a flakey friend.

Loneliness can lead to ill health, as I explain in Chapter 3. But having a physical or mental health condition can also increase your chances of becoming lonely (see Chapters 9 and 10). Some health conditions are particularly likely to increase your risk of loneliness. These include:

❑ Long-term health conditions such as diabetes, arthritis, and cancer

❑ Physical immobility and frailty

❑ Sensory impairment

❑ Urinary incontinence

❑ Mental health conditions

- ❑ Cognitive impairment, such as dementia
- ❑ Weight-related issues
- ❑ Alcoholism and substance misuse

TIP

It's understandable to feel lonely because of a physical or a mental health condition. Many health conditions can make you more vulnerable to being lonely and isolated. If this sounds like you, you can find more useful information in Chapters 9 and 10 and throughout this book.

Helplines and support groups for specific health conditions can give you advice and connect you with people facing similar issues. See the Appendix for some useful hotlines and resources.

CONFRONTING LONELINESS WHEN DEALING WITH HEALTH CONDITIONS

REAL WORLD EXAMPLE

Paul was experiencing depression and anxiety. As a result, through no fault of his own, he had to keep canceling meetings with friends at the last minute. After a while, Paul's friends stopped contacting him. And he didn't feel like he could contact them about a meetup because he couldn't be sure that he would feel well enough when the time came. Before long Paul became isolated and lonely.

If you're dealing with such health conditions, it can be difficult to leave the house. You can become homebound, physically unable to get out. You may also find it psychologically difficult to leave your own home. This can mean that maintaining existing relationships and making new connections is difficult. The result can be a reduction in confidence and self-esteem. Friends and family may not understand the full impact of your health condition and may feel that you're ignoring them.

In addition, some health conditions can be stigmatized. Examples include HIV, many mental health conditions, and substance addiction. If you're dealing with one of these health conditions, you might be reluctant to mention or explain it to friends and family. This can further damage your social relationships because friends and family don't understand why you're not engaging with them.

You might worry about making social arrangements because you know you might not be able to stick to them. If your health condition flares up, you might have to let friends down. It can lead to a negative spiral of loneliness.

If you have a health condition that's affecting your relationships, try to have an honest conversation with your friends and family. Explain to them how you feel and how your health condition limits you.

Being a caregiver

A caregiver is anyone who provides unpaid care for a friend or family member who can't cope without that support. People often need a caregiver due to illness, disability, mental health, or addiction. This type of care is different from mainstream childcare responsibilities. It's also different from being a paid caregiver, such as a home care worker or an aide working in a nursing home.

If you're an unpaid caregiver, you might find yourself helping someone dress, bathe, move about, or take their medication. You might also help with shopping, laundry, cleaning, cooking, mail, or bill paying.

Unpaid caregivers number in the millions globally. The US has approximately 53 million, the UK 6 million, Canada 3 million, and Australia 2.5 million. People don't always identity as being a caregiver; instead, they often say that they're simply "looking after someone." This means that, most likely, millions more unpaid caregivers exist. People who are unpaid caregivers are likely to be more at risk of feeling lonely. In the UK alone, it's thought that eight out of ten unpaid caregivers are lonely and socially isolated.

If you're an unpaid caregiver, you're more likely to feel lonely for several reasons:

- ❑ Being unable to get out of the house
- ❑ Not having time to meet friends and family
- ❑ Feeling guilty about leaving the person you're caring for
- ❑ Not having time to participate in social activities
- ❑ Feeling uncomfortable disclosing that you're a caregiver or talking to friends about what you do
- ❑ Feeling "invisible" because even when visitors come to the house they are often there to visit the cared for person, as opposed you, the caregiver

If you're a caregiver, your lifestyle usually changes to accommodate your responsibilities. You might find yourself withdrawing from your usual activities or leaving your paid job. If you manage to remain in paid work, you may be unable to meet colleagues socially outside of work, or you might meet them less frequently than you had previously. You might find that you have no time for your usual hobbies or social activities, so you have fewer opportunities to interact with people. Your own health can start to suffer as the burden of care takes its toll. This itself can make you feel lonelier.

SOCIALIZING WITHOUT GUILT WHEN CARING FOR A LOVED ONE

George is retired. He used to meet his friends at the local pub in the evenings and play pool on weekends.

A few years ago his wife Amelia's health condition deteriorated, and she needed more support. George became her primary caregiver. He helps her bathe and use the restroom. He does the shopping and prepares all her meals. He also deals with all the household domestic chores and finances.

Although George has some free time in the evenings after he has helped Amelia to bed, he usually feels too exhausted to meet his friends socially then. He also feels guilty going out when his wife is homebound. He's become very lonely since becoming the main caregiver for his wife.

TIP

If you're a caregiver like George and are feeling lonely, you'll find some tips throughout this book to help you feel better. In particular, check out Chapter 11. Many of the millions of unpaid caregivers are experiencing the same kinds of difficulties you are.

Depending on where you live, additional support may be available to you. I provide some links and helplines in the Appendix. Even if you don't identify as a caregiver, it can be a good idea to contact a local caregivers support center if your area has one.

Your local caregivers center can help you find local support. They often run groups so that caregivers can meet each other and share their experiences in a safe setting. These centers can also advise you on opportunities for respite care so you can get a break from your caring role for a short period of time while the person you care for is supported.

Social class and financial circumstances

Another risk factor for loneliness relates to social class and wealth. Overall, people who have lower incomes, are living in the most deprived areas, and are of a lower social class are more at risk of loneliness.

For a range of reasons, lower wealth and income lead to a greater risk of loneliness. Financial resources bring opportunities for socializing, visiting places where you feel a sense of belonging, and living where you feel safe and have plentiful local amenities and facilities. On the other hand, lower income and poverty can lead to inadequate housing in neighborhoods that feel unsafe and where community facilities are poor or absent.

WARNING

The financial anxiety that's often accompanied by low incomes can also damage or create challenges to building and maintaining relationships. It's much more difficult to meet up with friends or relatives for a meal or a coffee if you don't have sufficient funds to do so. It's also more challenging to visit that special place by the coast or lake that brings you a sense of belonging and reduces your feeling of loneliness (see Chapter 15).

TIP

If you find yourself strapped for cash and struggling to maintain existing relationships or create new ones, don't despair. You can continue to meet up with friends even when you're short on cash. You just need to be a bit more inventive. Some examples include meeting in the local library, having a picnic on a warm summer's day in a local park, attending local community activities which are often free of charge. If you're having financial difficulties and are looking for cost effective ways to meet new people, try chatting to people in the local shops, on public transportation, or simply sit on a bench in a public place and strike up a conversation with passersby who sit next to you.

Access to transportation

In contemporary western society, a lack of transportation often leaves you more vulnerable to feeling lonely. Being able to get out and about whenever you want is often essential to creating and maintaining social connections with others. It also enables you to engage in activities and visit places where you feel a sense of belonging.

Transportation tends to feature prominently in discussions I've had with people who feel lonely. This has particularly been the case with minority ethnic populations, with older people, and with people who have long-term physical and mental health conditions. Public transportation is often restrictive for people with certain health conditions, and those with low incomes can't always afford a car, taxi, Uber, or Lyft.

TIP

If you feel that a lack of transportation prevents you from engaging with others and leaves you feeling left out and lonely, it might be a good idea to try to access some local support groups that can help you. You can find local support groups by popping along to your local library, or doing an internet search.

Fortunately, you can keep in contact with friends or relatives in other ways. If you have access to the internet, you can connect to people electronically (see Chapter 7). You can also try writing a traditional letter or asking people to meet you near your house or apartment. These are just a few examples, but you'll read about many others throughout the book.

Life Events That Trigger Loneliness

A number of life changes can cause transient (temporary) loneliness. These changes are known as transitory life events. They're triggered by factors such as changing schools, going to college or university, retirement, bereavement, unemployment or layoffs, divorce or separation, and children leaving home.

These events can temporarily limit your opportunities for meaningful relationships with others. They can affect your sense of belonging somewhere or your ability to visit places where you have that sense of belonging. They can also alter the way you perceive or accept yourself. All of this can make you temporarily feel lonely. I explain more about some of these life transition points now.

TIP

If you find yourself in one of these transitory life phases, remember that it's nearly always temporary. Your feelings of loneliness are a prompt to make some adjustments to your life following the transitory life event that's just taken place.

Bereavement

Experiencing bereavement is a key life transition point that can trigger loneliness. When someone who's close to you passes away, it's understandable that you might feel lonely. You're likely to experience a whole series of different and difficult emotions. If you lost a spouse, a close loved one, or a special confidant, you might even feel as though you're lonelier than if you'd not had that supportive companion in the first place. Your relationship with that person might have acted as a buffer to protect you from feeling lonely, but now that they're gone, you might feel more exposed and vulnerable to loneliness. You're likely to feel a sense of loss of that relationship, but your relationships with other people can change too. Quite often after the death of a loved one, your wider family and friendship networks can be affected. Some bereaved individuals say that they have much less contact with family following their loss. This can especially be true if the person who has passed away was the one who took responsibility for organizing social activities and family get-togethers.

TIP

The feelings of loneliness due to bereavement are likely to reduce in intensity over time as you adjust to life without the person you've lost. However, if your bereavement was some time ago and you're still feeling as lonely as ever, you might be experiencing chronic loneliness. Whether your bereavement-related loneliness is temporary or feels like it's been around forever, you can overcome your feelings of loneliness and start living a fulfilled and happy life again. Chapter 8 discusses different options that are specifically designed for people who have experienced bereavement. Try those and the other tips in this book to keep loneliness at bay.

If you're struggling to deal with bereavement, it's helpful to talk to someone who understands. See the Appendix for some useful hotlines and resources.

Children leaving home

Another life transition point that often triggers loneliness and grief is experienced when your children move away for college or to live with a partner or spouse. This is sometimes called the empty nest syndrome. The syndrome often hits the hardest when the youngest child leaves home. It can lead to feelings of happiness and excitement for your children and their future, but also feelings of emptiness and sadness. You might experience depression, distress, or a loss of purpose and meaning in your life. If you're the main caregiver, you might experience these feelings more severely. Sometimes the empty nest syndrome strikes when you're going through another life change, such as menopause, a marriage breakdown, or the loss of your own parents. A combination of these life changes can make the transitionary loneliness of your children leaving home feel even worse.

TIP

If you're experiencing empty nest syndrome, try to appreciate the peace and quiet of your home once again and look forward to enjoying quality time with your children when they come to visit. It's easier now than ever before to keep in touch through technological advances such as social media and texting. Try to arrange regular times to FaceTime your children without cramping their style. Chapter 4 offers some useful tips and strategies designed specifically with you in mind. If your feelings of depression are severe and don't seem to be easing over time, it might be worth contacting one of the relevant hotlines in the Appendix.

Having a baby

Becoming a parent is a major life-changing event. Although it's usually a positive and rewarding experience, it can also be a trigger to isolation and feelings of loneliness. Becoming a new parent can make you feel a loss of identity and can change your existing relationships with your partner, family, and friends. You can feel too tired to go out and socialize or to take time for yourself. If you're a new mom, you also have to deal with changes to your body and a new role in life. All these changes can make you feel lonely, especially in the postpartum period.

Parenthood can trigger loneliness among all new parents, but some are more likely to be adversely affected by this transitory life event than others. Those more likely to be affected by loneliness are mothers, young parents, and parents with low incomes.

TIP

If you're a new mom or dad and are feeling lonely, it can be particularly difficult to admit your feelings. You might feel as though the safe arrival of your new baby should be enough to protect you from loneliness. But everyone needs social interaction, and your baby can't always provide you with the companionship you need. Don't feel guilty if you're feeling lonely as a new parent. Instead, recognize that your loneliness has been triggered by a life-changing event which has affected your social relationships. Things will soon settle down. Your existing relationships will resume again, and new relationships will undoubtedly form. You can join a local parent and toddler group to help you meet new parents who'll be in a similar position. Chapters 4 and 11 also offer some helpful tips while you're experiencing this temporary transition to help you feel less lonely and isolated. If you're feeling particularly depressed and sad, it might be worth contacting a relevant hotline listed in the Appendix.

Divorce and separation

Divorce and relationship breakdown can trigger loneliness and isolation, even if you weren't necessarily happy in the relationship. Feeling lonely after a relationship has ended is a normal part of the grieving process. It can take time to get used to being single, to living on your own, and to life without your partner. Sometimes you have to get used to life without your in-laws and extended family too. You also might have less contact with your children. It's important to take some time for yourself after a relationship breakdown. Spend time doing things that you enjoy and have meaning to you. Go to places where you feel a connection, a sense of belonging. Perhaps these are places you couldn't visit with your partner. Your feelings of loss and loneliness won't last forever despite how strong they feel now.

TIP

Your feelings of loneliness after a divorce or separation are normal and temporary. Turn to Chapter 4 which includes some useful tips. If you're feeling particularly depressed and sad and the tips in this book aren't working for you, you might need to get some additional support to help you on your way. Chapter 13 has some useful therapy techniques you can try, or you might want to contact a relevant hotline listed in the Appendix.

Moving house

Moving house can be a positive and happy experience for some, but for others, it can be a transition point triggering loneliness. However, as you adjust to your new environment, those initial feelings of loneliness often subside. Whether you experience loneliness after moving house can, to some extent, depend on whether your house move is by choice or forced upon you. If it's the latter, it's more likely to leave you vulnerable to loneliness. You're coming to terms with a new home, which you didn't necessarily want to move to, along with a new neighborhood and new people to adjust to. You might move home due to divorce, separation, or marriage; because your children have left home and you need to downsize; because you're having children and need to upsize; because you can no longer pay your mortgage or rent; or because you just landed a new job. Or maybe you've just decided you'd like a new home.

Sometimes your move is in the same neighborhood, but other times it involves moving to distant towns, cities, or even different countries. Of course, wars, conflicts, and natural disasters can also force you to move. Quite often a move is tied up with another transitory life change that can cause loneliness, such as divorce or a job change. Because of that, it's not always easy to determine which particular change is the cause of the loneliness. Quite often it's a combination of the life transitions.

Moving can lead to transitory loneliness for a range of reasons. You might feel a sense of loss and grief moving away from your previous home. Perhaps you don't feel a sense of belonging or connection to your new home or your new neighborhood, town, or country. Maybe you don't know anyone in your new area. If you're moving to a new country and you don't speak the language, you might not be able to communicate well to be able to forge new relationships and settle in.

Whatever your reasons for feeling lonely, you can use the tips in this book to overcome this transitory loneliness. Chapter 4 helps you create relationships in your home. Chapter 5 assists in forming meaningful relationships in your community. Chapter 14 facilitates building meaningful relationships with others. Chapter 15 offers tips on how to create and maintain a sense of belonging to place.

Changed employment status

As I explain in Chapter 6, your workplace can be a place for you to create meaningful relationships and a sense of belonging, both of which can help you fend off loneliness. However, if you change or leave your workplace, you can experience transitory loneliness until you adjust to your new environment. The loss of your work routine and the social structures that surround it can lead to a loss of purpose, a decline in self-worth, and a loss of confidence. You may also find it difficult to maintain relationships with ex-work colleagues who aren't available when you are and whom you may no longer identify with in the same way now that you're not working.

Employment changes can trigger loneliness for many. I provide strategies and tips on how to both avoid and reduce your feelings of loneliness when changing your employment status in Chapter 12.

Changing educational institutions

Similar to changing jobs, switching educational institutions can be a challenging time that can lead to loneliness, at least initially. Loneliness can be triggered by going to school for the first time, switching schools, or starting college. First-year university students who are moving away from home for the first time can be particularly vulnerable to loneliness. Sometimes you might sail through an educational transition without noticing that it even took place, and other times you'll feel intensely lonely as a result. The loneliness can stem from leaving your parents for a large part of the day for the first time; going to an unfamiliar place or building; mixing with new people you don't know; and seeing others getting along well and feeling left out. Whatever the specific reasons for your loneliness, adjusting to your new surroundings and peers takes time. Once you're adjusted, your loneliness should ease.

TIP

If your feelings of loneliness are lasting longer than you'd like, making you overly miserable, and causing you to dislike going to school or college, it might be a good idea to start taking action. I provide some useful tips in Chapter 12 and elsewhere in the book for you to try.

Global disasters, pandemics, and violence

Global disasters such as pandemics and conflicts can instantaneously trigger loneliness among vast sections of the population. The Covid-19 pandemic forced self-isolation, working from home, and distancing from friends, family, and work and school colleagues. The loss of direct social interaction with others and the inability to visit places that offer a sense of belonging caused many to feel intensely lonely and isolated for months on end. The enforced social isolation triggered mental health issues among large swaths of the world's population. Some still remain fearful and anxious about socializing despite the virus being much better controlled today.

REMEMBER

Alongside pandemics, wars and conflict can trigger loneliness on a large scale. Wars can lead to death and bereavement, leaving relatives and friends with a sense of loss, grief, and loneliness. Many are forced to flee their homes, communities, workplaces, and friends. Families are often segregated. Those who stay in the war zone can be isolated in their own homes, unable to go outside onto the streets because they're unsafe. Those who flee their homes are often displaced, with no place to call home. They may struggle to make friends and connect with people in their new settlement (sometimes due to a language barrier). Wars can lead to loneliness and other mental health issues such as depression, anxiety, fear, and increased substance abuse. Loneliness can affect those serving in the military and those left behind at home.

TIP

Global disasters such as wars and pandemics can be specific trigger points for loneliness. They can also lead to other disturbing and distressing challenges. Although these disasters are often temporary in nature, they can continue for many years, and their effects can last a lifetime. At times of such global disasters, organizations such as the International Red Cross provide support across the globe. These agencies provide humanitarian aid and support, including meaningful activities to reduce loneliness. Often, refugees and asylum seekers can get assistance from local support groups. See the Appendix for some useful hotlines and resources.

Measurement Tools for Loneliness

Most commonly, loneliness is measured quantitatively through statistical measurement scales. A scale is really just a way of numerically measuring an opinion or emotion. Two main loneliness scales have been tested and validated for assessing whether you're lonely and to what degree. The first one is the UCLA scale. The UCLA scale, as its name suggests, was developed by the University of California in Los Angeles. The second scale is the De Jong Gierveld scale, named after a Dutch professor who designed it. I'll show you both scales, and you can decide which one to use. You can also try both scales and see if there's any difference in your loneliness results.

The UCLA loneliness scale

REMEMBER

The UK Government's national loneliness strategy recommends using four questions to assess loneliness. The first three questions are from the University of California, Los Angeles (UCLA) three-item loneliness scale. The last is a direct question about how often people feel lonely, and it's currently used in the UK's Community Life Survey. Using the UCLA scale ensures that loneliness is being measured using a gauge that's been assessed as valid and reliable. The single question allows the respondent to say for themselves whether they feel lonely, which provides insight into the subjective feeling of loneliness.

TIP

To assess whether you're lonely, answer the following questions, circling the answer that best describes how you feel right now.

1. How often do you feel that you lack companionship?

Hardly ever or never; Some of the time; Often

2. How often do you feel left out?

Hardly ever or never; Some of the time; Often

3. How often do you feel isolated from others?

Hardly ever or never; Some of the time; Often

In order to score your answers, your responses should be coded as follows:

Hardly ever or never = 1; Some of the time = 2; Often = 3

Add the scores for each question together to give you a possible range of scores from 3 to 9. If you score 3–5, you're not lonely. If you score 6–9, you're classified as lonely.

Next, ask yourself the direct measure of loneliness:

4. How often do you feel lonely?

Often/always; Some of the time; Occasionally; Hardly ever; Never

If you score 6–9 on the first three questions and circle Often/always, Some of the time, or Occasionally for question 4, then you're classified as lonely. Don't worry if your score means that you're lonely. Your feelings of loneliness can change at different times of day and on different days of the week, so try answering these questions on a few different days and times to start with to see if your answers are always the same. If you find that you're lonely at certain times but not others, try to determine if there's a pattern to when you're more likely to feel lonely. Some people feel lonelier at night or on weekends or on holidays. Once you've worked out when you're more likely to feel lonely, you can try some of the tips in this book to reduce your feelings of loneliness on those days. If you find yourself lonely every day, start working through the tips in the book. Before long, your answers to the questions will start to change.

The De Jong Gierveld loneliness scale

REMEMBER

The De Jong scale separates out social and emotional loneliness and identifies whether you're experiencing either or both. Social loneliness occurs when you're lacking a wider social network, such as a network of friends or work colleagues. Emotional loneliness emerges when you lack an intimate relationship with a partner, spouse, or special friend. The De Jong scale has six questions; three are about emotional loneliness, and three are focused on social loneliness. This scale helps you work out why you're feeling lonely rather than just whether you are lonely. You'll learn whether you're lonely because you're lacking a wider network of friends or because you lack an intimate relationship.

TIP

To use the De Jong Gierveld loneliness scale, answer the following questions, circling your answer:

1. I experience a general sense of emptiness. [Emotional Loneliness]

   Yes; More or less; No.

2. I miss having people around me. [Emotional Loneliness]

   Yes; More or less; No.

3. I often feel rejected. [Emotional Loneliness]

   Yes; More or less; No.

4. There are plenty of people I can rely on when I have problems. [Social Loneliness]

   Yes; More or less; No.

5. There are many people I can trust completely. [Social Loneliness]

   Yes; More or less; No.

6. There are enough people I feel close to. [Social Loneliness]

   Yes; More or less; No.

To score your answers on the scale:

For Questions 1–3:

If you answer Yes or More or less on questions 1–3, give yourself a score of 1. Give yourself 0 for No.

For questions 4–6:

Give yourself a score of 1 for No or More or less, and give yourself a 0 for Yes.

Emotional Loneliness Score

This produces an emotional loneliness score, ranging from 0 (not emotionally lonely) to 3 (intensely emotionally lonely).

Social Loneliness Score

This produces a social loneliness score, ranging from 0 (not socially lonely) to 3 (intensely socially lonely).

Overall Loneliness Score

You can also total the scores for each question. This gives a possible range of scores from 0 to 6, which can be read as follows:

Least lonely 0 1 2 3 4 5 6 Most lonely

Once you've scored yourself on the De Jong Gierveld scale, you can assess whether you're lonely overall and, if you are, which kind of loneliness you're experiencing. You might be experiencing social loneliness, emotional loneliness, or both. Either way, don't be alarmed. I'm here to help. Depending on which loneliness you're experiencing, you can turn to an appropriate chapter to get some tips on how to make changes to your life to dispel those feelings of loneliness.

Chapter **3**

The Wide-ranging Costs of Chronic Loneliness

B esides being an unpleasant feeling, chronic loneliness has wider implications. It can affect the health and well-being of those who feel lonely, which in turn influences their ability to perform well and achieve their potential in education, at work, and in other aspects of their lives. This then results in wider costs for health and social care systems, for individual businesses, and for the economies of nations. In the United States, studies show that stress-related absenteeism attributed to loneliness costs employers approximately $154 billion annually, and that social isolation among older people costs the US government nearly $7 billion in additional health care costs per year.

In the UK the collective costs of chronic loneliness are calculated to be around £10,000 per person per year. This figure includes well-being, health, and work productivity costs that are associated with severe loneliness. What's more, it represents the cost per person to the UK economy and business only. If you add in the costs to the health and social care system and the monetarized costs of poor health to the individual, the total cost would be significantly higher.

The costs to the lonely individual relate to the damage to their health and well-being, their educational achievement, and their performance at work. Individual businesses face costs relating to lost productivity, absenteeism, and labor turnover. Heath services also experience costs because lonely people are more prone to certain health conditions. All of this leads to wider cumulative costs for the economies of nations.

In this chapter I discuss more about the implications of chronic loneliness to you as an individual and to the wider economy. I then discuss the ways in which governments have responded to what some have called the *loneliness epidemic* and outline some of the interventions and initiatives that are successfully tackling loneliness.

Personal Costs of Loneliness

Loneliness is often a temporary or transient feeling that should fade away when you reach out to people, reconnect with family and friends, make new connections, or visit places where you feel a sense of belonging.

But if this transient loneliness persists, it can become a chronic condition, where you feel lonely often or all the time. Chronic loneliness can last for a long time — sometimes for years. It can affect your health, harming both your physical and your mental health.

If you're feeling lonely, it's only natural to worry about how loneliness might be affecting your health. But remember that you can avoid and reverse these adverse health implications by addressing your feelings of loneliness head on. Once you've read through the various health implications of loneliness in this chapter, try some of the different strategies throughout the book, and before long you'll start feeling a greater sense of well-being. Any physical health conditions you may have related to your loneliness will start to ease.

TIP

If your loneliness is proving particularly difficult to eradicate, seek out some of the psychological options in Chapter 13.

Health impacts

Scientific research suggests that loneliness can affect your overall health and trigger some specific health conditions. Feeling lonely can make you hypervigilant so that you respond to threats more quickly than you would normally. Consequently, your stress hormones increase, which in turn can increase your blood pressure and weaken your immune system. People who are lonely or socially isolated can have a higher risk of premature death than individuals who aren't lonely or socially isolated.

AS HARMFUL AS 15 CIGARETTES A DAY

The most commonly cited research, and the one that tends to grab the headlines, is a study by Professor Julianne Holt-Lunstad, a professor of psychology and neuroscience at Brigham Young University. Along with colleagues, she published research in 2010 concluding that the health effect of loneliness is equivalent to smoking 15 cigarettes a day. Her team came to this conclusion by combining data from 148 studies through a meta-analysis.

The meta-analysis contained data on 300,000 participants who were studied over seven and a half years. The researchers explored the extent to which social relationships can influence the risk of premature death. Their research concluded that lonely people are 50 percent more likely to die prematurely than people with strong social relationships. They then used a statistical tool called random effects models and from this concluded that the influence of social relationships on the risk of death is comparable with a number of well-established risk factors for death, including smoking cigarettes. They also pointed out that the health risks of loneliness are similar to alcohol consumption (more than six drinks a day), physical inactivity, and obesity (measured by Body Mass Index).

REMEMBER

Loneliness can trigger three primary types of physical and mental health conditions:

>> **Depression:** A number of studies have found that loneliness can lead to a persistent depressed mood and depressive symptoms. It can also lead to related symptoms such as anxiety, a loss of energy and hope, and a higher propensity for suicide.

>> **Coronary heart disease and stroke:** Social isolation and loneliness are associated with a 29 percent higher risk of coronary heart disease and a 32 percent increased risk of stroke.

>> **Dementia:** Loneliness and dementia are associated. Individuals experiencing loneliness have a significantly higher risk of developing dementia than those who aren't experiencing loneliness. One study showed that the increased risk of developing dementia from a 1-point increase in loneliness (on a 1 to 5 scale) is 41 percent.

These health conditions can also lead to loneliness, which I discuss in more detail in Chapters 9 and 10.

If you think you may have any of these health conditions or you're worried about your health more generally, contact your doctor or health practitioner and explain your concerns. There are some useful hotlines in the Appendix if you need support with your feelings of loneliness, any of these specific health conditions, or if you have suicidal thoughts.

Concerns for general well-being

The links between loneliness and poor well-being are undisputable, but the relationship is complex and goes both ways. Poor well-being can cause loneliness, and loneliness can cause poor well-being. What's more, if you have poor well-being and are feeling lonely, it's not always easy to identify which condition is triggering which.

Feeling lonely can lower your well-being, and chronic loneliness can lead to a downward spiral. You may start to have a cynical outlook on your social connections with other people. You might see their actions or words more negatively and feel that your social surroundings are threatening. As a result, you might misinterpret other people's intentions toward you, which can lead you to become less sociable. You might start to remove yourself from social contact. You can even begin to actively sabotage your own social relationships. All this can exacerbate your feelings of loneliness and isolation and lead you to withdraw further. This can have a negative affect on your well-being.

Loneliness can damage your well-being in three ways. It can affect your:

>> **Psychological well-being:** This refers to your feelings about yourself and your life. When you're psychologically well, you have positive feelings about yourself, you're content with your life, and you feel optimistic about the future. Loneliness can adversely affect your psychological well-being, regardless of your age. It can increase your chances of experiencing depressive symptoms, low self-esteem, and suicidal thoughts. One in 8 UK adults have had suicidal thoughts and feelings due to being lonely.

>> **Social well-being:** This refers to your ability to participate, feel valued as a member of, and feel connected to a wider social network. It relates to the quality of your social connections. Loneliness has been found to negatively affect your social well-being. It can mean that you lack the necessary social skills and find it difficult to develop close social relationships. If you're lonely, you might also perceive the quality of your social network in a more negative light, which can further reduce your social well-being.

>> **Emotional well-being:** This refers to the state of your emotions, life satisfaction, sense of meaning and purpose, and ability to pursue self-defined goals. Loneliness can directly lead to diminished emotional well-being and result in feelings of hostility, sadness, and fear. One out of every two lonely people in the UK say that feelings of loneliness have made them feel sad.

If you feel lonely most or all of the time, it can have a major impact on your well-being, your mental health, and your ability to function effectively in society. If you're feeling lonely and you recognize some or all of the signs that it's affecting your well-being and mental health, now's the time to take action.

You might have difficulty admitting your loneliness or talking about it. You might feel ashamed and embarrassed or feel that there's something wrong with you. I understand completely how you feel. Many lonely people I've researched over the years have said the same. In fact, a quarter of UK adults say they feel ashamed about being lonely, and 35 percent say they would never admit to feeling lonely. Loneliness isn't your fault. Millions of people around the world are in a similar position to you. The more you talk about your loneliness, the more you normalize the feeling, and the easier it becomes to get help.

TIP

LOCAL LONELINESS SERVICES

Numerous services and support are available to help you feel less lonely. These services are often available in your local community or neighborhood, and they're usually provided by volunteer and community sector organizations, local charities, social enterprises, or your local government or health service providers.

- **Creative activity projects:** These involve creative activities you can do, usually as part of a group. Examples of available activities include arts and crafts, knitting, gardening, and DIY. You participate in activities you enjoy while meeting other people who have similar interests. Attending the classes can take your mind off being lonely. At the same time, you're likely to strike up friendships with others you can meet outside of the organized activities. For more help on how to use creative activities to reduce your feelings of loneliness, turn to Chapter 14.

- **Physical health interventions:** A number of different activities in your area focus on engaging in physical activities. These can include walking groups, chair-based exercise, running groups, Zumba classes, yoga, Pilates, Tai Chi sessions, and even nutrition sessions. These activities help you meet other like-minded people, improve your health and well-being, and often involve getting outside and breathing in fresh air, all of which give you a feel-good factor to reduce your feelings of loneliness. For more information on how physical activity can help you feel less lonely, see Chapters 14 and 15.

(continued)

(continued)

- **Technology-based interventions:** In recent years new technological innovations have emerged to help you maintain or widen your connections with other people electronically. That way even if you can't see people face to face, you can keep in touch. Technology can also help you virtually visit places where you feel a sense of belonging, which can prevent or reduce your loneliness. Some specific technological interventions have been developed to help with loneliness. You can access them in your own home through apps on your smartphone, tablet, laptop, or a smart TV. If you're not fully up to speed with new technology, various local groups can give you the skills and communal facilities to make the most of these inventions. If you want more information on how to use technological innovations to help you feel less lonely, read through the information in Chapter 7.

- **Psychological support:** Various psychological therapies and techniques can be particularly helpful if you've been lonely for a while or your loneliness is proving hard to shift. These can include Cognitive Behavioral Therapy (CBT), self-hypnosis, Eye Movement Desensitization and Reprocessing Therapy (EMDR), Emotional Freedom Technique (EFT), meditation, and many more. Some of these are self-help techniques, and some require support from a qualified practitioner. Turn to Chapter 13 for more details on which therapies are best for you and how to get started on them.

- **Befriending services:** In countries such as the UK, many organizations offer befriending services. These involve matching you up with another person you can identify with and lean on for support. A befriender might arrange regular calls or visits to see you and can offer you advice and support, assist you with visits to medical appointments, or simply join you for a coffee. Befriending services can also be offered in groups, where an individual facilitates regular meetings with a group of people who are facing similar issues and challenges. These are sometimes called *peer support groups*. You can find out more about befriending and peer support groups in Chapter 14.

Limited educational success

As I discuss in Chapter 2, loneliness is experienced most frequently in adolescence and young adulthood. Most adolescents and young adults are in school during those years. It's pertinent then that loneliness can impair academic performance and result in lower employment prospects. It can lead to poor recognition memory performance and lower grades.

Young people can experience loneliness because of an educational life transition. This might be starting school, moving schools because of a home relocation, transitioning from grade school to high school, leaving home to go to college, or moving abroad to study. These transitions often involve changes in social networks and a loss of, or less frequent, social contact with family and friends. See Chapter 12 for more information on loneliness due to educational changes and how to overcome it.

Young people who are lonely are more likely to have negative attitudes toward school, drop out of school, and obtain lower educational attainment by the age of 18 compared to those who aren't lonely. They're also more likely not to be in school or at a job or training. The negative impact on educational success is particularly strong for young people who have been experiencing chronic loneliness, especially if they've been feeling lonely since childhood.

REMEMBER

Loneliness might affect educational performance for a number of reasons:

>> **Poor sleep quality:** Loneliness can make it difficult for you to sleep or can cause disturbed sleep. This means your body doesn't repair, maintain, recover, and enhance physiological systems that are important for your brain development, cognitive function, and mood.

>> **Cognitive deficiencies:** Loneliness can affect your attention span, memory, perceptions, and decision-making.

>> **Stress, anxiety, and cortisol levels:** Loneliness can lead to higher levels of stress anxiety and cortisol levels, which can affect your emotional well-being and your academic performance.

>> **Ill health:** Loneliness can trigger ill health, which means you're more likely to be absent from school. As a result you're more likely to visit the doctor and to experience depression and symptoms such as headaches, backaches, and stomachaches than those who aren't lonely.

>> **Low self-esteem:** Loneliness often leads to low self-esteem, especially in young people. You can feel a low sense of self-worth and have a negative perception of yourself, which can lead to lower levels of confidence and adversely affect your academic performance.

>> **Compromising behaviors:** Loneliness can lead you to become involved in activities and behaviors that can adversely affect your health and your academic achievement. These can include substance abuse, self-medication, overeating, and unprotected sex.

If your feelings of loneliness are affecting your educational achievement, or your children's results are being damaged by their loneliness, don't panic. Chapter 12 has some useful tips and strategies to try. As soon as you start to reverse your feelings of loneliness, your grades will improve.

Stifling performance at work

You don't need to be a lone worker to feel lonely in the workplace. You can work in a crowded working environment and still feel lonely and disconnected from your coworkers. Loneliness at work can strike at any age and can affect your ability to perform well. For more information about loneliness in the workplace, see Chapters 6 and 12.

REMEMBER

Evidence suggests that your performance at work is affected by loneliness based on a number of factors:

>> **Levels of engagement in the workplace:** If you're lonely, you're likely to be less engaged and less committed, and therefore less productive at work. Engagement in the workplace is a human resources concept that refers to the level of enthusiasm and dedication you feel for your job.

>> **Job satisfaction:** If you're lonely, you might have a more negative attitude toward work and your job satisfaction can be lower. This can mean that you're less responsive to your employers' requirements and more likely to take time off work and seek employment elsewhere.

>> **Personal and organizational effectiveness:** Loneliness can adversely affect your reasoning and decision-making ability and can lead you to withdraw from your workplace commitments, all of which can adversely affect your personal and organizational effectiveness.

>> **Workplace affiliation and commitment:** Loneliness can reduce your workplace affiliation and commitment to job roles and tasks, adversely affecting your performance at work.

>> **Creativity:** Loneliness can lead to a loss of creativity at work, which can affect your ability to perform well.

>> **Teamwork:** If you feel lonely, particularly at work, you may feel disconnected from your work colleagues and not part of the team. As a result, you may feel unable to share your thoughts and ideas and find working cooperatively as part of a team challenging. Colleagues may find you less approachable and feel that you're less committed to the workplace. This can affect your individual performance but also the wider performance of the team.

>> **Absenteeism:** Loneliness can lead to a range of mental and physical health conditions. This can mean you're likely to have more days off work due to ill health, which can adversely affect your workplace performance.

TIP

If you feel lonely at work, or your loneliness is affecting your ability to perform well when you're at work, turn to Chapter 6, where you'll find some advice on how to deal with these feelings. Try some of the tips I've provided, and within no time you'll be back on track.

Choking creativity

Loneliness can have a significant effect on your ability to be creative. The negative emotional experiences that you experience when you're lonely can adversely affect your cognitive processes and emotional well-being, thus inhibiting your creative spirit. This can affect your creativity at home, in the workplace, in educational settings, and in any hobbies and social activities you engage in.

REMEMBER

Loneliness can affect your creativity in two main ways:

>> **Cognitive processes:** Loneliness can affect your cognitive processes, which are important for creativity. It can make it difficult for you to generate creative and innovate ideas. It can also affect your memory, so you might find it difficult to think creatively and retain any ideas that you manage to produce.

>> **Well-being:** Loneliness adversely affects your well-being and can lead to feelings of anxiety, worry, and sadness. It can also make you feel depressed and lower your self-esteem, self-worth, and confidence. You can also feel less motivated when you're lonely. When your emotional well-being is damaged in this way, it can be difficult to take risks, explore new ideas, and express yourself creatively.

TIP

Although all this sounds quite negative, many ideas throughout this book can reduce your feelings of loneliness so that you can regain that spark of creativity. What's more, loneliness doesn't always adversely affect creativity. In fact, in some instances loneliness can stimulate new ideas. In many cases, lonely people come up with inspiring and imaginative songs, poems, pieces of art, and literature. Also, becoming involved in creative activities is a good antidote to loneliness. So, if you're lonely and feel your creative juices are being affected, turn to Chapter 14, where you can find out more about using creative activities to combat your loneliness.

Costs to the Economy

Beyond the individual cost of loneliness, the wider economic costs of loneliness to health services, businesses, and economies are estimated to be escalating.

Staff turnover

One of the main ways in which loneliness among staff can affect individual businesses relates to turnover levels. Workers who are experiencing loneliness can feel left out of groups and teams, become disengaged from their workplace, and feel dissatisfied with their employment situation. This can lead them to seek employment elsewhere in an attempt to find a more socially connected workplace environment. Regardless of business size, increased staff turnover is costly. Indeed, it can cost employers around 33 percent of an employee's annual salary. This is due to the costs of replacement staff through recruitment, appointment, and training. Employers additionally lose out financially through lost productivity and missed deadlines. Employees who remain in the company can be burdened with additional workloads, which can dampen their morale, thus affecting their productivity too.

Absenteeism

Because loneliness can lead to physical and mental health conditions (see earlier and Chapters 9 and 10 for a more detailed discussion), workers who feel lonely are more likely to be absent from work due to sickness. This can be costly for businesses. Loneliness has an estimated annual cost to US employers of over $154B, accounting for approximately 5.7 additional days missed by lonely employees compared to those who are not lonely.

The cost of absenteeism of workers in the UK due to health-related loneliness is estimated to be £20 million per year. There are additional costs to employers when their employees become caregivers for people whose health conditions can be attributed to loneliness. In the UK the annual cost of absenteeism to employers is estimated to be around £220 million.

Reduced productivity

Employees who feel lonely are likely to be less productive than those who are more socially connected. This can be due to a number of factors, including weaker memory and recall, difficulties in decision-making, poorer judgment, and reduced creativity and motivation. Productively can also be affected by higher rates of absenteeism and increased labor turnover among lonely staff. The combined impact of loneliness on productivity has significant costs for employers. The estimated costs of the reduction in productivity attributable to loneliness in the UK per year are around £665 million. Comparable data aren't available at the moment for the USA, but the figure is likely to be much higher.

TIP

Whether you're an employer who's facing escalating business costs due to a lonely workforce or an employee who's experiencing loneliness and realizing that it's adversely affecting your performance at work, you can easily make changes to ensure that your working environment is less lonely, more productive, and thus more profitable. Chapter 6 shares a range of tips and strategies for both employers and employees. If you're an employer, by adopting the strategies that I outline, you'll find that you can tackle loneliness and have a more productive and resilient workforce, where there's a greater sense of organizational identity. This will help your business maintain performance and withstand economic challenges. If you're an employee, by trying out some of the tips in Chapter 6, you'll become a happier and more productive worker, which will in turn boost your levels of work satisfaction and career development. If an employment change is making you feel lonely, turn to Chapter 12.

NATIONAL RESPONSES

A growing international recognition of the escalating costs of loneliness has led some countries to develop national loneliness strategies. Lobbyist and campaign groups, with a mission to reduce loneliness and its negative impact, have also begun to emerge in several countries. I provide details here of some of the nations that have developed strategies to tackle loneliness. There's pressure in a number of other countries to follow suit.

- **The UK response:** In 2018 the UK was the first country to appoint a minister for loneliness. At the same time, it developed the first-ever national loneliness strategy, A Connected Society: A Strategy for Tackling Loneliness, laying the foundations for change. This strategy lay the groundwork for other countries to follow suit. The UK's national loneliness strategy set out three overarching objectives: 1. To reduce the stigma of loneliness by facilitating national conversations about it; 2. To get loneliness on the agenda of the policy-making and service delivery organizations; 3. To improve the evidence base on loneliness, measuring changes over time and as a result of service interventions. The UK government has made funds available for loneliness initiatives and services and carries out regular annual updates of progress made in tackling loneliness across the nation. The Campaign to End Loneliness is a kind of lobbyist group in the UK that's funded through various sources, including trusts, financial and in-kind donations from companies, and donations from the general public. The campaign has been instrumental in tackling loneliness in the UK since as far back as 2011. The vision for the campaign is that everyone can live a life free from chronic loneliness.

- **Australia's fight against loneliness:** Inspired by the Campaign to End Loneliness in the UK, Ending Loneliness Together (ELT) was set up in 2016 and is Australia's national organization working to tackle loneliness. It represents a national network of organizations and aims to raise awareness and reduce the negative effects of chronic loneliness and social isolation. Its current focus is on building the evidence on interventions to tackle loneliness. Although Australia doesn't currently have a national loneliness strategy, members of parliament are involved in ELT.

(continued)

(continued)

- **Fighting loneliness in Japan:** Following the UK's lead, Japan established a minister for loneliness in 2021. This was largely a response to the impact of Covid-19 on loneliness and social isolation and the increasing rates of suicides linked to loneliness. The ministerial appointment was shortly followed by the development of a governmental loneliness priority plan that includes a focus on creating a place of belonging and a national counseling system to support those who are lonely.

- **US reaction:** In 2023 the US Surgeon General responded to what has been called "the loneliness epidemic" by producing an advisory, Our Epidemic of Loneliness and Isolation: The U.S. Surgeon General's Advisory on the Healing Effects of Social Connection and Isolation. The Advisory explores how to build more connected lives and a more connected society and community. In the US, advisories are set aside for significant public health challenges that require the nation's immediate awareness and action. This advisory is a public statement that highlights loneliness as an urgent public health issue and provides recommendations for how to address it. It puts forward a national strategy to advance social connection that includes six pillars: 1. Strengthen social infrastructure in local communities; 2. Enact pro-connection public policies; 3. Mobilize the health sector; 4. Reform digital environments; 5. Deepen our knowledge; 6. Cultivate a culture of connection.

- **Dealing with loneliness in Demark:** The National Partnership Against Loneliness in Denmark is supported by the Danish government and brings together over a hundred key organizations. It puts forward Denmark's first strategy, Together Against Loneliness — A National 2040 Strategy for Reducing Loneliness, and action plan to tackle loneliness in 2023. The plan aims to reduce loneliness by half by 2040 and focuses on five key life areas in which loneliness should be prevented and addressed: home and living; daycare, school and education; leisure and communities; working life and employment; and health and care.

Social prescribing for loneliness

Social prescribing is also known as *community referral* and refers to a process whereby health professionals refer patients to support in the community to improve their health and well-being. Social prescribing has become fairly widespread in the UK and has started to become more prevalent in other countries in recent years. There have been movements toward social prescribing in the US, Canada, and Australia, and it's said to be in operation in more than 17 countries in Europe, Asia, Australia, and North America.

Social prescribing is a nonmedical referral that a range of health and social professionals use, including doctors, nurses, allied health medical staff, and social workers. You can also refer yourself to this kind of support. Quite often there's a social prescribing specialist or a link worker associated with health and social care professionals who can suggest which local services are available and suitable for you. Local volunteer and community sector groups often provide the local services.

If you're socially prescribed a loneliness service, it can include a range of options, including physical exercise classes, yoga or Tai Chi sessions, gardening or DIY activities, art or singing classes, befriending support or peer support groups, or respite care for a loved one. The list is endless.

If you're lonely and feel that it's starting to affect your health and well-being, make an appointment with your doctor or health care center and ask if they can recommend any local services. If your health care professionals don't use social prescribing or you can't be socially prescribed to any local services, you can find further tips on how to get support for many of these services in the relevant chapters of this book.

For more information on social prescribing see the Appendix.

2

Creating Havens of Social Connection and Belonging

IN THIS CHAPTER

» **Establishing a new pad**

» **Having kids and emptying the nest**

» **Experiencing loneliness in marriage**

» **(Re)connecting at home**

Chapter **4**
Making Connections at Home

Your home is assumed to be a place where you feel at ease and comfortable even when you don't feel like you fit in or belong elsewhere. The saying "Home Sweet Home" denotes that home is where you feel happy. Although this is often the case, home can also be a place where you feel lonely and isolated, even if you live with other people. You might feel lonely at home all the time, or you might have periods when you feel connected and comfortable at home, and other times when you feel completely isolated and lonely. Feeling lonely at home can hit you particularly hard.

REMEMBER

Loneliness can strike at any time and in any place. Although you may feel as though you shouldn't feel lonely in your own home, it's completely normal. Many people do, and everyone's likely to feel lonely there at some point in their life. This feeling of loneliness is unpleasant and uncomfortable, but you can break out of it and create a happy and connected home.

In this chapter I focus on feeling lonely at home when living with other people. I explain some of the reasons you might feel this way and offer tips and strategies to reverse it. First, I discuss the loneliness experienced when you set up your home with a partner for the first time. I then discuss how living with in-laws can lead to lonely feelings. I then talk about the impact that having children can have on your connections at home. Next, I discuss what to do when you feel lonely in your marriage or relationship, followed by a discussion about how caring for loved ones at home can make you feel lonely and isolated.

In each of these sections I share some useful tips and strategies to help you overcome your feelings of loneliness at home. I finish the chapter with some overall techniques you can use.

Moving In with a Partner

Setting up a new home can be an exciting time in your life whatever the circumstances. But moving also comes with some upheaval. You probably expect the lead-up and the aftermath of moving day to be stressful, yet the changes that moving can have on your social relationships may be unexpected.

When you first move in with a partner, whether cohabiting or following marriage, it can be a surprisingly lonely and isolating experience. You can be excited and optimistic about your future with your soul mate, but you can also feel lonely, especially in your new home, because living together takes time to get used to. If you've been dating for a while, you might think that you know your partner and are fully prepared for what you're letting yourself into. But quite often living with someone on a permanent basis can be challenging. You can feel lonely during the initial adjustment period. Little things about your partner's lifestyle might annoy you and cause temporary rifts in your relationship.

REAL WORLD EXAMPLE

Anita is 29 years old. She was in a relationship with a man for 10 years before recently moving in with her new partner, Thomas. They bought a house together and were both looking forward to settling down and having children. The house was 30 miles from where Anita had lived previously and where the rest of her family and friends were based. Not long after they moved in together, Anita started to feel lonely. She liked to go to bed at a reasonable time so she could be fresh for work the next day, but Thomas liked to stay up until the early hours of the morning playing on his game console and drinking beer. Anita soon started to feel as though she spent more time with Thomas when they weren't living together. Previously, her family and many of her friends were just a stone's throw from her house, so she could pop in for a chat whenever she felt like it. Now she felt alone and isolated in her new home.

If you feel lonely after setting up a home with your partner or spouse, the most important thing to remember is that this is likely to be a temporary feeling while you adjust to living together. You need to learn more about each other's lives, your different routines, and the rituals that have developed over time. You'll eventually start to adapt your behavior a little so that your lifestyles become more synchronized. If this doesn't happen or doesn't happen quickly enough for you and you're feeling lonely and isolated, you can take some simple steps to improve the quality of your relationship with you partner and develop additional relationships in your new neighborhood.

Here are some tips for newly cohabitating couples.

Scheduling time with one another

Agree with your partner about a specific time each week for spending some quality time together. This could involve cooking a meal and eating it together, gardening, or playing a game. Try to find an activity you can do together in your new home rather than outside of it. This will help you make meaningful connections in your new home so it becomes a less isolating and lonely place.

Introducing yourselves as a couple

This will help you create a wider social network so that you're not completely relying on your partner for a meaningful relationship. Your neighbors may eventually become good friends.

Once you've introduced yourselves to neighbors, invite a few of them over for dinner. Invite neighbors whom both you and your partner have things in common with. Spend time with your partner preparing the meal and identifying topics of conversation that you can broach with your neighbors. This will create a bond between you as a couple and help you form happy and positive memories in your home.

Keeping other connections

Keep in regular contact with your existing friends and family. Sometimes people feel that if they move in with a partner, they need to spend all their time together, but doing so can lead them to disconnect from their existing friends and family. Try not to let this happen. It's important to maintain your existing social networks. Even if you've moved to another town, city, or even country, keeping in touch is easier now than ever before. Use the many technological advances available today to stay in touch and maintain those quality relationships. I provide some useful ideas on how to do this in Chapter 7.

Making yourself a local

It's a good idea to carry out meaningful activities in your new neighborhood. Find a local club or activity that you can enjoy on your own and another that you can enjoy with your partner. That way you're creating opportunities for bonding activities with your partner but also creating activities for you to do alone so that you build up your own personal resilience and a buffer to protect yourself from loneliness. This will help you avoid both *emotional loneliness* (where you lack a personal intimate relationship) and *social loneliness* (where you lack a social network). If you're not sure which local clubs exist, ask around, do some research at your local library, or do an internet search. Sometimes you can find ads or posters in local shops too.

Volunteering in your local community

Volunteering is something you can do as a couple or on your own. It's a great way to get to know people in your local community, help others, and connect with new people. By helping other people, you'll feel more confident, gain a sense of purpose and self-worth, which will make you more resilient to loneliness. If you want some tips on how to get involved in volunteering, see Chapter 14.

Living with the In-Laws

You might find yourself living with your partner and your in-laws. Although it can be a successful and positive step for all concerned, it can also lead you to feel lonely and isolated, at least initially.

REMEMBER

In some cultures, living with the extended family after marriage is commonplace and even expected. In these circumstances you might anticipate that being surrounded by your extended family will act as a buffer to loneliness. Indeed, this is sometimes the case. Some South Asian women I talked to who moved in with their extended family following marriage felt socially connected. They told me the home was filled with lots of activity, and they were far from lonely. But other South Asian women felt lonelier after moving in with their extended family because they didn't necessarily gel or have much in common with their in-laws.

In other cultures, particularly in Western society, living with in-laws is rare and may even be a last resort. Couples might move in with the in-laws for financial, practical, or circumstantial reasons. Regardless of why you're living with your in-laws or how well you get along with them, it can create a tricky living situation. You might feel out of place, left out, like you don't belong there, and disconnected from your partner (who's the reason you're there in the first place). It can be difficult to maintain the privacy and intimacy of a meaningful relationship with your partner while living in the home of in-laws.

TIP

Regardless of the reason, if you're currently living with your in-laws and feel lonely, know that your feelings of loneliness and isolation are valid even if you're surrounded by lots of people. You can feel lonely in a crowd. I share some simple steps that you can try next. If you haven't yet moved in with your in-laws but are going to in the near future, perhaps you can start thinking about how to accomplish some of these steps in advance of the move. That way you're less likely to become lonely when you eventually move in.

When trying out ideas to help you feel less lonely or avoid becoming lonely, remember that there isn't one simple solution to everyone's challenges in this area. The kinds of solutions that will work for you depend on the relationship you have with your in-laws, as well as the relationship your partner has with them. It will also depend on the reasons you're living with your in-laws, whose choice it was to move in, and any cultural norms and expectations. The way you feel connected to the home and your fellow household members will be governed by the daily routines of those living in the household, the household dynamics, and the extent to which you have things in common with your in-laws.

Avoiding misunderstanding and conflict

Have an honest discussion with your spouse and then in-laws if cultures allow. If possible, do this before you move in so that you can air your concerns and make moving in as smooth as possible. That way you can avoid early conflict or misunderstandings, which can help you get along and reduce any feelings of isolation or loneliness you may feel if relationships become strained. Agree to a broad plan with your partner, and let them do the talking. Let your in-laws know that you really appreciate them welcoming you into their home, and you want to ensure that you all get along. Discuss as many details about the arrangement as possible, so that everyone is on the same page. In some families and cultures, this will be more difficult than in others, so you'll need to adapt your approach accordingly. Be guided by your partner. They should know what will and won't be acceptable to their family.

TIP

Be yourself, and accept yourself for who you are. This might feel difficult when living in someone's home, where routines and ways of behavior have already been informally agreed upon among household members. Although it's important to blend into the household that's inviting you into their home, it's equally important to be yourself without causing disrespect. I provide some helpful suggestions on how to be yourself in Chapter 13.

Being open and honest with your partner

Find time and space to talk to your partner and express how you feel. Explain that you're grateful for the hospitality of your in-laws (even if you don't feel they're being very welcoming). Make sure you explain to your partner how you're feeling; don't assume that they'll know. Ask your partner how they're feeling about the situation too. Maybe they're feeling lonely or isolated too. They may feel like they're trying to please you and their parents, which is a difficult position to be in.

Agree with your partner to spend some time with together alone on a regular basis, doing something as simple as going on a short walk together each day, eating out for dinner, or visiting a place where you both feel a sense of belonging. Use the time to be yourself and enjoy your partner's company.

Making meaningful connections with your in-laws

Find ways to make meaningful connections with your in-laws. Discover what they're interested in, and share your interests with them. If you're from different cultural backgrounds and it's appropriate, share your traditional food and celebrations with them and help them get to know you better.

Engage in some meaningful activities with your partner and in-laws in the home. This will help you bond and create positive meaningful relationships, but it will also help you feel more comfortable when living in their home. See if you can find some common ground that you can do together or talk about together. This might involve playing a game, having a special meal, or watching a film together. Run some ideas by your partner since they know what makes the in-laws tick.

Maintaining other relationships

Just as with any new cohabitating situation, make time to maintain your relationship with your family and friends. If you feel lonely at home, retaining contact with your wider social network can ease the impact of that loneliness. If you're a long way from family or friends, make connections through technology. (See Chapter 7 for some ideas on how to do this.)

Getting out of the house

Get out of the house regularly to do some meaningful activities you enjoy, or go to places where you feel a sense of belonging. You can do these alone, with your partner, or with the in-laws. Perhaps experiment doing these activities and visiting these places both on your own and with others in the household to see which helps most with your feelings of loneliness. There are some useful tips on these in Chapters 5, 14, and 15.

Having and Raising Children

Having a family of your own can be a rewarding and fulfilling experience and is often the way to ensure that you have family to connect with in later life. However, parenthood can also be a lonely and isolating experience. For some women, the feelings of isolation and loneliness start when they're pregnant as they deal with the physical and emotional changes associated with becoming a mother, especially if it's for the first time. For other mothers, loneliness can emerge in the postpartum period and can be tied up with post-natal depression. Fathers, too, face a changing role and, in particular, can be adversely affected by the attention of their partner moving away from them and being directed primarily toward their offspring. Parents who are most likely to be adversely affected by loneliness are mothers, young parents, and parents on low incomes.

REMEMBER

Parenthood, especially for the first time, leads to a major change in your identity, your relationships with your spouse or partner, your family and friends, your daily routine, and your overall way of life. Becoming a new parent can make you feel a loss of identity and can change your existing relationships with your partner, family, and friends. You can feel too tired to go out and socialize or to take time off for yourself. If you're a new mom, you additionally have to deal with changes to your body and your new role in life. These changes sometimes take time adjusting to. The changes are often accompanied by a mix of complex emotions that surface when you're not always best placed to deal with them. The demands of caring for your children can lead to a lack of sleep and exhaustion and a need to balance caring for children with household chores and paid work. The emotional challenges of parenthood can sometimes seem doubly hard.

In everyday life, you can experience loneliness as a parent in many ways:

>> **You might feel overwhelmed by tasks or overly worried about your child's health or your own health.** At times like this you need to seek out help, but you might feel embarrassed about seeking additional help or feel you're not allowed to ask for help. These circumstances can make you feel very lonely.

>> **You may feel as though all you ever do is tasks relating to the baby or children and that you don't have time to be anything other than a parent.** Regardless of how much you love your child or children, you might be fed up talking in baby language and yearn for some quality time or meaningful conversations with fellow adults that don't involve children.

>> **You may find that you've given up doing all the things you used to enjoy because all your time is devoted to child rearing and other domestic tasks.** This can make you feel lonely because you're missing meaningful activities in your life. You might not always make a conscious decision to give up these activities. Sometimes it just happens over time.

>> **You may have little time or energy to meet friends and family.** They might not be available to meet when you are, or they might want to engage in activities that no longer suit you as a parent. This can make you feel cut off and lonely, as though your role has simply become one of parent, not a person in your own right with your own needs.

Whatever the reason that you feel lonely or are isolated as a parent, you're not alone. Loneliness among parents is common. Fortunately, you can try some quick and easy solutions to ease the feeling.

The following are strategies for dealing with loneliness as a parent.

Sharing how you feel

Tell your partner, family, and friends how you're feeling. It can sometimes be difficult to admit your loneliness to yourself, let alone to others around you. However, if you're feeling lonely, admitting it is the first step to changing the situation. If you're not entirely sure if you're lonely, carry out the assessment in Chapter 2. If the results show you're lonely, it's time to accept it and talk to family and friends about it. Other parents can be particularly useful to talk to because, chances are, they've been through something similar themselves at some point. Just talking to others might make you realize that you're not alone in your feelings, that loneliness is a normal part of being a parent.

Contacting support groups

If you can't talk to family and friends, or even if you can, it's helpful to contact local parent support groups. These groups often offer activities for parents and their children and assist you in meeting other parents. They can be good opportunities to discuss your loneliness with other parents who are feeling the same, and to make new friends. You can also try online support groups that are available through social media groups. There are too many available to mention, but a quick search on your favorite social media platform will open up a whole world of online support. If you're not sure where to start, turn to Chapter 7 for some further tips.

Spending time with your partner, friends, and extended family

Parenthood can often be quite full on. You can be so busy looking after your children that you forget about your relationship with others. Be sure to allocate some regular slots for that. Go out for a walk. Get a babysitter and have a date night. If you can't get out, wait for the kids to go to bed and have a special meal in.

If you can, try to meet friends and family occasionally without your children so that you spend some time focusing just on you and your needs. If you can't easily find time away, you can talk to friends by phone, online, or through email, text, or social media apps (see Chapter 7). Try doing this after you've put your children to bed. Sometimes you might feel too tired to make the effort, even for a simple text message, but you'll feel much better for it if you do. You may even gain a renewed sense of energy because your mind is diverted onto other issues for a brief while.

Engaging with the world beyond parenthood

Make small talk when you're out and about. Whether you're taking a walk in the local park with the kids, standing at a bus stop, or passing people in the parking lot at the grocery store, try smiling and saying hello to passersby. Not everyone will respond, but many will. This small act will make you and them feel better, and it might even lead to longer conversations, which could eventually lead to newfound friendships.

Allocate some time to visiting places where you feel a sense of belonging. When you're a parent, especially a new or first-time parent, it's often difficult to find time to do anything for yourself. But if there's a particular place that makes you feel happy, it's worth taking a trip there. Take your child along with you if you can't get there without them. Being in your special place will undoubtedly make you feel more relaxed, connected, and refreshed.

Try to find time to make regular trips to your special place. It could be by the coast, a lake, or a mountain. Maybe it's a local park, a sports stadium, or just a special bench in your garden. If your special place is some distance away or you just can't get there at the moment because of your childcare responsibilities, try visiting it virtually. You can do this in various ways, all from the comfort of your own home (see Chapter 7).

WARNING

Sometimes you can feel lonelier if you visit a place virtually that you can't physically get to at the moment. If this happens to you, wait a while before you visit it virtually again. Sometimes when you return a second time, the feelings of loneliness or sadness are replaced by feelings of belonging. If you continuously feel lonelier when visiting a place that you can't get to physically, cease visiting it virtually and try some of the other techniques I've provided.

Getting outside and staying active

Get outside as much as possible for physical activities. This will enable you to engage in meaningful activities, supply you with endorphins so you feel less depressed, and give you an opportunity to meet other people to chat with. You might want to try enrolling in a local gym (some have childcare facilities). Or you could seek out a park run on a Saturday morning. The distance is always 5k, and you can either walk it or run it. There are park runs in operation all over the world, but you can find the ones in the US at https://www.parkrun.us/. They're free to join and are a great way to meet other people while keeping fit and healthy. You can take your children and push them in their stroller or get the older kids to run or walk with you.

TIP

Being outside is good for your well-being, but if it's rainy or cold, it can be nice to have indoor options to keep physically active and boost your endorphins. You can follow lots of exercise, dance, yoga, and meditation classes online. Many are free of charge, and you can experiment to find the ones that suit you best. Once you've found the session or app that fits your style, try to allocate a set time for this activity on a regular weekly basis. Some of them have chat functions so you can communicate with other like-minded people.

Exploring new, meaningful activities

If you can find time, try to prioritize participating in a hobby or an activity that's of interest to you. It could be joining a choir, learning to play a musical instrument, creating arts and crafts projects, or learning a foreign language — anything that interests you and gives you a sense of purpose. As a parent, your free time for spending on hobbies or other activities of interest is often limited and maybe even nonexistent. If this is the case for you, try an online app that you can use in the comfort of your own home. If you decide on this option, make sure you allocate a few minutes each day to engage in the activity. When one of my friends had young children, she spent just five minutes a day learning German on an online app. It gave her a renewed sense of purpose and something to look forward to on a daily basis.

WARNING

If you're a new mother and are feeling lonely, isolated, anxious, or depressed and the techniques listed here aren't helping you, you may have post-natal depression. Don't worry if this sounds like you. Many women experience it, but it usually eases over time. However, if your symptoms have been around for a while and aren't improving, arrange an appointment with your doctor, who can refer you to specialist services. Your doctor might refer you for psychological support or counseling. You can find some useful information about the different options available in Chapter 13. I had post-natal depression following the birth of my first child and felt sad and lonely most days. However, once I found a suitable solution, which for me was homeopathy, I felt like a new person, eager to engage in life again.

There are some helpful hotlines and resources in the Appendix too.

Managing as empty nesters

Another key life transition point that can lead to loneliness is when your children grow up and leave home. They might be moving away for college or moving in with a partner or spouse following marriage. This is sometimes referred to as the empty nest syndrome. It's often experienced when your last offspring moves out of the family home. You can feel it even when other relatives are living in the house. It can lead to mixed emotions. You can feel proud and excited for the future happiness of your children as they become independent adults, but at the same time you can experience loneliness, a sense of loss, and grief. You might also experience symptoms such as depression, sleeplessness, loss of appetite, sadness, and anxiety. You may find that you have difficulty concentrating or have bouts of temporary confusion.

REMEMBER

The main caregiver tends to feel the empty nest syndrome more strongly. Often this is the mother. Sometimes parents respond quite differently to their children leaving home, which can contribute to them feeling less connected as a couple. This in turn can intensify the feelings of loneliness and isolation in the home once the children have gone.

Many parents every year experience empty nest syndrome. The good news is that, for most, it's a temporary experience. Once you've adjusted to the peace and quiet, you can actually enjoy spending more time with your partner or more time doing things for yourself. What's more, you can keep in touch with your offspring easily and can start enjoying more quality time with them now that you're not nagging them about keeping the noise down, leaving dirty laundry around the house, or putting their dishes in the sink instead of in the dishwasher.

TIP

If you're feeling lonely because your children have grown up and moved out, don't worry. The following sections provide tips for making the transition to being an empty-nester. Regardless of how you spend your time, keeping busy after your last child flies the coop is key to adjusting to the change with minimal loneliness. This can be especially helpful in the early days after your children leave. Throw yourself into your work or a new hobby, get fit, or take up a sport. Think about all the things you've wanted to do in the past few years as your children have been growing up and throw yourself into them.

Acknowledging how you feel

You may well be experiencing the empty nest syndrome if you're feeling lonely and isolated after your children have left home. You might get some warning that you're going to feel lonely when your last child leaves home, or you might feel that you're handling it well but then be suddenly hit by a wave of loneliness or sadness. These feelings can be triggered by specific things, such as hearing your child's favorite music on the radio or finding an item of their clothing in the house. The adjustment time to your offspring leaving home can vary depending on your relationship and the specific circumstances. Just acknowledge and accept your feelings and allow yourself time to adjust to your new living circumstances.

Preparing and planning for life after the nest is empty

As soon as you know that your child is moving out of the family home, start preparing, even if you still have other children living at home, and even if you don't feel as though you're going to be affected by their departure. The better prepared and ready for the move you are, the less of a shock it will be when moving day arrives. Use this time to teach your child any necessary skills they may not have for independent living, such as financial management, cooking skills, painting, and decorating. Also use it as a time to start developing a list of things you've put on hold while your children have been growing up and that you're now able to do. If you have a partner or spouse living with you, involve them in the discussions and plan some nice things to do together that you've not been able to do in the past few years.

Remaining calm

Don't panic if you can't plan for your child leaving home. Sometimes there might be a last-minute decision or a sudden change of plans. If this occurs, keep calm, and take a few deep breaths. Tell your child you're happy for them, and when you get a few spare minutes to yourself, write a list of the benefits to your child of leaving home and another list of all the things you'll be able to do once they've moved out. Like all major changes in life, if you approach it with a positive mindset, you're more likely to adapt to the change more smoothly and easily.

Agreeing to expectations with your child

Discuss with your child the ways that you're going to keep in touch. Try to keep a balance between allowing your child to branch out and live an independent life as an adult, while retaining some forms of communication between you as a family. Explore with your child and any other siblings the preferred modes of communication — text, video calls, phone calls, voice messages. Keep in mind that they might have different communication styles and preferences than you do. Be sensitive to their wishes. At the same time, if your child asks for a communication method that you don't understand or know how to use, ask them to give you some simple training on it before they leave home. Determine whether you're going to keep in touch on an ad hoc basis or are going to have a regular time each day or each week when you're going to make contact. That way you'll all know what to expect and won't be waiting around for your offspring to contact you.

Strengthening connections with your partner

As your children are growing up, it's easy to neglect your relationship with your partner. Once your kids have moved out, it's a good time to reconnect with your partner and do things together that you enjoy. Sometimes it can take a while to reconnect with your partner, so give it time. Take the initiative and arrange a date night to the cinema, for a meal, or to the local bar. You could also do something more active, like bowling or trying a high ropes course. Or perhaps you can plan home improvements now that the children have moved out. You might decide to go to that vacation destination you've always longed to visit but have been unable to afford. Of course, you might find that once your children flee the nest, you have very little in common with your partner and have grown apart over the years. If you or your partner feel like this, you might want to try couples counseling. But quite often if something connected you in the first place, you can reignite the flame.

Embracing the peacefulness

Appreciate the peace and quiet of your home once again, and enjoy spending some quality time on your own at home. You might decide to read a good novel, listen to some music, or just chill out with your favorite drink, enjoying the tranquility of your own home. Remember, it might not be long before your home is busy again with grandchildren coming to stay, so make the most of the peace and quiet while you can!

If you're feeling particularly depressed following your children leaving home or are having difficulties in your marriage or partnership with your children gone, a number of helplines listed in the Appendix can offer you support.

WARNING

Don't be tempted to make a major decision until you've come through the empty nest syndrome. You might feel as though you want to move to a smaller home or even separate from your partner, but wait a while until you've adjusted to your new living arrangements before making any rash decisions.

Finding Yourself Trapped in a Lonely Relationship

If you're in a long-term relationship and that relationship is making you feel lonely, you're probably experiencing a form of emotional loneliness.

Emotional loneliness is when you lack a close emotional attachment to someone, usually a romantic partner. If you're single or have been previously married or in a long-term relationship, emotional loneliness is pretty common. But you can also experience it when you're in a long-term relationship that isn't giving you the kind of emotional attachment you need or desire. In these cases, this kind of loneliness can actually feel stronger than if you don't have a partner at all.

Feeling lonely in a marriage or in a long-term relationship isn't uncommon. There are reports that around a third of married people in some countries feel lonely in their marriage. So if you feel lonely in your marriage or relationship and are worrying that your feeling isn't normal, be assured that it's not unusual. Plenty of other people are facing similar situations.

TIP

A first step is to look for signs that you might be feeling lonely in your marriage. Ask yourself if you feel or experience any of the following, and put a tick next to the ones that apply to you:

>> You don't feel as though you have a meaningful connection with your partner. You don't talk about things that are meaningful. Your conversations are merely superficial, focusing on trivial topics like what you're having for dinner, household repairs or chores, and the weather.

>> You feel lonely even when you're with your partner. In fact, sometimes you feel lonelier when you're with them.

>> You find reasons not to spend time with your partner and enjoy the company of other people more.

>> You don't have many romantic or sexual experiences with your partner, and when you do, you don't feel an intimate connection with them.

If more than one of these resonates with your relationship, you might be feeling lonely in your marriage.

TIP

For a full assessment of whether you feel lonely, complete the loneliness measurement scales in Chapter 2.

QUIZ: ARE YOU EMOTIONALLY LONELY WITH YOUR PARTNER?

Here's a quick quiz to determine if you're feeling emotionally lonely. Ask yourself the following questions:

1. Do I experience a general sense of emptiness when with my partner?

Yes; More or less; No.

2. Do I miss having people around me when I'm with my partner?

Yes; More or less; No.

3. Do I often feel rejected by my partner?

Yes; More or less; No.

If you answer yes or more or less on questions, give yourself a score of 1, and give yourself a score of 0 for no. Then total your scores.

If you score 0, you're not emotionally lonely in your marriage/relationship.

If you score 1, you're a little emotionally lonely in your marriage/relationship.

If you score 2, you're emotionally lonely in your marriage/relationship.

If you score 3, you're intensely emotionally lonely in your marriage/relationship.

If after totaling your scores you find you're emotionally lonely in your marriage, don't worry. I provide some information on why you might be feeling like this and how to reduce these feelings of loneliness.

I explain in Chapter 2 that marriage tends to be associated with a decrease in loneliness and is one of the main and strongest protective factors against loneliness. It's not surprising then, that if you feel lonely in your marriage, it can come as quite a shock.

REMEMBER

You might feel lonely in your marriage or relationship for a whole range of reasons:

>> You don't have as much in common as you first thought, or your respective interests have moved in different directions over time.

- One or both of you is experiencing stress due to work, family issues, a traumatic event, or bereavement.

- You don't have enough quality time to spend together due to work or family pressures.

- You and your partner have different expectations of the relationship.

- You don't have a close intimate connection, or sex is unsatisfying.

- You feel your partner's behavior is insensitive.

- You perceive your relationship to be inferior to those of others around you, your friends and family, people on social media, and celebrities.

Boris's experience is a good example of someone who feels lonely in his marriage. I came across Boris in some research I carried out a while ago.

Boris is a 45-year-old married man. He married the love of his life, Fatima, when he was 23. He frequently says that his wedding was the happiest day of his life. He and Fatima both work in highly pressurized jobs and have three children together. In the past few years Boris has started to feel increasingly lonely. Fatima no longer spends much time with him because she's always busy taking the kids to and from school and to activities after school. Their daughter is a keen soccer player, and Fatima spends most Saturdays supporting her daughter, while Boris looks after the other children. On Sundays Fatima spends most of the day resting and catching up with domestic chores. They rarely have sex because Fatima is usually too tired. Boris can't understand why Fatima doesn't want to spend time with him. All his friends are married with children, but they seem to spend time with their spouses. Boris feels neglected and lonely.

TIP

Although feeling lonely in a marriage or a relationship can be unpleasant and deeply unsatisfying, it's also quite normal and to be expected from time to time, especially when leading a busy and stressful life. However, that doesn't mean that loneliness in marriage is an inevitable consequence. You can take some easy steps to connect more with your partner, which I discuss here.

Sharing your feelings

If you feel lonely in your relationship, explain how you feel to your partner, and ask them how they feel. They might be feeling the same. Before you talk to them, plan carefully what you're going to say, how you are going to say it, and when. Select a time when you're feeling calm and rational, not when you're upset or full of emotions. Most importantly, don't blame your partner.

Making time to be together

Organize some regular quality time together where you can have meaningful interaction. Try to plan it together so it's something that you both want to do. It doesn't have to be an elaborate plan. It could simply involve going on a walk together or preparing and eating a meal together after the kids have gone to bed.

Once you've started talking and spending quality time together, introduce happy memories from your shared past. Maybe it's the first time you got together, your first holiday, or your wedding day. Look through old photos or video clips of both of you together. You could do this while listening to music that's significant to you as a couple, such as a hit from the time you first met or a song that was played at your wedding.

Plan a day trip, or an overnight stay if that's possible. Select somewhere that's meaningful to you as a couple. It could be a bar or restaurant where you first met, the site of your first date, or maybe your wedding venue. The location should evoke happy memories for both of you.

Try to spend a little bit of time each day focusing on your partner and your relationship with them. This doesn't have to take up too much time. It could simply involve a loving greeting when waking up, going to bed, or leaving the house. It could involve a small gesture, like making them a cup of tea or coffee. Perhaps it's buying them a small gift or maybe adding an item to the shopping cart that you know they'll appreciate.

Confiding in a friend of family member

Talk with a close friend or family member whom you can trust about the feelings you're having. Chances are, they'll have experienced something similar in their relationship or know someone who has.

WARNING

Don't be alarmed or upset if any of these strategies don't work immediately. It can sometimes take a bit of time to reconnect. However, if you've tried all these things and are still struggling with loneliness in your marriage, it might be worth exploring couples therapy or marriage counseling. Sometimes underlying issues are acting as a barrier to your connection. Expert counselors can identify these issues and help you deal with them.

There are some helplines listed in the Appendix which you can contact if you need further support.

Adjusting to Marriage by Arrangement

In some cultures, most notably South Asia, Southeast Asia, the Middle East, and parts of Africa, parents and family members play a key role in identifying a suitable spouse for their offspring. Families who come from these traditions but live in the Western World quite often continue the practice of parental involvement in arranging marriages. With the advent of technological advances, the way in which these marriages are arranged and organized has evolved quite a bit in recent years.

REMEMBER

An arranged marriage is a type of marital union where family members, such as parents, play a role in selecting the bride and groom. The widely held perception of a bride and groom meeting each other for the first time at their wedding isn't necessarily accurate, especially in contemporary society. Although in some cultures family, and in particular parents, continue to play a major role in selecting a bride or groom for their offspring, there seems to be a general movement toward children having more say in who their future spouse is.

TIP

Anyone can feel lonely in their marriage, both those who have selected their own spouse and those who have had their spouse selected for them. There hasn't been much research on whether you're more likely to feel lonely in an arranged marriage versus one you've chosen yourself. However, some research from Turkey suggests that self-selected marriages lead to lower loneliness than arranged marriages.

My research team recently spoke to some South Asian women who had marriages arranged by their parents. Many of them said they felt lonely following their marriage. They mentioned the difficulties transitioning from single to married life and explained that during the initial stage of marriage they felt lonely for two main reasons. First, they didn't really know their husband very well and needed time to get to know them and to adjust to their new life together. Second, they were often expected to move in with their husband's family, whom they didn't have a connection with yet. Sometimes they had to move miles away from their family and friends. The combination of being uprooted from their familiar environment, missing their home and their family and friends, and feeling like an outsider in their new home led to feelings of loneliness and isolation.

Nasreen, 22, had an arranged marriage a year ago. The marriage was arranged by her own parents and her husband's parents. Nasreen lived in a northern town in the UK with lots of family and friends close-by. Upon marriage, she was expected to move to London — more than 200 miles away from her home — to live with her husband and his family. She has felt very lonely since getting married. She feels left out and unable to connect in a meaningful way at home, to her husband, or his family.

TIP

If you're in an arranged marriage and are feeling lonely like Nasreen, remember that it's a perfectly understandable feeling, especially if you haven't had a chance to form a meaningful connection with your spouse, or if your marriage has meant moving away from friends or relatives and living with a new family whom you barely know. Forming meaningful bonds can take time.

Regardless of your particular marital situation and living arrangements, if you've had a marriage arranged for you and you're feeling lonely, here are some tips to help you feel less isolated.

Making an effort to connect with your partner

Chat regularly with your partner so that you can get to know them better. Tell each other what you're thinking and feeling, what you're enjoying about your married life, and what things are upsetting you. Regular communication can help you develop a meaningful relationship, which will reduce your feelings of loneliness in your marriage.

Make small gestures of appreciation on a regular basis. It's sometimes easy in a relationship to take each other for granted or to overlook all the things that your partner does for you, focusing solely on the tasks you do for them or the sacrifices you feel you're making. Try to take some time each day to show your appreciation to your partner.

Spend some time doing activities together. Discuss as a couple what these could be. List all the things each of you likes doing, and try to identify one or two that you can do together.

Share a meal together. Food is a great way to encourage people to bond. Find time and space to eat together alone with your spouse. If you can't do this at home, go out and have a meal in a café or restaurant. Or if the weather is nice, perhaps have a picnic. Pack some of your spouse's favorite foods to show you're thinking about them.

Balancing who you spend your time with

Keep in regular contact with your family and friends. Being married doesn't mean giving up time for yourself. If you've moved away from your family and friends, keep in touch by text or social media. Try to arrange regular weekly times when you can have a video chat.

Make an effort to get to know your extended family. If you're living together, it can be particularly helpful to form a bond with them so that you can feel a meaningful connection to them, and to your home. Both of these will help you feel less lonely. There are some more tips on how to do this earlier in the chapter in the section "Making meaningful connections with your in-laws."

Seeking support in your faith or in a local group

Ask God or a spiritual leader to help you in your relationship. If you're particularly spiritual or have a strong religious devotion, it can help to talk to, and ask for assistance from, God.

Go to your local support group. Most communities have support groups for different population groups, and they usually offer activities for like-minded people. These can be great places to meet people like yourself and discuss issues you're finding particularly difficult in your life right now. You can locate details of where and when support groups meet by looking online, at your local library, or at the community resource center.

Join a relevant social media support group online or through a social media app. It's a way to get advice and meet others, virtually, who are in a similar position to you.

Experiencing Domestic Abuse

People who have been subject to domestic abuse are often referred to as *domestic abuse survivors*. People of all ages, genders, gender identities, sexualities, and ethnicities experience domestic abuse. Both men and women and people identifying as LGBTQIA+ can be survivors of domestic abuse, although women are more likely to be affected than men.

Domestic abuse is more common than you might think. In the United States, more than 10 million adults experience domestic violence annually. One in four women, and one in ten men experience sexual violence, physical violence and/or stalking by an intimate partner during their lifetime. In the UK 2.4 million people face domestic abuse each year, with one in three being male. Survivors of domestic abuse face many challenging life circumstances, including physical and mental health implications, increased anxiety, depression and stress, a sense of helplessness, fear, and social withdrawal. They're also at heightened risk of feeling isolated and lonely.

Domestic abuse is any incident of threatening behavior, violence, or abuse between adults who are, or have been, intimate partners or family members, regardless of gender or sexuality.

Behavior is abusive if it consists of any of the following:

>> Physical or sexual abuse

>> Violent or threatening behavior

>> Controlling or coercive behavior

>> Economic abuse

>> Psychological, emotional, or other abuse

It doesn't matter if the behavior consists of a single incident or has occurred over a series of incidents. Abuse is rarely a one-off event, and domestic abuse behavior tends to get worse over time.

Survivors of domestic abuse are at risk of feeling isolated and lonely for a number of reasons:

>> **Perpetrators of abuse often try to isolate their victims from their family and friends.** The perpetrator can use this tactic to make the victim feel more vulnerable, lose confidence and self-esteem, and become more dependent on the abuser.

>> **Family and friends can sometimes actively exclude the survivor, making them feel even more isolated and lonely.** This often happens when family and friends get frustrated or annoyed that the survivor hasn't left the perpetrator. When this occurs, it's often because friends and family don't fully understand all the circumstances.

>> **The survivor can isolate themselves from family and friends.** There's often a perceived stigma attached to domestic abuse, and survivors might not feel able to admit it to themselves or their close friends and family. Survivors often experience depression, anxiety, and low self-esteem, and this can carry on long after the survivor has left the abusive relationship. All these factors can mean that survivors choose to isolate themselves from friends and family.

>> **Existing friendships can be severed.** When people are abused, they sometimes behave in ways that their friends don't understand and find difficult. Friends can make negative judgments, especially if they're not aware of the abuse or don't fully understand it. This can then damage relationships between survivors of domestic abuse and their friends.

TIP

If you're a domestic abuse survivor, whether you're being abused currently or have been in the past and feel lonely, it's important to remember that feeling lonely in these circumstances is entirely understandable. It's also important to remember that the abuse isn't your fault. I provide some tips here to help you feel less lonely and to start rebuilding your life. Just take one step at a time.

Finding support

Contact your local domestic abuse support group or center. Most localities have a group or helpline that can offer advice and a whole host of support mechanisms. These can include group activities, reading groups, coffee mornings, walking groups, exercise classes, befriending services, and access to counseling support. All of these initiatives can help you make connections with people who've been through a similar experience or who understand how you feel. This can help you make new friends and access the kind of support you need.

Reaching out to other people

Reconnect with family and friends you may have lost meaningful contact with. Chapters 5 and 14 discuss various ways to help you reconnect with friends and family. But following an abusive relationship, you might need some additional support to help you do this. You might need to open up about the abuse. Your family and friends might hold negative judgments about some of your behavior, which you'll need to work through. Or the perpetrator might have turned them against you. However, with support, you can make progress toward rebuilding connections with family and friends. You can access help through the support groups mentioned earlier, national helplines, or social media support groups. Do a quick internet search for the support available near you, or look for ads in your local library, health center, or at the doctor's surgery. Useful information for survivors of domestic abuse is often displayed in public restrooms too.

Seeking out psychological support

I provide details about the different types of psychological support available for loneliness in Chapter 13. It might help to read through the options to decide which suits you. You can then look for a relevant therapist. Many therapists specialize in supporting survivors of domestic abuse. Depending on which country you're living in and what support is available, you might find that such support will involve a fee. However, if you're unable to pay, ask your local domestic abuse support group or your doctor for a referral. There's a useful list of helplines and support agencies in the Appendix.

Reengaging with activities from the past

Think about the activities you used to enjoy prior to connecting with the abusive partner, and spend some time engaging in those again. If you can't remember what you used to like doing or haven't been outside an abusive relationship, try some different activities and see which you enjoy. You could try gardening, learning a foreign language or a musical instrument, joining a gym or choir, volunteering. . . the list of possibilities is endless. Have a read through Chapter 14 for some ideas. Carrying out meaningful enjoyable activities is helpful to distract you from any negative influences in your life. It can also connect you with like-minded people with whom you can form a relationship over time.

WARNING

If you're experiencing domestic abuse or have been subjected to patterns of bullying or controlling behaviors, it's important that you get support. If you're concerned that you're suffering abuse or have left an abusive relationship and are struggling to cope with the aftermath, contact the relevant helplines listed in the Appendix. If you're in immediate danger call 911 in the US.

Creating a Connected Home

As I've discussed in this chapter, you might feel lonely in your own home for a whole range of reasons, such as setting up a home for the first time with a new partner, becoming a parent, becoming an empty nester, or having difficulties in your marriage. I've provided some tips for each of these in the appropriate sections of this chapter. In this section I offer you more solutions to try if you're feeling lonely and isolated at home. You can give these a try whatever the reason you're lonely at home.

Bonding through food

Food is a great way to bring people together to foster and maintain meaningful relationships, thus staving off loneliness. Both cooking together and eating together promote bonding. They encourage sharing of cultures and heritage, build bonds between generations, stimulate meaningful conversations, and promote a greater sense of empathy and trust between the individuals involved. Cooking and eating together can be particularly effective for bonding purposes, especially if done on a regular basis.

TIP

If you feel lonely, try cooking a meal for your household, or if you live alone, invite people around for a meal. Prepare a menu that you know will appeal to the rest of the household or your dinner guests. Think about some mealtime discussion topics in advance so that you can get the conversation started, if need be. If you're not very confident in the kitchen, you can suggest preparing a meal with other household members. That way the cooking experience can be a bonding mechanism, and you can all enjoy eating the fruits of your labor.

Playing together

There's a well-known saying: the family that plays together stays together. When families spend quality time engaging in activities together, such as playing games, they create strong and lasting bonds.

REMEMBER

Engaging in shared lighthearted activities such as playing board games, cards, electronic games, or traditional games like Charades can help families, individuals, or groups of individuals bond and create meaningful relationships. Playing games can build communication skills between individuals, help people work together to form solutions, and build patience and empathy.

TIP

Making time to play games and have fun with the rest of your household, whether it's one individual or a large extended family, can help you feel closer, more satisfied, and less lonely. If you live alone, consider inviting others over for a games night. You don't need to have close friends to do this. You could invite work colleagues or neighbors. Playing games is a good way to foster intergenerational bonds, such as between grandparents and grandchildren. It can also lighten the mood when there's tension, for example, between couples or between parents and teenagers. If the time you have together is limited, plan the games night in advance, when everyone can be there. If you're feeling adventurous, try combining a household meal with a games night to follow.

Scheduling date nights

It's easy to lose connection with your partner when there are so many other things going on in life that seem to take priority, whether that's looking after the children, going to work, doing household chores, or other activities that seem to consume a lot of time out of the day. You can find yourself so busy and exhausted with everyday life that you forget to spend time with each other. And this can contribute to you feeling lonely.

TIP

It can be a good idea to schedule regular date nights in your calendar so that there's an allocated time to help you rekindle and strengthen the relationship between you and your partner. Date nights can simply be a reminder to allow time to connect with your partner amid the chaos and stress of everyday life. And it doesn't have to be expensive. A date night could involve staying at home to watch a movie or listening to music together. Or it could be a little more adventurous, like going out for a meal at your favorite restaurant, strolling around the park or your neighborhood, or trying out a new venue. Most importantly, date nights help you maintain a connection with your partner.

Realizing the power of pets

Spending time around companion animals can provide mental health benefits and help with feelings of loneliness. According to the British Small Animal Veterinary Association (https://www.bsava.com/), companion animals are classified as "any domestic-bred or wild-caught animals, permanently living in a community and kept by people for company, enjoyment, work (e.g., support for blind or deaf people, police, or military dogs) or psychological support, including, but not limited to dogs, cats, horses, rabbits, ferrets, guinea pigs, reptiles, birds, and ornamental fish."

Companion pets can reduce loneliness by:

>> Offering companionship to their owners. This can be especially helpful if you live alone. Many pet owners talk to their pets.

>> Being a physical presence that demands routine and accountability, through feeding, playtime, and care.

>> Giving you a sense of purpose. Feeding your pet and taking care of it can be a good reason to get out of bed.

>> Helping fulfill the basic human need for touch. Stroking a dog, cat, or other animal and caring for them can help make you feel needed and wanted and can act as a form of stress relief.

>> Keeping you physically active and exposing you to other people. Some pets, such as dogs, need regular time walking outdoors. This keeps you physically active but can also increase your opportunities for meeting other dog owners and help you strike up conversations.

>> Reducing your anxiety and building your self-confidence. Pets tend to live in the moment and can help you appreciate the here and now instead of worrying about the future. This can be especially helpful if you're anxious about going out and meeting people.

TIP

If you think that having a pet is the way forward for you:

>> **Decide which kind of pet would best suit your lifestyle and home.** Do some research to make sure that you know what you're letting yourself in for. Some pets need more care and attention than others, so get one that you can commit to looking after.

>> **Visit animals shelters in your community.** After doing some research, you might feel that you don't have the time, money, or ability to own a pet. The good news is that you can experience the benefits of being around animals in other ways. One thing you can do is visit a local shelters.

>> **Look after someone else's pet.** That way you gain the companionship and benefits of a pet without all the responsibility. You can look out for dog walking or animal sitting opportunities online.

REMEMBER

It's important to research fully so you understand everything that caring for a pet entails. Getting a pet is a major commitment for the lifetime of the pet, which could be for 15 or more years. Ensure that you fully consider the implications before getting a pet. If in doubt, try looking after a pet as a first step.

Chapter 5

Belonging in Your Community

The neighborhood or community where you live can play a key role in determining whether you feel lonely and to what degree. Some communities enable social connections to thrive and facilitate positive social interaction and a true sense of belonging. Other can stifle social connections and generate a sense of disconnection.

A combination of factors relating to the social fabric, design, community facilities, and demographics of your neighborhood can make the difference between you feeling either socially connected and belonging, or disconnected and detached. Your local community is often where you carry out day-to-day activities and do the things you enjoy and that matter the most. It's important that you feel comfortable and accepted in your community and are able to engage in meaningful social encounters with others.

It's also helpful if you feel comfortable visiting and immersing yourself in the various places and spaces that exist locally. In this chapter I explore the factors that can lead you to feel lonely, isolated, and disconnected in your communities. I then outline some strategies you can adopt to feel more connected.

Feeling Disconnected in the Community

You might feel lonely and disconnected in your community for a variety of reasons. Your experience of loneliness in your neighborhood is determined by a mixture of your personal characteristics and circumstances, the demographics of the local population, and the facilities and social fabric of the community where you live.

In the following sections, I explore some of the factors that can contribute to making a community feel more or less lonely.

Rural retreats or city life

The extent to which you feel lonely in your community can depend on whether you live in a rural area or a large city. Both can have benefits and drawbacks, depending on who you are and what your personal circumstances are like.

If you live in a rural area or small town, you can find that your community is close-knit, and people tend to know each other. Passersby are more likely to engage in fleeting encounters like saying hello or asking how you're doing. Fellow citizens are also more likely to strike up conversations in local shops or community buildings, such as libraries or leisure facilities. All these can lead you to feel less lonely if you live in a rural area.

WARNING

However, rural communities and small towns are often more homogenous and less welcoming of people who are different due to their ethnicity or sexual orientation. It can also take newcomers some time to be accepted. I live in a semi-rural village in the UK, and when I moved there around 16 years ago, I was told in earnest by the locals that I was an "incomer" and that it would take me at least eight years to be accepted. Eight years!

Small towns can also sometimes feel a bit like a goldfish bowl because everyone knows your business. This can be stifling if you're introverted or fit into a marginalized group because of your eccentric behavior, ethnicity, religion, or something else.

All of these ingredients of rural life can be a recipe for greater loneliness for some people. What's more, your loneliness can feel amplified in a smaller town or rural community, where everyone knows each other. You can easily feel left out and isolated because there's simply no one else to turn to for friendship. Public transportation and social infrastructure can also be lacking, so it might be difficult to get out and about and meet other people whom you might have a meaningful interaction with.

If you live in a city, on the other hand, you're more likely to be living in a more densely populated area, and people are less likely to make small talk in the streets as they go about their everyday busy lives. There's less likely to be a sense of community or common values. You're more likely to be living in a heterogeneous community, where people from all walks of life are present. People are less likely to know each other, and you can sometimes feel anonymous.

For some, this can make city life feel isolating and lonely. For others it can feel more welcoming and accepting, especially for those who feel different due to their disability, their ethnicity, their sexual orientation, or something else entirely.

Cities are also more likely to offer a range of social and community infrastructure with a wider range of shops and leisure activities so that you can engage in meaningful activities and have opportunities for meeting other people. Public transportation is also likely to better serve urban populations, so accessing facilities is easier. It's easy to see then why, for some, city life can feel less lonely and isolating, while others can feel lonelier there.

TIP

If you feel lonely and think it might be triggered by the community you live in, write a list of all the attributes your community has and a separate list alongside it of all the negative features of your community. Then next to each of the positive attributes put a C if that feature makes you feel connected. Next to all the negative attributes, put an L if it makes you feel lonely. Total the number of Cs and Ls. If you have more Ls than Cs, it's likely that your community is contributing to your loneliness.

Regardless of whether your loneliness is caused by your living in a large urban metropolis or a small rural settlement, there are ways to combat these feelings. I provide some key strategies and techniques that you can try in the second half of this chapter.

Type of housing

Alongside the type of community you live in, the kind of housing you inhabit plays a role in how lonely you might feel. Across the globe, people live in all kinds of housing arrangements, including private detached houses, semi-detached or terraced private housing, apartments, and semi-permanent structures, trailers, squatter settlements, and slums. The type and design of housing can heavily influence your ability to connect with other people in your neighborhood and thus your experience of loneliness.

REMEMBER

Some research suggests that people who live in high-rise and one-story apartments are more likely to feel lonely and have a lower rate of well-being and mental health than those who live in single or low-rise multiple-story private accommodations. But it's not quite so simple as that.

If you live in a house that sits back from the street and you park your car in a garage, you might get few opportunities for chance meetings and interactions with your neighbors. You might not even know who your neighbors are. On the other hand, you might live in a high-rise property that has lots of well-designed communal areas and offers social activities that enable you to meet and socialize with your neighbors regularly. In essence then, the design and accompanying social infrastructure of your housing, as well as the type of housing, affects your experience of loneliness.

TIP

The following list offers some key housing features that may contribute to or ease your loneliness:

>> **Dark and narrow staircases, lifts, and corridors in apartment blocks:** These are likely to reduce social interactions, whereas wide and brightly lit corridors, staircases, and welcoming lobbies with comfortable seating are more likely to facilitate people using communal spaces and engaging in social networking.

>> **Communal spaces close to high-rise buildings:** These, along with shared entrances, can be associated with anti-social behavior, a lack of control, and security concerns. Those who are more vulnerable, especially older people, can feel uneasy about leaving their homes after dark. They might feel unsafe lingering in, and inhabiting, the very spaces that enable them to meet and interact with others.

>> **Streetscapes (the view from the streets):** Some research suggests that if you live in an area that has high-rise streetscapes, you're likely to have a reduced sense of control and perceive higher levels of anti-social behavior. This can make you feel unsafe and affect your ability and willingness to connect with others.

>> **Floor level in apartment buildings:** Some research suggests that living on a high floor in an apartment building can lead to more social contact, less loneliness, and better well-being. Those living on the ground floor might have concerns over privacy, safety, and a lack of control, thus influencing their ability to connect with others.

>> **Private houses with shared spaces:** Private dwellings that have shared spaces with neighbors can facilitate chance and fleeting encounters with others, which can reduce loneliness. Shared spaces might include walkways,

courtyards, and outdoor seating areas. In contrast, houses that are set back from a pedestrian route or road and have garages are less likely to enable chance or fleeting encounters.

>> **Intergenerational cohousing or community-led housing:** This is not available everywhere, but is increasingly becoming popular in various countries. This kind of housing is specifically developed to include multi-generations of residents with the inclusion of shared indoor and outdoor spaces so people can bump into each other in their everyday activities. Such spaces can include shared laundries, kitchen areas, and vegetable gardens. Often residents are involved in designing and running the housing developments. Research has indicated that people living in this kind of housing are less likely to feel lonely than people living in more conventional homes and neighborhoods.

TIP

If you feel that your housing type is contributing to your feelings of loneliness, try incorporating some of the techniques listed later in this chapter to help you interact more with your neighbors.

Neighborhood design

It's not just the design of your housing that can influence whether you feel lonely. Indeed, the design of your wider neighborhood can also play a significant role.

REMEMBER

The environment around you determines the range and quality of public spaces, both open and indoor. When these spaces are plentiful, welcoming, and accessible, it's easier to use them to interact with others.

These spaces facilitate meetups with people who you're already connected to and chance encounters with people you've never met. What's more, the way your community is designed not only influences your relationships with other people but affects your sense of belonging to the place where you live.

If you feel comfortable spending time in spaces and places within your community, it boosts your connection there, which in turn lifts your mood, thoughts, well-being, and health.

In general, less lonely neighborhoods tend to have a good mix of community buildings and friendly, shared places that residents want to use and feel comfortable frequenting. These might include more facilities such as community spaces, libraries, green spaces, health facilities, and children's play areas. They might also include cafés, bars, shops, and cultural venues such as cinemas, theatres, museums, and sports stadiums.

TIP

Some key design features foster social connections and can help communities and neighborhoods feel less lonely. See how many of these are present in your neighborhood. If your community has none or very few of these, it could partly explain why you feel lonely in your neighborhood.

» **Traffic-free safe spaces** that encourage pedestrians to walk, linger, sit, chat, eat, and enable children to play.

» **Communal gardens and parks** that encourage residents to bond with nature, and with each other. They enable you to spend time in the open air engaging in physical activities such as dog walking, jogging, or running. They're free green spaces where you can meet up with friends and family or have chance encounters with strangers.

» **Communal facilities** such as community centers, libraries, shops and post offices, health care centers, gyms, sports and leisure centers, sports stadia, theaters, cinemas, cafés, restaurants, bars, and clubs. All these offer places to engage in social interaction with other people.

» **Communal seating areas,** including picnic benches and indoor seating. These design features enable people of all abilities and ages to spend time in communal areas.

» **Public toilets** enable you to spend longer spans of time outdoors, which means your chances of social interaction increase.

Crime and fear for safety

If you feel unsafe and insecure in your neighborhood, you experience a lesser sense of belonging, and you're less likely to spend time in communal or public spaces. This in turn means you're less likely to meet other people. In fact, if your neighborhood feels particularly unsafe, you might actively avoid meeting other people.

Some places can feel more unsafe and unwelcoming than others. And the perceptions of safety in a particular place won't be the same for everyone. Areas of deprivation can feel particularly unsafe for certain inhabitants. Older people can feel unsafe in communal areas after dark. Women can feel unsafe walking alone at night. If you feel unsafe, it can deter you from leaving your house and engaging in your community, which can adversely affect your ability to interact with your neighbors.

REMEMBER

A neighborhood's walkability influences its levels of loneliness, especially among more vulnerable sections of the community. Walkability is felt to be particularly high when there's a network of easily navigable, safe, and attractive walking routes that are connected and well-lit at night. These walking routes can mitigate loneliness because they enable people to get out and about in their neighborhood.

TIP

If your feeling of unsafety is preventing you from going out and socializing in your neighborhood, you can try a few of the following strategies, all of which can help you make connections and feel less lonely:

>> **Connect with your neighbors:** Introduce yourself to your neighbors or get to know them better. Make small talk as you encounter them in the street or corridors, and offer to be a source of help for them in case of emergencies. Chances are, your neighbors will be feeling the same way as you. Striking up a friendship and finding a source of local support might help you feel safer, and your new neighbors just might become your new friends.

>> **Organize a neighborhood safety scheme:** Talk to your neighbors about your fears of crime and safety and consider as a group starting a neighborhood watch of sorts. It can reduce crime by means of improved home security, greater vigilance, reporting of suspicious incidents, and fostering a community spirit. These groups often work in partnership with the police and local organizations that want to improve their communities. A watch group brings neighbors together to create strong, friendly, and active communities ready to tackle crime. Besides making you feel safer, a group like this can better connect you to your neighbors.

See the Appendix for useful links and resources.

Bridging Gaps in Your Community to Encourage Belonging

As a member of your community, regardless of its size or how long you've lived there, you can influence how friendly or lonely it is to live there. Don't let the fact that other neighbors don't seem to engage with one another keep you from taking steps to improve the community spirit.

Here are some ways that community conditions can make you feel lonely, and some tips to help you foster a greater sense of belonging despite these circumstances.

Feeling accepted

REMEMBER

The extent to which you feel welcomed and accepted in your community plays an important role in if, and how, you're able to connect with others in your local area. It also influences whether you have a sense of belonging to your neighborhood. If you feel unwelcome, sense that you can't be yourself in public, and lack identification with your locality, it can lead to feelings of loneliness and disconnection. In some of the research I've carried out, people have said that they can't be themselves in their neighborhoods because of their religion, their ethnicity, or their sexual orientation. A lesbian couple living in a white homogeneous neighborhood told me, for example, that although they live together as a couple, if asked by neighbors, they say they're just friends. They feel unable to show each other any form of affection in public. As a result, although they aren't lonely in their home, they're quite lonely in their community.

TIP

If you feel unaccepted and unwelcome in your community because of a protected characteristic such as your age, sexual orientation, ethnicity, religion, or sex, recognize that it's not your fault. You're not the problem. A number of techniques, listed here, might be helpful for you:

>> **Accept yourself.** If you feel unwelcome by people in your neighborhood because you're different from them, accept yourself for who you are. Be comfortable with being you. This is easier said than done, of course, but I dedicate the whole of Chapter 13 to providing information about therapeutic techniques and skills that can help you be more accepting of yourself. Some of these are self-help techniques, and some require a qualified therapist.

>> **Join a community of interest group.** Many community groups and lobbyist groups serve communities of interest. Find one that suits you by looking in your local library or on the internet, and join it. It doesn't matter whether the group is based in your local neighborhood. You'll be able to meet other like-minded people who have faced similar challenges to you and get some helpful advice. You'll also have opportunities to make new friends or to volunteer, both of which will help you feel less lonely. For more information on the benefits of volunteering, turn to Chapter 14.

>> **Report any discriminatory behavior.** In some countries it's against the law to discriminate against someone because of a protected characteristic, such as age, disability, gender reassignment, marriage and civil partnership, pregnancy and maternity, race, religion, sex, or sexual orientation. If you feel you're being discriminated against for one of these reasons, you should report it. There are some helplines and online resources in the Appendix.

Cultivating neighborliness

REMEMBER

The *neighborliness* of a community — that is, the act of being friendly or kind to your neighbors — is often seen as an indicator of the level of loneliness in that community. A greater level of neighborliness means less loneliness among the population. However, neighborliness is subjective and can mean different things to different people.

What some people may find as a neighborly act, others can interpret as interference. In the past, people were generally considered more neighborly. They knew the names of those living on their street, and they could pop over to borrow a cup of sugar or an egg. They looked out for each other's properties while they were on vacation, watering plants and feeding pets. Contemporary society is generally more individualized. Particularly with the advent of new technology, people are spending more time alone on their gadgets.

Now rather than knocking on a neighbor's door, we order that missing item for our meal from an app to be delivered immediately. We tend to move around more for school and work and overall spend less time in one community. Consequently, it might be more difficult to build strong relationships with neighbors than it was in the past.

TIP

Nevertheless, even in today's more mobile and fluid society, you can gain a number of benefits from living in a community that's more neighborly, all of which can reduce loneliness and enhance your sense of belonging to the place where you live:

>> A neighborly community can facilitate reciprocity and support between people. Acts of neighborliness such as saying hello as you pass on the street or chatting in the local shop can develop an atmosphere that makes neighbors feel comfortable offering and asking for help from each other.

>> Neighborliness can improve your well-being. Living in a neighborhood where there's regular contact between neighbors and where people work together to improve their local community can have a positive impact on the well-being of individuals and communities alike.

>> Neighborliness means that residents know each other and are more likely to look out for one another. This can reduce crime and make people feel safer in their local community and better able to interact with others.

TIP

If you're feeling that a lack of neighborliness is one of the main causes for your loneliness, why not improve the neighborly spirit yourself?

>> Try making small talk with your neighbors instead of just rushing past because you're too busy.

>> When you get an opportunity, prolong a conversation with your neighbors and invite them for a coffee or a meal.

>> Get together with a few neighbors and organize block activities. Have a street party, or celebrate an upcoming festival together.

>> If crime and fear for safety are issues, get together with a few like-minded neighbors to create a neighborhood watch or similar initiative — keeping a lookout together for criminal activity in the area.

Connecting around shared interests

A good way to connect with people is to seek out those who have similar interests to you. Think about the activities you like doing or would like to do, and look for groups that offer them in your local area. The interests could involve all kinds of things, from politics, lobbyist causes, books, and gardening to choirs, dancing, bands, amateur dramatics, sports, walking clubs, and DIY.

Discover which groups are available by searching on the internet, visiting your local library, or looking at posters and leaflets displayed in your neighborhood. Once you've found one or two that interest you, try them out and see which you enjoy. It's a good way to meet like-minded people who live locally. Over time you may get to know these people better and start meeting outside of the group activities. If you can't find a local group of interest, you could set one up yourself or perhaps look further afield.

You might prefer to volunteer for a local group instead of using their services. That's a good way to help others while meeting new people. See Chapter 14 for more information on getting involved in local interests to create meaningful relationships with others, and on the benefits and how-tos of volunteering.

Sharing friendship through food

REMEMBER

Research suggests that communal eating can promote social bonding, improve your mood, promote feelings of well-being, and reduce loneliness. It can enhance your sense of contentedness with others and your sense of belonging to your community. This is because you tend to feel closer to those you eat with. You're more likely to feel better about yourself and more likely to have a wider social network capable of providing social and emotional support if you eat with others socially.

TIP

If you feel lonely or disconnected in your community, why not see if food is the route to greater friendship? Try some of these tips to get started:

>> Invite your neighbors for coffee and cake. Use the opportunity to get to know them better, and identify which neighbors you share commonality with.

>> Once you've established which neighbors you have commonality with, invite them for a meal. Sharing a meal together is a great way to create new and maintain existing relationships.

>> Get together with a few neighbors and suggest a block party in which everyone brings a home-cooked dish and you eat together. It's a good way of bringing neighbors together. It fosters the community spirit and sense of belonging and enables you to get to know your neighbors better.

Harnessing Connectedness and Community in Public Spaces

Regardless of why you feel lonely in your community, you can improve your social connections and develop a better sense of belonging with the neighborhood where you live. Both will ensure that you feel less lonely and disconnected.

Using green spaces

A good way to enhance your well-being, get out of the house, increase your chances of meeting other people, and improve your sense of belonging to your community is to use green spaces in your neighborhood.

Research suggests that the more exposure you get to green space, the less lonely you'll feel. Just two hours a week spent surrounded by nature can be enough to improve your sense of well-being. Adults in neighborhoods where at least 30 percent of nearby land is parks, reserves, and woodlands have a lower chance of becoming lonely compared to those living in areas with less than 10 percent of green space. What's more, the positive impact of green space on loneliness is even greater for people who live alone. Using green spaces doesn't just reduce loneliness among those who already feel lonely, but offers a protective factor against feeling lonely in the first place. Green spaces can lower blood pressure and cortisol levels (the stress hormone), which in turn can calm the body's fight-or-flight response.

Spending time in green spaces can also enhance your mood, reduce depression, and restore cognitive functioning. Alongside the health and psychological benefits, regular use of green spaces can help you come into contact with other people and increase your chances of meaningful interaction with others.

You don't have to live in a rural area to benefit from green spaces. Making regular use of local parks, urban farms, gardens, tree-lined streets, sports fields, golf courses, rivers, and green trails can reduce your chances of being lonely. If you're homebound, even momentary views of greenery through a window can offer benefits. Regardless of where you live, maximize your use of green spaces on a regular basis to keep feelings of loneliness at bay:

>> Try spending some regular time in green spaces. If you have green spaces nearby, take advantage of them for about 20 minutes each day. It could be your garden, a nearby park, a wooded area, a sports field, or a river or reservoir. Take a look around your neighborhood and see what gives you the greatest sense of well-being and the highest chances of meeting other people.

>> If you don't have a garden but have a back yard or balcony, try placing some greenery there. A few outdoor plants with leafy foliage should help. Failing that, increase the greenery in your home by buying some indoor potted plants. Indoor plants can be especially helpful if you live in an urban area that lacks green spaces, if you're too busy to visit green spaces on a daily basis, or you're homebound due to illness, disability, or age.

>> If you're homebound or find it difficult to get outside but have a green space to look out to, consider rearranging your furniture so that you can have a comfy chair facing out of the window onto a garden or tree-lined street. You can ask someone to help you move the furniture if you can't lift it alone.

>> If you have a dog, be sure to take it for walks into green spaces and parks rather than around urban streets and roads. This will give you a greater sense of well-being and increase your chances of meeting other dog walkers you can strike up a conversation with. Your dog will enjoy it more too.

>> Grow your own fruits and vegetables. You'll need to spend regular time in the garden getting rid of the weeds and attending to the plants, so you'll gain a greater sense of well-being. You'll also produce some healthy produce that you can eat or share with neighbors.

>> Join a local community organization that's linked to a green space. Check the internet or your local library for details. You can often find "friends of" organizations that are linked to local green spaces or organizations attached to local rivers and canals. Joining as a member allows you to make use of their services and activities, meet other people, and enjoy nature. You can also offer your services as a volunteer. See Chapter 14 for more information.

Conversing on benches and buses

Park benches and buses aren't just for sitting and traveling. They're places you can strike up conversations with others, which can ease your loneliness and might lead to the formation of more meaningful interactions over time.

REMEMBER

Public benches can be beneficial for combatting loneliness in a number of ways. They're resting places if you have limited mobility but still want to engage in public spaces. They're gathering places for meetups in open spaces without a financial cost. They're contributors to health and well-being because they allow you to spend longer time outside. And they enable you to make chance connections with others. If you're lonely, try sitting on a public bench for a while, and strike up a conversation with others who join you there.

Buses are similarly beneficial for dealing with loneliness. Buses can connect you with other people and places. The very act traveling on a bus can help you interact with others in your community or beyond. Some people deliberately catch a bus to interact with others.

TIP

Pop over to your local bus stop and take a bus journey to an area of your community you've not visited before. Take every opportunity to make contact with other people you encounter at the bus stop, whilst traveling, and at your final destination. Start with simple gestures, such as a smile or saying hello. If you get a positive response, try to develop the conversation. Make small talk about the weather, ask them where they're going, and tell them where you're heading. Not everyone will respond, but it's likely that some will strike up a conversation with you. Who knows what interesting people you'll meet along the way!

In the UK a specific bus service called Chatty Bus has even been developed as a more organized way of meeting people. This is designed to use space on the bus as a place for connections to thrive. Chatty Buses are in operation in different parts of the UK and each region offers a slightly different service.

Interacting in community facilities

If you feel particularly lonely in your community, your local library, post office, and shops can be a hub for social interactions.

TIP

See what's going on at your local library. It's a warm place to sit and browse through books or newspapers or to use the internet without charge. It's a great source of information and knowledge about your local community and the activities going on there. But it's also where you can interact with others. Some libraries also host community activities you can register for.

Choose your local post office over other parcel delivery options. You can strike up a conversation with one of the clerks and might even run into someone you know while waiting in line.

Shop locally on a regular basis, even if it's just for a newspaper or a gallon of milk. Try to avoid doing all your grocery shopping online or in large supermarkets. By frequenting the smaller shops, you'll get to know the owner and possibly bump into other regulars whom you can strike up conversations with.

Chapter 6

Finding Your Place at Work

D epending on your place of work and your personal characteristics and circumstances, your workplace can be a haven of social connection or a hellhole of loneliness. Many people spend a large proportion of their lives at work, so outside of their family home, it's often where they get the most opportunities for connecting with others. Some people feel a deep sense of belonging to their workplace that can also help them feel connected. But the workplace can make others feel lonelier. They can feel uncomfortable, that they don't fit in, and they can struggle to connect with fellow employees. When they see others at work getting along, it can make their mood even worse.

If people struggle to fit in at work or don't get opportunities to develop meaningful relationships with work colleagues, their mental health can suffer. They might start to dread Monday mornings, unable to face the working week again. This can affect anyone at any level of the organization, from those at the bottom of the employment hierarchy to the highest flying executives. If this sounds like you and you feel lonely at work, you're not alone. Many feel lonely in their jobs. This chapter has tips to help you.

If you're an employer or a manager who's keen to reduce loneliness and improve the well-being of your staff, this chapter can help you too. A lonely workforce can reduce worker creativity and performance and cause worker disengagement. It can lead to greater levels of absenteeism and high levels of labor turnover as employees move jobs to seek a more socially connected environment. All this can affect productivity and profits, so it's in everyone's interests to find solutions.

This chapter explains what workplace loneliness is. It helps you assess whether you or your workforce are lonely. It also explains the impact that workplace loneliness can have. From there, it discusses how workplace culture and practices can influence how lonely you feel. Finally, it provides some useful strategies to make your place of work an oasis of social connection.

What Is Workplace Loneliness?

Loneliness at work often comes about because you don't experience meaningfulness. You might lack meaningful relationships with your work colleagues. Or perhaps you feel that you don't have a meaningful relationship with the organization you work for, so you lack a sense of belonging there.

Defining loneliness at work

Loneliness at work can make you feel alienated or disconnected from other employees. In Chapter 1, I explain that you can feel lonely in a crowd, and the same is true if you feel lonely at work. You can experience workplace loneliness even when you're surrounded by work colleagues. You might feel even more lonely in these situations if you don't have positive relationships with your coworkers and feel as though you don't fit in.

Workplace loneliness is an unpleasant feeling that emerges when you have a lack of desired meaningful relationships at work. Like general loneliness, which I discuss in Chapter 1, workplace loneliness is a subjective feeling based on your own perceptions. If you feel lonely at work, it's often because the actual relationships you have there aren't the same as those you desire. Or your relationships might not be as positive and plentiful as those you see among your work colleagues. Loneliness can be experienced by employees but also by managers, executives, and directors.

REMEMBER

If you feel lonely at work, you're not alone. Around three out of five employees feel lonely at their jobs. Both the US and the UK governments recognize loneliness in the workplace as an issue and have included action plans to tackle it in their national strategies. If you're an employee, a key starting point is recognizing that you feel lonely at work. If you're an employer, it's important to start by acknowledging that some of your workforce are likely to feel lonely, and you might even feel lonely yourself.

Whatever your position in the employment hierarchy, you can experience loneliness.

Ask yourself this: How often do you feel lonely at work?

>> If your answer is never or hardly ever, you're unlikely to be suffering from workplace loneliness.

>> If your answer is occasionally or some of the time, you're experiencing some workplace loneliness, but it's not a major problem.

>> If your answer is often/always, you're definitely lonely at work, and it's time to take action.

TIP

Loneliness can strike at any time, whatever your position. I provide a whole range of suggestions and tips later in this chapter to help you.

Understanding the implications of workplace loneliness

Loneliness at work can have adverse implications for both people and organizations. It can damage the health and well-being of staff and the productivity of companies and economies. If you feel lonely at work, whether you're a worker, a manager, or a high-flying executive, your mental health can be damaged. If you feel lonely at work, you might experience any of the following:

>> Lack of control

>> Lower self-esteem

>> Poor job-related well-being

>> Feeling anxious and emotionally exhausted

>> Employment-related burnout, especially if you're a manager

>> Physical health conditions, such as headaches

>> A need to take more days off sick

As a result, your creativity and performance at work may start to suffer. You might be less able to make sound judgments in decision-making, and you may start to resent your workplace, employer, and coworkers.

As with loneliness more generally (see Chapter 1), feeling lonely at work can lead to a downward negative spiral. You can start to view work colleagues' behavior negatively, which can make you feel lonelier. It can impede your ability to develop workplace relationships even more. This can be accompanied by a lack of belonging at work and a lack of commitment to your employer. You might then ultimately start seeking employment elsewhere. None of these outcomes are beneficial for either you or the organization you work for.

With the right approach you can break the cycle of loneliness and reap the benefits of positive interpersonal relationships at work. I help you find the right solution later in this chapter. Once you've found the best way forward, you can establish satisfactory workplace relationships. Your well-being is likely to improve, along with your commitment, affinity, and sense of belonging. And when you feel good at work, you're likely to be more productive, and your employer will gain too.

Calculating loneliness in your workforce

If you're an employer, manager, chief executive, or director, it's helpful not only to assess how lonely you personally feel at work but how lonely your workforce is too. Calculating loneliness can help you decide if and what kind of action to take. Remember, loneliness at work is damaging for your company's productivity, its profitability, and its staff's well-being.

To carry out a quick deep dive into how lonely your staff are, ask staff members to answer anonymously how often they're lonely. Explain that you're trying to find out if loneliness is a problem in your company so that you can make improvements.

If a third or more of your workforce respond saying they're lonely often/always, some of the time, or occasionally, you might want to take action. If a third or more of your employees say that they're often or always lonely at work, I strongly advise you to take action. I provide some useful strategies later in this chapter. Even if your workforce doesn't report loneliness at the current time, you might find some of these ideas useful to implement in your workplace, These techniques may well prevent loneliness from being a problem in the future.

The question to assess loneliness at work is sufficient to get a rough estimate of the prevalence of workplace loneliness. But if you want a more comprehensive picture of loneliness in your workplace, I suggest you use the UCLA 3 item loneliness scale. See Chapter 2 for more details on how to do this.

The Influence of Workplace Culture on Loneliness

One of the factors that can contribute to your loneliness at work is the culture of your workplace. I'm referring to the attitudes, beliefs, and behaviors that make up your work environment. Workplace culture varies from one organization to the next. It's determined by a whole range of interconnecting factors, such as the business sector, the style of management, the perceived norms of behavior, the values and attitudes of employees, and the diversity of the workforce.

REMEMBER

Workplace culture affects if and how lonely you feel at work. A workplace culture is more likely to lead to loneliness when it:

>> Emphasizes individualism

>> Rewards personal success

>> Focuses on internal competition between employees

>> Has a controlling management style

This kind of culture tends to go against the basic human needs for belonging and positive social relationships.

On the other hand, a workplace culture is less likely to lead to loneliness, where:

>> Employees are encouraged to work together and support each other.

>> Managers articulate a clear vision that feels safe to contribute to.

>> Tasks are clear and innovation is supported.

These kinds of workplace cultures are more likely to lead to greater levels of trust, high-quality workplace relationships, and less loneliness.

Alignment with your values

When the culture of the workplace doesn't align well with your personal values, you can feel alienated and lonely at work. If you feel this way, there's nothing wrong with you. The workplace culture just doesn't suit your background, needs, or personal circumstances.

REMEMBER

Workplace cultures vary. And a workplace culture that leads to a sense of belonging, connectedness, and positive social relationships for one person can lead to alienation, isolation, and loneliness for another.

This can be seen in the case of Martin and Jodie, managers who work for the same research consultancy company but have completely different experiences. The company has a highly competitive culture, where bonuses are paid for individual performance. At the weekly staff meetings, employees are eager to outdo each other and demonstrate their knowledge and skills.

Martin and Jodie are equally successful in their work achievements, but Jodie feels lonely and alienated at work, whereas Martin doesn't. Martin thrives in this individualistic culture; he enjoys going to work, competing for the most contracts, and telling his colleagues just how good a consultant he is. Jodie, on the other hand, dislikes going to work; she works at home as much as possible, avoids the weekly team meetings whenever she can, and doesn't feel that she has anything in common with her coworkers. Jodie has tried to open up conversations about different topics, but her coworkers are only interested in talking about work and how good they are at their jobs.

If you find that you're feeling lonely at work, carry out this simple activity to identify if workplace culture is the culprit. Ask yourself four questions:

1. What are the key words associated with your workplace culture?

2. What key words represent your personal values?

3. Look through both lists and circle any words you've listed in your answers to both questions. The words don't have to be identical; also circle words that have a similar meaning.

4. If you find that only a few or no words are circled, your workplace loneliness may well be due to the culture of the organization you work for. If this is the case, you can try to implement some of the techniques at work listed later in this chapter. If you're not in a position to influence change in your workplace or management is reluctant to adopt change, you might want to consider a change of employer.

WARNING

Before changing your job or changing your employer, consider the benefits and drawbacks. If you or your family rely on your income, make sure you gain employment elsewhere before handing in your notice.

Demographics: Feeling you don't "fit in"

REMEMBER

The workplace culture might also make you feel lonely if your personal characteristics and circumstances differ from the dominant composition of the workforce. This can happen when your social class, age, gender, ethnicity, religion, and sexual orientation differ from the majority of the workforce. It can also happen if you have a disability. In these circumstances you can start to feel marginalized, excluded, alienated, and disconnected from the dominant culture, which can reduce the quantity and quality of your relationships with coworkers and diminish your sense of belonging to the organization or workplace.

Imogen, a young working-class woman working in the TV industry, fell afoul of this very issue. An actor from a working-class family, she went to drama school in the north of England. After graduating she got a job in the TV industry. The majority of her coworkers were middle class. A large number of them were Oxbridge graduates. Imogen found herself completely alienated at work. Everything about her was different: her accent, the food she ate, her hobbies, and her music. Although Imogen was initially excited to have achieved her lifetime ambition of a job in the TV industry, she felt alienated. She didn't have anything in common with her coworkers and found it difficult to form relationships with them.

TIP

If you can identify with Imogen and find yourself in a similar position, maybe because of your ethnicity, gender, sexual orientation, or some other personal characteristics, it's okay. I offer some tips later in this chapter for you.

WARNING

If you're finding yourself excluded and alienated in the workplace because of your personal characteristics, raise this issue with your line manager or Human Resource department. A dominant workplace culture can lead to discrimination, and your employer has a responsibility to address this. Employment legislation varies internationally. In many countries, it's against the law to discriminate against someone because of a protected characteristic such as the following:

>> Age

>> Disability

>> Gender reassignment

>> Marriage and civil partnership

>> Pregnancy and maternity

>> Race

>> Religion or belief

>> Sex

>> Sexual orientation

Loneliness at the top

REMEMBER

Workplace culture doesn't just contribute to loneliness among the workforce; it can affect those at the top of the organization too, including employers, managers, chief executive officers, and boardroom directors. Research suggests that those at the top can be as lonely as the rest of the workforce. If you're in charge, you might find yourself feeling lonely at work for a variety of reasons:

>> You might perform tasks alone and have less daily contact with peers at work, making it more difficult to generate workplace relationships.

>> Because of your heightened status and power, others at work may keep their distance from you socially.

>> To maintain social control as a manager, you may feel that you need to keep a degree of detachment from your employees, especially when you have to make difficult decisions.

>> You may have extensive work-related social networks external to your organization but feel unable to create real social bonds due to the competitive nature of those relationships.

TIP

When you're at the top of an organization, you might feel that you shouldn't feel lonely, that you should be invincible. But loneliness can happen whatever your status. Try introducing to your organization some of the strategies I discuss later in this chapter. Not only will they help you feel less lonely, they'll help your employees feel less lonely too. And less lonely managers and employees will be happier and more productive.

Impact of Employment Practices on Loneliness

Alongside the workplace culture, which I mentioned earlier, the practices of your employer can play a key role in determining how lonely you feel at work. The relationship between employment practices and workplace culture goes two ways. The workplace culture is likely to determine the working practices dominating your place of employment. Likewise, the working practices of your employer affect the workplace culture.

Designing your workplace

REMEMBER

The design of your workplace can play a big role in the extent to which you feel lonely at work. The design can either enable or discourage social relationships to form between coworkers. Workplaces with structures and features that enable people to come together are less likely to feel lonely and isolating to employees. Several design features can help informal relationships thrive, which then allows for high-quality meaningful connections to develop. Examples of helpful design features include:

>> Informal communal spaces for meeting and chatting

>> Communal eating areas

>> Installation of water fountains and drink stations

>> A room that can include board games, ping pong, or foosball

>> Meeting rooms and offices with glass doors and windows

>> Communal outdoor spaces and seating

I've worked in a number of environments, some of which have encouraged social interaction and team working, and some of which have actively discouraged it. I provide two quite different examples of places I've worked to show how design can affect loneliness among staff.

Workplace 1: A lonely place to be

In this workplace, everyone had separate office spaces, each positioned along either side of a corridor. The doors were wooden, and the corridor side lacked office windows. Communal spaces were limited, and most people had a way to make coffee and tea directly in their offices, which meant coworkers had little informal interaction. Staff primarily remained seated in their offices, working alone. It was difficult to know who was in the building because you couldn't see through the offices, as there were no corridor-facing windows. If you knocked on an office door to try to strike up a conversation, you felt as though you were interrupting their work. The culture of this particular workplace was elitist and individualistic. There was a strong hierarchical distinction between those at the top of the organization and those further down. The combination of the workplace culture and the building design meant that it was a lonely place to work.

Workplace 2: A more socially interactive space

In this workplace was a mixture of single and small group offices. Like workplace 1, the offices were situated on each side of a corridor. The offices had glass walls and doors so you could tell who was in the building on any given day. A communal kitchen and eating area had an informal meeting space with comfy chairs, as well as space for working. The communal space was brightly colored, had a selection of magazines and newspapers, and was an enjoyable and comfortable place to spend time. Although the workplace was also hierarchical, like workplace 1, the staff were encouraged to share input into decision-making, and management made efforts to make staff feel valued. The employer's logo was embedded on the glass office walls to give a sense of identity and belonging. The building design meant that coworkers regularly used the communal space and interacted socially. I really enjoyed working in this building and didn't feel lonely at work at all.

TIP

It's not always easy to change the workplace design, especially if you're not in a position of power. However, if you feel that the design is making it a lonely place to be, you can try a few simple things that I talk about later in this chapter. If you're an employer or manager, you'll find tips for you too.

Working alone

REMEMBER

Many jobs involve working by yourself, which can be quite isolating and feel lonely. Some jobs involve much more time alone than others. In my work, as an academic, I sometimes spend large amounts of time researching and writing on my own. But at other times I work with teams of people, attending group meetings, focus groups, workshops, and presentations. Some jobs involve spending the majority of time working alone or with few people around. Classic examples include truck drivers, cleaners, security workers, self-employed people who work alone, pet sitters, house sitters, artists, and transcriptionists. If you have a job that requires working alone or perhaps a job that doesn't bring you in contact with many other people, you might feel lonely at work. It's natural. Sometimes when I'm writing at my desk, day after day, I feel lonely too. However, some people prefer the solitude, peace, and quiet that lone working brings. They may not feel lonely at all. The desire for social interactions at work varies.

TIP

I provide some tips to help you feel less lonely at work later in this chapter. But if you're a lone worker, unless you're in a senior position, you might not be able to easily change your employment circumstances. If this sounds like you, it might be best to focus on making the other areas of your life feel less lonely. Perhaps you can do this by working on your meaningful relationships at home (Chapter 4) or in your community (Chapters 5 and 14). Or perhaps you can spend time when you're not at work in places where you feel a sense of belonging (Chapter 15).

Working remotely

REMEMBER

Working remotely has increased significantly in recent years and was particularly accelerated by the Covid-19 pandemic. Technological innovation (see Chapter 7) has made remote working much more feasible because workers can meet online, from the comfort of their own homes, through a whole range of software apps. Remote working can have many benefits to both employees and employers. It can reduce travel time and travel costs. You can carry out work more flexibly around your home and family life. It can lead to cost savings for the employer, reducing the need for expensive building rental, lighting, and heating bills. However, remote working can also lead to loneliness. It can reduce the opportunity for interactions and relationships in everyday work life. Communication isn't always the same through the lens of a computer screen, as I explain in Chapter 7.

TIP

In today's climate, unless you're a frontline service provider, it's likely that you'll spend at least some time working remotely. This may well make you feel lonely. If you work for an employer where remote working is encouraged or commonplace or you're an employer pursuing such practices, look for some tips later in this chapter. I help you think about how to manage remote working while retaining and encouraging strong social connections.

Dealing with precarious contracts

REMEMBER

Precarious work involves uncertain employment and an unpredictable income. Examples include temporary contracts that are time limited or, even more precarious, zero-hours contracts, where employers provide no guaranteed minimum of paid work or stable source of income. Work can be given or taken away by the employer at short notice. These kinds of precarious contracts are becoming more ubiquitous in certain sectors of the economy, especially in the service sector. Like remote working, precarious contracts have risen in recent years.

TIP

If you're employed on a precarious contract, you might have difficulties forming and maintaining relationships. You might also struggle to experience meaningfulness and pride in your work. Perhaps you encounter heightened anxiety because your income isn't guaranteed or because you're permanently seeking the next contract. All these things tend to be at odds with building positive social relationships and can create workplace loneliness. In the next section I provide some useful tips for overcoming loneliness at work.

Addressing Workplace Loneliness

Workplace loneliness can be damaging for the productivity and profits of businesses, as well as for the mental health and well-being of employees (see earlier and Chapter 10 for more details). So it's in everyone's interests to tackle loneliness and to find ways to support workers at all levels to be more engaged. This section has some useful suggestions to help employers tackle loneliness in their workplace. It also offers tips to employees for taking action to overcome their loneliness.

Talking about loneliness at work

Whether you're an employer or an employee, and whether you're directly affected by loneliness at work or not, it's helpful to raise the issue of workplace loneliness and get colleagues and coworkers talking about it.

REMEMBER

Loneliness is often perceived as a stigma in contemporary society. As a result, it can be trivialized or ignored, especially in the workplace. However, it's important to start talking about loneliness more in all aspects of life, including in the workplace. The first step to coping with, and overcoming, loneliness is to admit that you're lonely to yourself and to others.

TIP

If you're an employer, encourage your staff to talk about loneliness. Create a psychologically safe place where workers feel able to express themselves without fear that others will think less of them. Use team meetings and informal gatherings to discuss loneliness in groups. Also, try raising the topic in annual staff reviews so you can talk on a one-on-one basis. Take the lead as a manager and encourage conversations about loneliness so that employees feel comfortable sharing their experiences and vulnerabilities as well as expressing concerns, asking questions, and putting forward ideas. By understanding employees' experiences of loneliness, you'll be in a better position to show compassion and empathy towards your staff. If you feel able to, provide examples of when you've felt lonely at work. Before long, your team will open up about their experiences. And with your lead they'll start seeking and offering support to each other. This will then build higher quality, meaningful relationships among coworkers.

TIP

If you're an employee who's concerned about loneliness, you don't have to wait for your employer to become enlightened and take action. You can start to make some subtle changes yourself. When you get an opportunity, perhaps with colleagues you feel more relaxed with, bring up loneliness as a topic of conversation. Perhaps provide an example of someone you know who's feeling lonely at work and say that sometimes you've felt like this too. It's likely that they'll be feeling the same or have felt that way in the past. If you're on a precarious contract, discuss your feelings with others in the same position as you. If you're a lone worker, try broaching the topic of loneliness with others at home or in your neighborhood. The more you encourage discussions about loneliness in the workplace, the more likely you are to create a more compassionate and caring workplace culture.

Lunching together

REMEMBER

Sharing meals together is known to be effective in overcoming loneliness, whether at home, in your community, or in your place of work. Having dedicated time in the working day where people are encouraged to talk about nonwork issues can help workers be seen as individual human beings, beyond their professional role. At these gatherings, try sharing ideas and having informal discussions. It's a great way to encourage the formation of meaningful relationships between coworkers. It also creates a sense of belonging among staff, which assists in alleviating workplace loneliness.

TIP

If you're an employer, try suggesting a regular shared lunch, perhaps once a week or once a month, depending on your workplace circumstances. The lunch could be in a communal space in your workplace or in a local café. If your staff work remotely, suggest a weekly online lunch catch-up, where everyone eats at the same time and chats informally through an online app. Or if eating while being displayed onscreen feels odd, try weekly online coffee chats instead.

TIP

If you're an employee, you can similarly suggest a regular shared meal or coffee among your coworkers. They're likely to jump at the chance to get out of the office and have an informal chat over lunch. If you work remotely and live some distance from your fellow coworkers, perhaps suggest a lunchtime meetup online. If you're a lone worker, try to identify people you know from nonwork aspects of your life whom you could arrange a lunch date with.

Volunteering through work

Many employers provide opportunities for corporate volunteering, or *employee volunteering*, as it's sometimes called. This is a workplace-based initiative where employers offer support or encouragement for workers to volunteer. The voluntary work is often for the local community or for a good cause. This kind of voluntary work can have many benefits to both employees and employers and can fend off loneliness at work.

Corporate volunteering can help you become more engaged at work. It's beneficial for employees and employers alike. It can create a greater sense of meaningfulness at work and help you feel a wider sense of purpose and feeling of self-worth. It can also help you develop new and additional social relationships outside the workplace. All of these tackle workplace loneliness while helping a good cause. Corporate volunteering also has wider benefits in terms of creating greater worker job satisfaction and higher company productivity.

If you're an employee, ask your manager or contact your Human Resources department to find out what corporate volunteering opportunities are available. If none exist, ask your employer about possibilities to get involved. You can mention the wider benefits to the organization, such as the positive impact it can have on the company's profit margins and productivity.

If you're on a precarious contact, such as zero hours, it's unlikely that your employer will be willing to offer corporate volunteering opportunities. However, you could carry out voluntary work separate from your paid employment. This will give you a renewed sense of purpose and self-worth, which should help you be more resilient to any workplace loneliness you feel.

To search for volunteering opportunities, look for ads in your local neighborhood or library or try the links and resources in the Appendix. Chapter 14 also has some useful advice on how to get involved in volunteering opportunities.

Taking advantage of peer support groups

Many employers, especially larger ones, have support groups for specific groups of workers who are often marginalized. They can be for LGBTQIA+ workers, informal family caregivers, women, ethnic minority staff, and employees with disabilities. Some employers have support groups for staff on temporary contracts. These support groups are sometimes referred to as *peer support groups* and can be led by Human Resource leaders, team managers, or, quite often, volunteer employees. Such groups should ideally be for both employers and employees, focused on bringing together workers who have some common personal characteristics. The groups can be particularly helpful if you don't feel that you fit into your workplace culture because of your personal characteristics.

Hearing that others have experienced, or are experiencing, similar thoughts and feelings can help you feel more comfortable with your thoughts and support you to keep sharing those thoughts. The very act of expressing your feelings or thoughts among people who are similar to you can help you feel less lonely and isolated. Attending peer support groups also helps you create meaningful relationships with coworkers and gain a greater sense of belonging to your workplace, thus staving off those feelings of loneliness.

TIP

Peer support groups should be focused on enabling workers to share their workplace feelings and experiences. They should be convened regularly to build up trust and help workers feel safe sharing their emotions. This helps attendees understand their coworkers much better. If you're an employer and workplace loneliness is a problem in your workplace, direct your employees to appropriate workplace support groups. If you don't have any, think about starting some. Lead by example, start a group or two, and get involved in one that meets your personal characteristics.

Likewise, if you're an employee, ask your manager or Human Resources department what peer support groups exist. If none exist, try setting up one yourself.

Engaging with remote workers

REMEMBER

In today's society, remote working is much more common than ever before. You might be working for long stretches of time, isolated in your own home, seemingly cut off from your coworkers and workplace. To avoid or reduce these feelings of isolation and loneliness when working remotely, take action to engage with your fellow coworkers.

TIP

Whether you're an employer or an employee, try to initiate regular real-time communication at least once a day with a coworker. Use a range of methods, such as video conferencing, chat functions, and the telephone. I provide more detail about how you can use technology to support communication and reduce loneliness in Chapter 7.

If you're an employer, regular check-ins with your employees can be effective in reducing their workplace loneliness. Encourage your remote workers to discuss any concerns they have or challenges they're experiencing. Video chats and phone calls are more personal than emails and texts and can be an effective way of reassuring remote employees that they're valued.

Training and mentoring

REMEMBER

The type of workplace culture, and in particular management style, can play a role in how engaged people are in the workplace. I explain a bit more about this earlier in this chapter. A management style that encourages and values worker-led ideas can lead to worker empowerment. This can then facilitate greater self-confidence among workers. It can support more communication between employees and decrease loneliness. Management style, therefore, plays an important part in how lonely people feel at work. If a manager is a source of support and encouragement, employees are more likely to make sense of and find meaning in their work. And meaningfulness at work can keep loneliness at bay.

TIP

A program of training can be helpful in supporting those at the top of organizations apply a management style that's conducive to worker engagement. It can also improve employees' capacity to perform their roles and build their confidence and sense of worth. So whether you're an employer or an employee, explore the available training options at work. Just attending the training session itself will facilitate communication with colleagues and help with your workplace loneliness.

Chapter **7**

Interacting Through Technology

The word *technology* often means different things to different people, partly because technology is in a constant state of flux. Technology is a way of using scientific knowledge to help achieve practical aims of human life and this can involve changing or manipulating our environment. When I was growing up, the VHS recorder, the Atari game console, and the Sony Walkman were the most significant, new technologies which influenced me. Later on, computers and mobile phones completely changed my life.

Technological advances can influence the way you live, your interactions with other people, and the extent to which you feel lonely. Some research suggests that technology can make you feel less lonely, and some concludes that technology can actually make you feel lonelier. When you're engaging with technology, you need to be careful. Select the type of technology you engage with wisely, and think about how you're going to use it.

In this chapter I explain how you can use technology in a positive way to help you feel less lonely, without relying on it as a primary or sole means of interaction. I also offer some tips to help you avoid the pitfalls of using technology in a way that can make you feel lonelier. When loneliness is temporary, perhaps due to a recent relocation or loss, technology can get you through a challenging time. It can expand your world and the connections you make in it.

I show you how to maintain and create new relationships through phone and video calls, texts and social media, and friendship apps. I also provide an easy-to-follow guide for making the most of technology that's been around a long time: TV and radio. And I explain how you can benefit from immersing yourself in a virtual world. Even if you're a technophobe, this chapter shows you easy ways to use technology to ease your loneliness.

Using Technology to Find and Connect with Friends

As I discuss in Chapter 14, one of the best ways to reduce your feelings of loneliness on a long-term basis is to develop meaningful relationships with other people. One way to both maintain existing relationships and create new ones is through the use of technology.

In today's world, families and work colleagues are often dispersed geographically, and technology has become normalized as a way of connecting with people. Recent technological innovations make connecting with other people much easier and quicker than ever before, often with the click of a button. Yet at the same time society is arguably more disconnected than ever before. Technology can have both a beneficial and a detrimental effect on loneliness.

I provide a step-by-step guide to using different types of technology in a way that can help you connect more easily to other people and feel less lonely. I also include some tips and warnings on how to avoid the pitfalls of engaging with technological innovations.

Live phone calls and video chats

Today the telephone is nothing like its original inception in 1876, when Alexander Graham Bell invented it. Then it was a wired mechanism for having voice conversations. Now phones are mobile, wireless, and used to transmit written messages, take and share photographs, access the internet, play games, watch movies, listen to music, and occasionally talk to someone.

Research has shown that to ease loneliness, regular ten-minute calls are helpful, as are a small number of quality conversations, as opposed to many superficial conversations. A live phone or video call is one of the quickest and easiest ways to connect with another person and feel less lonely.

Calling someone you feel close to and engaging in a meaningful conversation over the phone can alleviate loneliness and help you reconnect to people whom you've not had contact with for a while. It can also improve your well-being and promote a sense of fulfillment that can continue long after the call has finished.

Live calls can help you explore ideas and topics of mutual interest in more detail. They can also reduce the chances of misunderstandings that often occur in written mediums, such as emails or text messages. Calls allow you to ask the other person to explain or clarify what they mean instantly. How many times have you become annoyed by the content of a text or email without checking whether the person really meant the message in the way you interpreted it?

Live phone and video calls can make you feel good. When you have live conversations, you pick up cues through the *prosodic voice*, which is the rhythm of the voice, the way it rises and falls. This can make you feel safe and generate warm and comfy feelings.

The added benefit of a video chat is that you can see the person you're talking to, not just hear their voice. It's easier to read body language when you have a visual. Video chats can also build a closer connection, especially if you haven't seen the person for a while.

Live phone or video calls are perhaps the best way to reduce your feelings of loneliness quickly. Making a live call might seem easy to you, or it might feel difficult. I was brought up using the telephone. It was the only way to contact my friends and family, short of visiting them directly, so I find live calls easy and straightforward. However, my kids have grown up in a different era. The thought of a live telephone call often scares them stiff!

TIPS FOR THE LIVE-CALL AVERSE

During the lockdowns associated with the Covid-19 pandemic in 2020 my daughter regularly had video calls with her granddad. She didn't feel comfortable just talking to him, so she organized art activities for the two of them to do together via a video call. The calls kept them in contact with each other when they couldn't meet face to face, gave them something to talk about, and developed their art skills.

Depending on your age and job and whether you're used to making calls or having video chats, you might find making a live call scary. Here are some simple-to-follow ideas to get you going.

- **Decide who you're going to call or have a video chat with.** If you're not sure or don't think there's anyone you know who'd want to communicate this way, try

(continued)

(continued)

doing the lifeline or sociogram exercises in Chapter 14 to help you identify a chat partner.

- **Decide whether you'd prefer a voice or a video call.** A video call can be a great way to see a friend or family member you feel comfortable with. It can socially connect you and make it easier to take cues from their facial expressions and body language. But if you haven't seen someone for a long time or you're not particularly close to this person, you might want to start with a phone call instead. Also, if you're not feeling very good about your appearance, haven't had time to do your hair or makeup, or haven't emerged out of your PJs, you might not want to be seen on camera. In that case, opt for a phone call in the first instance.

- **Decide whether to schedule the call with the other person in advance or make a surprise call.** Some people love surprises, and others hate them, so think about the person you're intending to call and what they'd be most likely enjoy. If you're not sure, err on the side of caution. Send a text message first saying that you're planning to ring them later and ask when a good time would be.

- **Decide in advance what you're going to talk about.** It can help if you think of some key topics or themes you'd like to discuss. Think about things you have in common and scribble down a few ideas. Most likely, you won't need to use your list because once you get started, the conversation will flow naturally. Remember that the other person might not be confident using the phone and could appear a little shy or quiet. Having a few topics of common interest should help you both come out of your shells.

- **Arrange to do activities together on the live calls.** If you're worried about what to say when on a video chat, you can agree on some activities to share on your call that don't involve merely talking. You and your chat partner might choose to spend your shared time watching a film online, playing a game, doing some artwork, or cooking and then eating a meal together. This way the conversation will be determined by the activities and will flow much easier. Before long you'll be talking freely and easily.

Text and voice messages

If you don't feel ready yet to make a phone or video call, perhaps you can try a text or voice message to start with. Then once you're comfortable with that, progress to a telephone or video call. Text and voice messages are virtual interactions that can reduce loneliness and improve your feelings of well-being. Sometimes a quick text or voice message can actually be the simplest way to connect or reconnect.

REMEMBER

A voice message allows you to instantly communicate with people. You can use it to deliver a voice message without talking to the person live. It's quicker than typing a message, and the recipient can simply listen to the message. Although it might not be as effective as a live call, it can help you connect to other people, and the person receiving the message can benefit by hearing your voice.

TIP

Likewise, if you get a reciprocal voice message, you'll gain by hearing their voice, which can help you feel less lonely. Just remember that you might send a voice message and not get one in return. If this happens, don't be alarmed, and don't assume that the person doesn't want to know you. It might be because they don't like leaving voice messages or don't feel comfortable doing so. If you're unsure what medium the recipient will be most comfortable with, ask them first in a text.

Text and voice messages can be useful in a variety of circumstances.

>> **If people have different lifestyles:** Maybe they work an unusual shift or live in a different time zone than you do.

>> **For connecting with people who are busy:** Maybe you want to connect but don't want to bother them. If you send a voice or text message, they can reply when they have more time. Remember to ask them to get back to you if you want a reply. They might not realize your need.

>> **If you don't feel so confident speaking over the phone:** Text and voice messages can feel more comfortable if you lack confidence.

>> **If your calling recipient might not feel comfortable on live voice or video calls:** Maybe you're comfortable, but your friend isn't. A text or voice message is a good alternative.

>> **If you want to send photos with a short text or voice message:** This can also be a good way to connect with people. Sharing snippets of your life, such as a holiday snap or a photo of your house or local neighborhood, can generate a greater sense of connection while giving you something to discuss if you do eventually talk in person, by phone or video.

>> **If you want your relationship to be meaningful:** Try to share emotions and personal experiences in your messages so that you connect on a deeper level and increase your chances of creating or sustaining a meaningful relationship.

>> **If you want to keep the dialogue going:** Remember to ask questions so that you get a response to your messages and stimulate further dialogue.

>> **If you want to leave voice or text messages about things that matter:** These could be topics of mutual interest, such as sports, music, your family, or work.

>> **If you don't have anyone to text:** You can use one of the many friendship apps that are designed to connect people. I explain more about these later in this chapter.

Social media

What is social media, and how should it be defined? Social media is generally seen as interactive technology which enables people and groups to create and share information virtually. This is done through virtual networks and communities. It's sometimes described as an online facilitator or enhancer of human networks that can support social connectivity. The information that people and groups share through social media can include written messages, photographs, videos, and links to online information. Almost anything really.

Social media has expanded rapidly and now plays a key part in many people's daily lives. Whether you're a seasoned user of social media or have never dabbled in it before, this section helps you use social media in a way that connects you to other people.

Social media is a great tool to use if you feel lonely. It enables you to reach many people whom you've had a connection with in the past or whom you might want to connect with for the first time. Facebook is a good place to start. With billions of users worldwide, it's one of the world's most popular social media sites. With such vast numbers of people on it, you're bound to find someone to connect with.

How social media can help against loneliness

Social media can reduce loneliness by broadening your range of connections. You can rekindle relationships that might have drifted in the past or find new relationships with those who share your hobbies, values or life circumstances.

REAL WORLD EXAMPLE

Here's a simple scenario. Ella is 25. She was feeling particularly lonely because she split up from her boyfriend at the same time that she decided to stop communicating with her abusive father. Although she still had a good relationship with her mother, she felt extremely lonely. Ella decided to use social media to track down an old friend, Michelle, whom she hadn't seen since college. The two old friends connected via Instagram and started exchanging messages. After a while they met up face to face, and now they're best buddies again.

REAL WORLD EXAMPLE

Julian is 70 years old. His wife recently died, and his son migrated to the other side of the world for work. His house suddenly felt really empty because he'd shared it for the past 40 years with his wife and son, and now they were gone. Many of his old friends had died or moved away, and he'd lost contact with them. Julian had never used social media before but decided to try Facebook. Because he used to be a keen runner, he joined a few athletics and running groups, and before long he was engaging in discussions with people online about his favorite sport. Although all these encounters were virtual, he started to feel motivated about life once again.

Identifying which social media platforms to use

You can choose from an assortment of social media websites and apps. If you're using them to connect with other people and to feel less lonely, consider which ones are the best for you.

TIP

You might want to start with one or two of the more popular social media websites. Those with more than 100 million registered users include Twitter (now X), Facebook (and its connected Messenger app), Instagram, LinkedIn, WeChat, ShareChat, QZone, Weibo, VK, Tumblr, and Baidu Tieba. Why not do an internet search and see which social media websites you like the look of?

When you're looking through the websites, think about how you prefer to communicate with other people. If you prefer to share links and brief messages, you might like a site such as Twitter. If you prefer to share photographs and videos, Instagram might be good for you. If you're trying to make connections with work colleagues on a professional level, LinkedIn might be your best choice because you can display content from your resume.

WARNING

Choose your social media website carefully. You have numerous options, but if you're using social media to connect with other people, stick to an outlet that helps you develop authentic social connections in a community that feels welcoming and supportive.

Having selected your social media platform, start searching for people whom you might know currently or have known in the past. Try to form a relationship with them by liking a post they shared, inviting them to connect with you, or sending them a personal message.

You can share your own posts and photographs once you get the hang of things. Try tagging some of your connections in your posts to expand your network quicker. If you don't know many people on your social media outlet and are having difficulties connecting with people, try to join a group. Social media groups cover all sorts of topics, so there's bound to be something you're interested in.

Once you join a group, you'll start seeing posts and messages about topics of interest, and you can reply and start making connections with people who have similar interests. I primarily use Facebook, for example, and am a member of various groups connected to Sheffield Wednesday, which is the football team I support. As a result, I frequently see posts about new signings, views on the latest match, and conversations about the team's chances of promotion. I can chat online with others about any of these topics.

KNOWING WHEN TO DISCONNECT

Social media can enable you to interact with many people online. Although that's often a good thing, it can also create challenges. It's easy to compare your life to what others are posting online. You might feel that they have more friends, a better social life, a better body shape, are more attractive, go on more expensive vacations to more exotic locations, or just generally have more money. This can exacerbate mental ill-health, make you feel lonelier, depressed or anxious. If you do start to feel worse by engaging in social media, reduce your daily usage to 30 minutes, and remind yourself that people only post on social media what they want you to see.

Often others aren't as happy or fulfilled as you might think based on their posts. Also, be careful of anyone on social media asking you to exchange money, personal information, or inappropriate photographs or images. If you have any doubt about the intentions of a request, report it immediately to the platform's moderator, and block the user from your account.

You can also join a social media group that can support you when you're feeling lonely. There are groups for all kinds of emotional and physical health conditions, including loneliness. Search through some of the support groups you might want to join. You can connect with like-minded people but also get help and support.

If you're particularly keen to connecting with others who live in your community, some of the social media sites have local groups you can join. Many schools have social media groups; they're often set up by past pupils or students and are great ways to reconnect with old school pals. I've reconnected with a few school friends this way, first by chatting online, and then by arranging to meet up in person.

WARNING

Although social media is a great way to reduce your feelings of loneliness, if you use social media too much, it can actually make you feel more lonely. In terms of social media usage, less is definitely more. Some research shows that limiting the time you spend on social media can be beneficial and that if social media is making you feel lonelier, restricting your time on it to 30 minutes a day can help alleviate these feelings.

Friendship apps

If you've tried to connect with people you already know by calling them, texting them, or contacting them on social media without luck, don't despair. Connecting to new people has never been easier with digital technology. One way to find new like-minded people to connect with is through friendship apps.

REMEMBER

Friendship apps are like dating apps, but they're designed to help you make platonic relationships. And they're becoming increasingly popular. You can find a number of friendship apps on the market, and because it's an area of growing interest and popularity, I imagine many more will emerge in the coming years. Some of the key friendship apps at the moment include Meetup, Hey! VINA, TalkLife, Youper, Predictable, Happify, Yubo, Peanut, Pally, Bumble BFF, and Bloom community.

Some of these apps target the general population who want to make friends, and others target specific population groups. So, for example, Hey! VINA targets women, Peanut focuses on pregnant women and new mothers, and Yubo targets young adults. Bloom Community is more of an events-based app that organizes in-person group experiences; it's especially concerned with helping people from marginalized communities, such as LGBTQIA+ people. Some of the apps allow you to find your own companions by searching through photos of individuals, whereas others apply social psychology to match users.

TIP

If you feel especially nervous starting a conversation with someone you don't know, a friendship app makes it easier. People using friendship apps are open to having new friends, so you should get a positive reception if you reach out to them. Here are a few tips to help you if you're using a friendship app for the first time, or haven't had much success when using one previously:

>> Think about the type of person you want to connect with in advance of using the app. You can be selective.

>> Be spontaneous. Sometimes it's best to go with your gut feeling rather than analyzing the kind of person you want to connect with too much. This might open your world to new types of people whom you wouldn't normally connect with.

>> Use the apps to chat with a whole range of people until you find someone who's compatible.

>> If you don't find anyone you get along with straight away, don't fret. Give it a little more time, or try a different app.

WARNING

It's always best to check the safeguarding measures that the apps use. Follow their guidelines on how and when to meet people face to face and take any of the recommended precautions. Be careful not to exchange personal information, money, inappropriate images, or photographs. If you're in any doubt about the intentions of a request, report it immediately to the platform's moderator. When you meet someone in person for the first time, it's safest to do so in a public place. Tell someone where and when you're meeting the person, and if you feel in any danger at any time, call for help.

If you don't like the idea of friendship apps, you can find some tips about how to create new relationships in Chapter 14.

Distracting Yourself with "Surrogate Relationships"

When you feel lonely, especially if it's a temporary or transitory loneliness following a change in your life, it's a good idea to initially use distraction techniques to take your mind away from feeling lonely.

You can do this in a number of ways. You can take yourself to a place where you feel a sense of belonging, such as a park or a beach (Chapter 15), you can keep busy by throwing yourself into your work (Chapter 6), or you might even adopt a pet (Chapter 4).

Another strategy you can use is to immerse yourself in entertainment or informational media, such as the TV or radio. These are old items of technology, but they're still useful tools today, and they're easily available. They can not only act as a distraction from your feelings of loneliness but can provide you with a surrogate — a replacement or pseudo-social connection. Of course, the more modern versions of entertainment and informational media today are streaming services and podcasts, and they also work quite well to curb loneliness.

There are a few ways you can try using the TV and radio to combat your feelings of loneliness.

>> When you're alone in the house and feeling especially lonely, turn on the radio or TV at a low volume for some background noise.

>> Try different radio or TV channels until you find the ones that you enjoy and that distract you from your feelings of loneliness.

>> If you have a strong sense of belonging to a particular place, tune into a radio or TV channel that is broadcast from there. It could be a location in the same country or elsewhere in the world. Or it could be a program about a particular place or interest you have.

>> Listen or watch channels that play your favorite style of music and boost your mood.

>> If you're feeling particularly brave, enter a radio quiz or game show, or engage in a phone-in to spark some interaction and conversation.

>> Listen to podcasts based on topics you're interested in.

WARNING

Although both the TV and the radio can be good distractions and provide you with surrogate social connections when you feel lonely, think of them as short-term measures. Once you begin to feel a little less lonely by distracting yourself or connecting with your favorite TV characters or radio presenters, start trying some of the other activities in the different chapters of this book. That will help you complement your pseudo-social friends with real ones. These surrogate relationships are really intended to be temporary bridges and not permanent solutions to long-term loneliness. In particular, it's important to remain active and get out of the house, especially as you get older.

TV and streaming services

A traditional form of technological-based distraction and friendship replacer is the TV. When I was younger, it was my main source of technological distraction, and I gained many TV "friends" from the popular soap operas of the time. The TV is still a key source of entertainment today, whether it's watched on a traditional TV set or on a laptop, smartphone, or tablet. People of all ages find TV stimulating and distracting from their everyday strains and stresses. They also find it to be a source of comfort and companionship. Many older people and people who are homebound say that the TV is their main source of companionship.

REMEMBER

It might seem too simple to be true, but watching TV can help you feel less lonely. Alongside being a distraction, the TV can compensate for a lack of social interaction and provide pseudo-social connections. A pseudo-social connection is a kind of superficial but not actual connection. These pseudo-social connections can provide fictional bonds with TV characters to aide in companionship — in the short term at least.

As a short-term solution, watching TV is reported to supply the same kind of emotional relief that you can get from being with real people. It can help you create parasocial relationships. *Parasocial relationships* are one-sided relationships you can develop with people or characters whom you see on the screen. You can gain these parasocial relationships by watching fictional characters on your favorite TV shows and becoming involved with their personal lives as their stories unfold. These parasocial relationships evolve the more you watch the characters, just like a relationship with a real friend evolves. The good thing about these parasocial relationships is that when you feel lonely you can find them quickly and easily simply by putting your favorite show on the TV. And because these characters aren't real, quite often their lives are much more interesting!

TIP

So if you're feeling particularly lonely and want a quick and easy remedy, switch on the TV and watch your favorite show. You'll soon find that you've forgotten all about your loneliness and are strengthening the fictional bond you have with the characters on screen. This can be especially helpful if you have a long-term health condition, you're getting older and can't easily get out of the house as much as you used to, or you're experiencing a transitory loneliness (see Chapter 2) due to a particular change such as switching schools, migrating, or transitioning to a new job.

Radio and podcasts

Callum is a 35-year-old gay man. He recently split up from his partner of 10 years and felt very lonely. Life at home had become isolating after Marcus moved out of their apartment. Marcus was loud and noisy, and now the rooms felt silent and lonely. Since Marcus left, all Callum could hear was the clock ticking away. When Marcus was around, Callum never even realized the clock made a noise. Callum started listening to the local radio station. At first he used it to silence the noise of the clock ticking, but it immediately made him feel less lonely. Then he started tuning into different radio stations that played good music. His mood really lifted.

Like TV, the radio can help you feel less lonely. Having been around for well over a century, the radio is an old form of technology, but it still plays an important role in today's society. Around three billion people worldwide are reported to listen to the radio every week at home, in their cars, and at work. It can distract you from your feelings of loneliness and help you connect to other people. In surveys that aim to understand people's experience of loneliness, people often report that listening to the radio helps them feel less lonely.

Tuning into the radio can help you feel less lonely in a number of ways:

>> **Providing distraction:** The sounds emanating from the radio, whether through music or voices, can distract you from your feelings of loneliness. The sounds can fill a void in your thoughts and environment that can make the loneliness feel less overwhelming.

>> **Deadening the silence:** The radio is a quick and easy way to fill the house with noise. When you feel lonely and alone, the house suddenly feels quiet, and you might notice that you have only your internal thoughts for company. Radio presenters can make the house feel less empty. You don't even need to turn the volume up high. Just having the radio on quietly can provide background noise and voices to make you feel less alone. It's an effective coping mechanism.

>> **Engaging the mind:** Depending on which channel you tune into, the radio can stimulate your mind. As you're listening to discussions about topics that are important to you, your mind is both informed and entertained. Podcasts

can be particularly good at engaging your mind, and their conversational approach can create a sense of connection between you and the speaker.

>> **Connecting to the wider world:** The radio is a great way of connecting you to places and spaces around the world through discussions and conversations, plays, music, or simply the news. Besides being informative, this can connect you to places and spaces that you feel a sense of belonging to (see Chapter 15).

>> **Facilitating social connection:** In the same way that the TV can give you a pseudo-social connection to a fictional character, the radio can help you develop a pseudo-social connection to a presenter. The familiarity of the voice can help you feel less lonely. Radio listeners can develop strong bonds with the presenters who they tune into, and often they maintain these relationships by following the presenter even if they change to a different time slot or switch channels. These pseudo-social relationships can offer surrogates for social interaction when people feel lonely.

>> **Supporting active engagement:** Radio phone-ins and game and quiz shows can enable people to actively engage in discussions and dialogue with others in a fairly controlled, though public, way. Even if you're not brave enough to pick up the phone and call in yourself, just listening to others engaging in dialogue can give you a sense of social connections and take the loneliness away for a while.

>> **Providing companionship:** Because the radio is such an intimate medium, it often feels like the person on the radio is talking just to you. By listening, you feel like you're part of a conversation even if you're not actually speaking.

>> **Boosting your mood:** The music played on the radio can boost your mood and give you a sense of well-being that will make you feel less lonely. It might also make you feel more able to engage in real-life social contact.

Immersing in a Virtual World

If you're experiencing a temporary or transitory loneliness, where something has triggered you to feel lonely, immersing yourself in a virtual world might be just what you need as a short-term solution to take your mind off your feelings of loneliness. But the benefits of virtual reality aren't limited to mere distractions from everyday life. Immersing yourself in virtual reality can connect you to other people and connect you to places and spaces (see Chapter 15) that you feel a sense of belonging to, both of which can help you feel less lonely.

Toying with virtual reality and augmented reality

REMEMBER

Virtual reality refers to a setting that's simulated entirely by a computer. All the objects you see are virtual. If you use virtual reality, you see computer-simulated graphics in real time, which allows you to have an immersive digital experience. Augmented reality, on the other hand, uses the real physical world but enhances it by using computer graphics in real time.

Both virtual reality and augmented reality have been around for a while, but recent technological advances have meant that an immersive environment is now more widely available. If you decide to try either virtual reality or augmented reality, you can use headsets, hand controllers, or wearable devices. When compared to other technologies such as laptops or tablets, these will give you a sensation of being there. You'll feel like you're really at a place or really with a person. This means you can experience a flight over the Alps, a visit to the Pyramids, a trip back in time to a place you remember as a child, or perhaps a walk around a local lake or beauty spot. You'll feel as though you're actually there.

You might even dream up a fantasy-based location and then go and visit it. Other options include engaging in virtual activities like dancing, taking part in interactive art, or playing an endless list of different games. You can use virtual reality experiences on your own, perhaps as an escape from everyday challenges or to forget about feeling lonely for a while. You can use it to connect with a place where you feel a sense of belonging, which can put you at ease. You can also use virtual reality to connect with other people and enjoy the experience together, or you can try competing with someone through a game. Virtual reality can be particularly useful if you have an illness or are homebound because it can allow you to visit places and see people that you wouldn't normally be able to.

WARNING

The research on the impact of virtual reality in the context of loneliness is currently at an early stage. It's important not to replace human contact completely with virtual reality and to limit the amount of time you spend each day immersed in a virtual world. Sometimes going to places in a virtual world, where you've visited before, can improve your mood. But other times it can make you feel upset and sad, especially if you're not able to get there or if you used to visit the place with someone who's no longer in your life. So if you find yourself getting more upset and lonelier, perhaps try visiting somewhere completely different. If you feel particularly lonely or depressed after using virtual reality, there are some helplines in the Appendix which you can contact.

Gaming

Although gaming can be done through virtual reality, it doesn't have to be played that way. You can engage in electronic-based games without immersing yourself in a virtual world. Like the distraction of virtual reality, gaming can take your mind away from your feelings of loneliness for a while.

REMEMBER

You can get involved in gaming activities by purchasing a game console such as Xbox or PlayStation, or you can play games on your tablet, laptop, or smart phone. Games are available for all different tastes and preferences, including word games, card games, sporting games such as football and golf, and action-packed games. You can often connect to other people who are playing the same game, at the same time, anywhere in the world. When you're ready, you can expand beyond playing the game alone to making connections with others through the gaming experience. Multiplayer platforms can be especially helpful in increasing social connection, forming community, and reducing loneliness.

Gaming can also benefit your emotional health and well-being, which are both intertwined with feelings of loneliness. Gaming can create a sense of achievement and purpose. In fact, game developers are now designing games to address psychological issues and improve mental well-being. A game called *Sea of Solitude* even has loneliness as its main theme. It was created by someone after a relationship breakdown and is based on their real-life experiences. In the game, Kay, the heroine, has to fight humans who have turned into monsters because they became lonely. To save herself from becoming one of them, Kay has to fight her own loneliness.

Some games that involve a number of different people playing simultaneously are strategy-style games. Up to 50 or more players engage in complex missions that are only successful if the players communicate effectively and work together. Games that encourage people to interact instead of play in solitude can be good for helping with loneliness.

Many games also enable the establishment of a communication channel outside the game to discuss game strategy and delegate tasks. Although discussions often start with the game, they can move onto other issues. Sometimes these kinds of interactions can allow players to express themselves in ways they might not feel able to in their real lives. This can foster the development of meaningful relationships between game players. (See Chapter 14 for more help with developing meaningful relationships.)

TIP

Do some research on the internet and decide which types of hardware you want to use for gaming. Are you going to buy a dedicated gaming console or use an existing device, such as a laptop, mobile phone, or tablet? If you're new to gaming, you might want to try out an existing device before splurging on a games console.

Decide which kinds of games you're going to play based on your interests. Do you prefer action-based games or more sedate word games, such as Scrabble? If you're not sure, download a few and see which styles suit you best. You might find that you prefer different types of games at different times of the day or week or depending on your mood.

If you're keen to engage with other people as well as distract yourself from feeling lonely, it's a good idea to play a game that engages with others. Again, do some research to find the best multiplayer games in your area of interest.

Try to engage in chats and discussions with other gamers outside of the game-playing sphere to create meaningful connections. You can start by conversing about the game and strategy and then move onto other topics, such as what activities they enjoy when they're not gaming. Before you know it, you'll have a new group of virtual gaming friends that you might want to meet in person.

WARNING

Make sure you don't spend too much time gaming because it can be addictive. Even if you gain friends through gaming, try to have face-to-face interaction too. (Chapter 14 has further advice.) Too much gaming can lead to a sedentary lifestyle, and it's especially important to get some physical exercise to improve your health and well-being. Also, read about a game before playing it. Some involve violent, sexist, racist, or homophobic behavior that can be upsetting.

Social robots

Social robots, or robotic friends, have recently started to emerge as an alternative for social companionship, especially when it's difficult to gain interaction with other humans. The main use of social robots to date has been to support older people living in residential care homes. They've also been used to support older people who may be homebound. These robots can help older people and their relatives or caregivers manage their health better.

REMEMBER

There are different kinds of robots. For example, Fribo is one that can help friends and family keep an eye on older people who is living in their own home. It can ensure that older people are keeping physically active. It works by creating a virtual living space between a group of houses and by listening for activity in people's houses and encouraging those connected to talk via chat apps. Microphones and sensors on Fribo can recognize activities like when someone comes home, or leaves home, turns on or off a light, or opens a door or fridge. This information is then shared anonymously with the rest of the group. Anyone in the group who hears the message can then text others in the group or send a message to Fribo which then passes a message onto the person being cared for.

Some robots can hold simple conversations and learn people's interests. They've been found to boost mental health and reduce loneliness in nursing home settings. One group of social robots based on mobile robotic telepresence (MRT) systems facilitated positive social interactions with older people. They're essentially video screens, raised to head height, and on wheels. They can be controlled remotely using a smartphone app. These systems allow relatives and caregivers to visit — remotely — their loved ones more often even if they live far away. In these examples, although the communication essentially takes place through a computer screen, the robot's physical presence mimics face-to-face interaction. Research has shown that lonely people react more positively to talking through an MRT robot than through a video call.

Other examples of social robots include pet-like companions. Popular ones include Aibo, Paro, and MiRo. Although pet robots offer limited interaction, research has shown that they're as effective as real pets in reducing loneliness (see Chapter 4), especially for older people living in residential care.

Social robots are a growing area, and although their use at the moment is primarily for supporting older people, in the future I imagine more social and companion robots will emerge, which is likely to affect your experiences of loneliness. Keep an eye on this space!

WARNING

Social robots shouldn't be used as a replacement for human interaction. Doing so can damage a person's mental health and lead to more, rather than less, loneliness. If you have an older relative in a care home who's using companion or social robot, don't forget to maintain personal human interaction too.

3

Dealing with Loneliness During Life Transitions

Chapter **8**

Overcoming Bereavement

Like everyone, you're likely to be affected by bereavement at some point in your life. It can strike at any time and at any age. The older you get, the more likely you are to encounter it. The bereavement associated with the loss of a loved one is a key life transition that can trigger loneliness.

Loneliness can occur regardless of how old the person was who passed away, whether it was expected or a shock, and whatever their relationship to you. You can feel lonely after the death of anyone you've had a connection to, even if you'd lost contact with that person, and even if the relationship you had wasn't a positive one.

You might feel lonely because of the missed opportunity of a relationship you never had. Loneliness can arise following the death of a spouse or partner, parent, child, friend, sibling, other relative, or work colleague. What's more, loneliness triggered by bereavement can strike at any time. It can arise immediately after the death of the person, or it can occur days, weeks, or months later.

One of the reasons loneliness strikes at different times following the death of a loved one is because grieving occurs in different ways. There's no right or wrong way to grieve; it's a personal and individualized experience. If you don't feel lonely after someone close to you has died, it doesn't mean that they weren't important to you. Likewise, if you do feel lonely, that unpleasant feeling won't necessarily last forever.

In this chapter I help you understand why you might be feeling lonely following the loss of a loved one. Then I provide some tips on how to deal with the loneliness that can emerge and offer some strategies for resuming life again when you feel ready.

The Loneliness of Grief

Grief affects everyone differently. It can take so many forms that it doesn't really have a normal or right way. Grieving can make you feel numb, sad, angry, depressed, anxious, worried, physically ill, unable to sleep or eat, or more sleepy or hungry.

It's widely acknowledged that bereavement has five stages:

>> **Denial:** You might feel unable to believe or accept that the person has died. This might lead to feelings of shock, disbelief, panic, or confusion.

>> **Anger:** You might feel extremely angry and annoyed that the person has been taken from you or about the way in which they died. This might lead you to blame people for their death. You might blame the person who died, yourself, or others.

>> **Depression:** You may experience a somber mood that affects your everyday life. It might come and go, or it might last for a while. Depression can make you feel like there's no joy or pleasure in life.

>> **Bargaining:** You try to find a way to avoid or reverse the loss or to reduce the pain. You can start making promises to yourself or to a higher power hoping you'll feel better. This phase can also lead to feelings of guilt. You might think that if you'd acted differently, things could have been different.

>> **Acceptance:** You start to accept the loss and understand what it means for you and your life going forward. This doesn't mean that you like what happened. In this stage you accept the loss even though you may still feel bad about it. You're starting to see the way ahead.

Although these are generally accepted as the most frequently experienced stages of grief, everyone experiences grief differently. You're likely to go through each of these stages at some point following bereavement, but you won't necessarily go through them smoothly from one to the next, and you won't necessarily experience the stages in this order.

One of the feelings that you can experience at any or all of these stages is loneliness. For some people this can be an overwhelming sense that you haven't experienced before. I know it sounds like a cliché, and it's hard to believe when you're right in the thick of grieving for a loved one, but these unpleasant, intense feelings will diminish over time. When you're feeling particularly lonely, try to remind yourself that these feelings, however bad they are right now, won't stay the same or last forever. I provide some tips later in this chapter to help you deal with the loneliness resulting from bereavement.

REMEMBER

You might feel particularly lonely following the loss of a loved one for a number of reasons. Understanding what the triggers are for your specific feelings can help you through the bereavement stages.

Loss of companionship

If your main companion passes away, you might feel that you've lost your soul mate or confidant, which can be a particularly lonely experience. You might have lost a key attachment figure, such as a romantic partner, whom you were emotionally close to.

Loneliness is one of the biggest challenges that those who are widowed have to overcome on a daily basis. If you lived with the person who passed away, you might find yourself living alone, perhaps for the first time. This loss of a supportive companion can mean that, at least in the short term, you feel more of a sense of loss and loneliness than if you'd not had that supportive companion in the first place.

If you spent most of your time with that person, you might not have many friends or family to connect with. Or the loss of your main companion might make you feel lonely even when you're with friends and family.

John was an older man I spoke to for a research project. He and his wife had been married and living together for more than 50 years, and following his wife's death he felt intensely lonely. He and his wife did everything together, and not even regular visits from his children and grandchildren could soothe his feelings of loneliness.

TIP

Losing a major companion can take time to come to terms with. It's important to recognize that things will feel better over time, and you won't always be this lonely. When you're ready, try some of the tips later in this chapter. And remember that reaching out for support and companionship doesn't mean that you care any less for the person who passed.

Breakdown of your social network

Following the death of a loved one, you might feel a loss of companionship not only from the person who died, but from your wider social network. If that starts to dissipate, you can experience *social loneliness*. This is when you lack a wider network of social support, such as friends or work colleagues.

A breakdown of your social network can occur following the death of a loved one for a range of reasons. Your deceased partner might have been the one who arranged social gatherings with friends, and they're no longer around to do that. Or your social circle may have revolved primarily around your deceased partner's friends and family.

In some cases the death can strain your wider social network, and relationships can break down. Such a breakdown in family or friendship networks following bereavement is quite common and was mentioned by many research participants in a project that looked specifically at loneliness and bereavement.

TIP

If your social network has broken down following a bereavement, you'll find some useful tips later in this chapter on how to resume them. Chapters 5 and 14 include more detail on how to forge new relationships.

When others move on

Quite often right after someone close to you dies, you're in contact with a lot of people. You'll undoubtedly have contact with a range of individuals who need to be notified, such as health professionals, funeral directors, financial institutions, and so on. Friends and family often make contact immediately following a death and on the lead-up to the funeral.

However, you might find that soon after the funeral, people stop reaching out as much. Jenny, a recently bereaved widow, felt lonely when her husband died. Initially, acquaintances and family were around to see if she was coping. But after a while she felt like people had forgotten all about her and her husband and assumed she was fine. Months after her husband's death, she saw very few people and thus continued to feel lonely.

TIP

If it feels that friends and family have forgotten about you since your loss, try taking the initiative and contacting them. Ask them if they want to meet up over coffee, or look at some of the tips I provide in Chapter 14 on reconnecting with others. Sometimes when you're grieving, you can be reluctant to ask for support and feel as though others should contact you. But now's not the time to be too proud to ask for help. And, in any case, your friends and family are unlikely to be intentionally ignoring you; they're just unsure how to help you through your grieving process.

When I was 17, my friend Paula told me that her mother had died during summer vacation. I was completely shocked and didn't know what to say, so I didn't say anything. I didn't ask how she was or invite her to my house after school. It wasn't because I didn't care. I just didn't know how to deal with the situation myself.

Losing your caregiving role

If you were the caregiver for the person who passed on, it can be a particularly difficult time, with many mixed emotions haunting your thoughts. Caregiving for loved ones can, itself, trigger loneliness. However, when your caregiving role ends, it can leave a big void. Not only do you lose the companionship of the person you were caring for, but you're suddenly left with many hours to fill that you previously spent looking after that person.

If your caregiving responsibilities were particularly intense, you might not have had much time for yourself or for any other relationships apart from the person you were caring for. You may not have had time or energy to maintain your wider social network of friends, family, and work colleagues. You may have had to give up paid employment and social activities. Maybe it's been a long time since you've socialized with anyone other than the person you cared for. It's understandable, then, that this can trigger loneliness.

TIP

I discuss the loneliness arising specifically from a change to your caregiving role in Chapter 11, so if you've been a caregiver and the person you cared for has passed away, it might be helpful to read this chapter and Chapter 11 in conjunction.

Changed sense of belonging

I mention elsewhere in this book, in particular in Chapter 15, the important role that a sense of belonging can play in warding off or reducing loneliness. When someone passes away who connected you to a place where you have a sense of belonging, being there can reduce your sense of loneliness and make you feel more connected to the person who passed on. This was the case for an older woman named Serena. She had a strong sense of belonging to the house she lived in with her late husband. The house was now too big for her, but it was filled with happy memories of her life with her husband, which she said helped her overcome her loneliness.

For others, places where a sense of belonging is felt can have the opposite effect and actually trigger loneliness. This often occurs when the place you feel a sense of belonging to was shared with, or reminds you of, the loved one who passed away. In this situation you might find yourself feeling lonelier when visiting a place that, in previous circumstances, made you feel less lonely. A good example of this was relayed to me by a football fan friend of mine named Natasha. She used to support her local team with her friend Lucy. A few years ago Lucy died of cancer, and Natasha stopped going to the games. She said it was too painful and lonely to continue supporting her team because it reminded her of her times there with her friend.

TIP

Grief affects everyone differently. If you feel less or more lonely being in places where you had a shared sense of belonging, or shared memories with the person who has passed away, it doesn't mean that you cared more or less about them. It simply means that you're experiencing your grief differently. The important thing is to notice how certain places make you feel. If they make you feel lonelier, avoid them for now. You might find that over time you can resume visiting these places that once gave you a source of comfort.

Practical obstacles

After a loved one dies, you might face practical barriers that can isolate you and contribute to your loneliness. Maybe you relied on the person who passed away financially, or they were your caregiver. Perhaps they drove you around or organized social events and holidays. If any of these situations applies to you, the loss of your loved one might have created practical obstacles that make connecting with others more difficult.

TIP

If you're not used to organizing get-togethers with family or friends, I offer some useful tips in Chapters 4, 5, and 14.

If you need support with your care, read through Chapter 11, and see the Appendix for some useful resources and helplines.

Dealing with Loss in Your Own Way (and Time)

The loneliness that accompanies grief affects everyone differently. Like grief itself, there's no right or wrong way to deal with it, or any specific time period when you'll start to feel less lonely. Allow yourself time to grieve, and remember that you won't feel like this forever. With time you'll start to accept your loss and gradually feel less lonely. Once you feel like you want to move on, it can be helpful to adopt a flexible approach to coping, which involves processing the loss, moving beyond it, and considering any positive consequences.

For example, when my father-in-law lost his wife, he was able to travel to Austria. He'd been stationed there during the Second World War and had always longed to return. Enjoying his trip to this mountainous country, where he felt a sense of belonging, distracted him from his loneliness but didn't mean that he missed his wife any less.

There are a number of ways you can deal with your loss to help you feel less lonely. I explore some of those options now.

Visiting death cafés

Death cafés represent a community-based approach of supporting individuals, families, and communities to prepare for illness, death, grieving, and the associated loneliness that often accompanies the process. Participating in death cafés allows you to share your experiences connected with dying and grief with strangers, which can reduce your loneliness and improve your well-being. A death café might sound depressing, but people generally report leaving them feeling uplifted.

REMEMBER

Death cafés are present in more than 80 countries across the world and are a global social franchise. Public events are organized locally in cafés, restaurants, libraries, or other public spaces, and a volunteer hosts and facilitates discussion about all aspects of death and dying, including loneliness. The main rule for death cafés is that cake or other culturally appropriate foods are provided to honor "our finite lives." The death café approach brings people in communities together. By allowing people to share intimate stories and experiences with others who are going through similar experiences, it can aide in dealing with the loneliness of dying and the loss of a loved one.

TIP

If you want to attend a death café as a participant, go to https://deathcafe.com. Alternatively, if you can't locate one in your local area, or you prefer to host a death café as a volunteer, you can find a useful guide on how to do it here: https://deathcafe.com/how/. You can also check out death cafés on Facebook at https://www.facebook.com/deathcafe. See the Appendix for more details.

Talking to family and friends

Maintaining a relationship with your family and friends following a bereavement is critical. You might not feel much like talking to them initially, but it's helpful to retain your connection with them so that when you do want to talk to someone, you can.

REMEMBER

Being able to talk to family and friends gives you the opportunity to share how you feel. Just getting your feelings off your chest can help. Talking about the person who died can make you feel closer to them. If this is the case, be sure to tell your friends and family that talking about your loved one is helpful for you. Sometimes people avoid discussing the person who died for fear of making you feel worse or lonelier.

If you can, select the friends and family whom you confide in carefully. Some people find talking about grief uncomfortable. If that's the case, they might avoid you, say things that you find hurtful, or become impatient about the time it's taking you to heal.

TIP

Identify people who are good listeners. These might not necessarily be those who are closest to you. It's important not to isolate yourself from other people. If you don't feel you have any suitable friends or family who can support you as you need, try attending a death café, or seek to widen your social network. (See Chapters 5 and 14 for some tips on how to do this.)

Peer and bereavement support

Sharing your grief and accompanied feelings of loneliness with other people who have had similar experiences can be beneficial. You can feel less alone in your feelings, and you can get some useful tips on coping by listening to others share their stories. One way you can gain this kind of support is through specialized peer bereavement support. This is usually offered in person or by phone. It can take the form of group support, where a trained volunteer who has experienced bereavement themselves facilitates a group of bereaved people. Or it can be a one-on-one service in which a trained volunteer talks just to you and offers you individual support. Both group and one-on-one bereavement support are usually provided by charitable organizations in your local community.

TIP

I've provided some useful links in the Appendix, but you can also find your local bereavement charity through an internet search or by visiting your local library. Alternatively, you might want to try social media bereavement groups so you can connect to others who have experienced bereavement. Search for a group that suits you on your favorite social media platform.

Counseling and therapy

REMEMBER

Following bereavement, you might find it easier to talk to a professional counselor or therapist who has specialized skills to help you deal with your loss and the accompanying loneliness. Bereavement counseling is offered by a trained counselor who's qualified to help with your feelings of grief and loneliness.

Bereavement counselors can help you process the feelings you have as you go through the stages of grief and the loneliness that can accompany it. You can talk to them about the person who died, how their death is affecting you, and how you're coping. The bereavement counselor will help you understand your feelings and begin to adapt to life without your loved one.

TIP

The way to get bereavement counseling varies depending on the country you're living in and your health care system. If you work for a large employer, they may have access to bereavement counseling support. Or if your loved one used hospice care, you can often access bereavement counseling support through that route. Some charitable organizations offer bereavement counseling, or you can find a counselor privately and pay for sessions. Costs will vary. Many therapists have their own websites explaining how they work and what to expect.

Journaling

REMEMBER

Journaling involves writing about your thoughts and feelings on a regular basis. It's a type of expressive coping method, which is a technique that helps you process negative thoughts, feelings, or experiences by releasing them. As you express your thoughts by writing them down you feel as though you're more in control of them, and that they have less power over you.

Journaling is an effective and powerful way to process different emotions that you might be feeling as a result of a whole range of issues, including grief, stress, and trauma. It has been demonstrated that Journaling can improve your mental health by:

>> reducing stress and anxiety.

>> helping you regulate your emotions.

>> improving your self-awareness.

>> supporting you to relax and sleep.

>> helping you to solve problems and make sound decisions.

You can spend as little or as much time Journaling as you wish. It can be done in a few minutes a day, or you can spend much longer on it. It can involve writing just a few words, or a long piece, or you can use it as a creative experience to produce images and art. You can start journaling straight away by purchasing a purchasing a book or journal that you use specifically for expressing your feelings. There are also a whole range of pre-designed journals for you to choose from. If you're not sure how to get started, or what to write why not start by using one of these questions as a prompt:

>> What are your main challenges at the moment?

>> What are you grateful for today?

>> What would you like to do right now if you could and had no restrictions?

>> Where would you like to be in 5 years?

If you prefer you can also opt for guided journaling, which is what my colleague, Fiona did to help her with the grief of multiple pregnancy losses.

REAL WORLD EXAMPLE

Fiona endured nine pregnancy losses of varying types, and one successful pregnancy over a 7-year period from age 37 to 43. She found the isolation and loneliness that resulted from her fertility journey multi-layered. Friends and acquaintances distanced themselves. They didn't contact her as much as they didn't want to intrude, they didn't know what to say, and they were worried about reminding her of her loss.

Fiona also found herself withdrawing from social contact too, and lost friends in the process. She used to have friends with whom she spent maternity leave and she found it harder and harder to spend time with them, as they were trying to conceive again. Baby news was something she found hard to be around. It was a difficult trigger: reminding her how her life was stuck in limbo while theirs had moved on. This also impacted her self-identity and as a result her confidence in who she was and her values.

Initially to deal with the grief of the pregnancy losses, Fiona joined a weekly online journaling group and this has been her lifesaver. The guided journaling sessions are led by a trained life coach and have been pivotal for her self-development; acknowledging and processing her grief; recognizing the associated trauma around pregnancy loss and its effect on her; and building her resilience and emotional literacy. Through the journaling, she has reconnected with her self-identity and knows what her values are and how to align her life with them again. In addition, the group members have become firm friends and although the meetings are usually virtual this does translate to real-world meetings from time to time as well, which are an absolute joy.

Resuming Your Life

Resuming your life doesn't mean that you should forget about the person who passed away. It simply means that you can start to live your life again without them. You can still keep a connection with the person who died as you're resuming your life.

TIP

Talking about their loved one, making a photo album of them, or looking through photographs or videos of them might help you move on. You'll probably feel sad immediately after doing any of these things, but these actions can also help you feel closer to the one you lost and more able to carry out the normal day-to-day activities you enjoy.

Getting out and about again

When you feel able to, start getting out and about again and doing the activities you enjoy. There's no right or wrong time when you should resume these activities. You might feel that you need to resume life as quickly as possible, or you might need longer to adjust. Both responses are okay, and neither means that you don't care about the person who died. A 52-year-old woman I spoke to recently whose partner had just died a few weeks earlier said that she had to get on with her life again as soon as possible as an "act of self-preservation." She needed to start doing the things she loved to do again so she, too, wouldn't "go under."

TIP

Maybe it's been a while since you've engaged in activities you enjoy, especially if the person you're mourning had a long illness or you were their caregiver. You might want to make a list of all the activities you used to enjoy doing and all those activities you've always wanted to do, or places you'd like to visit but haven't yet. List anything you want, from going to the gym or attending more live theatre, to traveling overseas, revisiting a childhood haunt, or getting tickets for your favorite band. Work your way through the list one at a time. If an activity or place makes you feel more upset or lonely, move onto the next activity. If you find an activity you enjoy, do it again. You might even meet new like-minded people while you're there. (See Chapter 14 for help on connecting with others in a meaningful way.)

Challenging yourself

There's nothing like challenging yourself to keep you busy and distract you from your loneliness. You could get involved in fundraising for a charity that supports the health condition your loved one died from so that you're doing some wider good at the same time. Many charities offer opportunities to get involved in challenging fundraising activities, such as marathons, runs or walks, zip lines, or mountain climbing.

TIP

Do an internet search to see if there's a charitable challenge you like the looks of or that contributes to an important cause. Some employers offer ways to get involved in charitable challenges. A challenge offers a way to meet other people you can connect with. You can also set your own challenge.

Making small steps to (re)connection

After losing a loved one, it can feel difficult to (re)connect with other people again. You might have isolated yourself following your bereavement, or your family and friends might have carried on with their lives, seemingly forgetting about your grief. Your social circle may have been intrinsically linked to the person who died, or they may have been responsible for arranging your social events. Whatever your situation, the key thing is to take small steps to reconnect with other people again. And if you can't reconnect, find new people whom you might be able to develop meaningful relationships with. Chapters 5 and 14 include some detailed tips on how to do this, but here are a few ideas to get you started:

>> **Get involved in a local community group or charity.** Many organizations hold community meals and other activities tackling loneliness.

>> **Join a club or activity.** If you're ready, join a new club or activity. This could be anything from sports, to crafts, or even a new faith group. The website Meetup (https://www.meetup.com) is a great way to find people in your area with similar hobbies.

>> **Volunteer.** Volunteering is a great way to meet new people in your local area. The opportunities are numerous. Check out which exist in your local area by visiting your local library or doing an internet search. Your employer may also offer volunteering opportunities.

>> **Exercise.** Physical exercise is a good way to improve your well-being, which will in turn help you deal with your grief and feelings of loneliness. Try going for a walk or run regularly, or better yet join a walking or running group. Your local park might have a run too. (See Chapter 14 for more details.) You can also join your local gym; before you know it, you'll be chatting with a fellow member as you're both out of breath on the exercise equipment.

IN THIS CHAPTER

» Managing loneliness and reaching out

» Dealing with the impact of disability

» coping with ailments . . .

» Managing through severe illness

Chapter **9**

The Loneliness of Health Conditions and Disabilities

B eing ill and being lonely often go hand in hand, creating a loop of causation. Loneliness can lead to ill-health, and ill-health can lead to loneliness. Chapter 3 describes how loneliness can increase your risk of some physical health conditions, such as heart disease and dementia. However, many physical health conditions can also, themselves, be a trigger for loneliness. For some, the diagnosis alone leads to loneliness, particularly for conditions such as cancer and HIV. For others, the symptoms of the condition can lead to loneliness. Or it could a combination of the two.

Experiences of loneliness that are triggered by one or more health conditions can fluctuate depending on the type of illness. Some diseases can create symptoms that flare up at particular times. So too can your feelings of loneliness, which can mirror these peaks of ill health. This means that your feelings of loneliness may vary over a day, a week, a month, or a year. If you have a long-term health condition or multiple conditions, you might find that the impact on your ability to maintain and create new meaningful connections with people or places is particularly severely affected, which may make you especially vulnerable to loneliness.

In this chapter I look at ways in which you can limit any loneliness which emerges due to ill-health or a disability. I then explore three broad groups of health conditions that can contribute to loneliness: disabilities; disorders that can affect your self-image, such as skin conditions; and serious health conditions, such as HIV and cancer.

Of course, I could have explored several other health conditions that can influence if and how lonely you feel, but you'll get the gist of how physical conditions relate to loneliness based on what I *have* covered.

Preventing Loneliness Due to a Physical Illness or Disability

Regardless of the individual circumstances, you can apply many tips and strategies provided in this section to prevent a physical health condition or a disability from causing or exacerbating loneliness.

Finding or creating outlets for support

If you have a disability or another kind of health condition, it can be tempting to say that you're okay when asked, even if you're not. Often you don't want to be a burden to other people, so you don't tell them the whole truth.

However, it's important to share how you feel; otherwise, family, friends, and caregivers won't know. Sometimes people around can focus on providing you with practical support, but it might be more important to you that they sit down and converse instead.

If you have a disability or long-term health condition there are various avenues for support.

Maintain contact with friends and family

Maintaining contact with friends and family can be a challenge, especially if you have difficulties getting out of your home. Invite friends and family over, arrange routine online calls, FaceTime them, or have frequent phone conversations.

REMEMBER

Text messages are popular because they're a quick and easy way to communicate, but hearing someone's voice can be a more effective way of keeping your loneliness at bay. It's more personal.

Open up

Talk to people about how you feel. They could be family, friends, or work colleagues or maybe just someone who's a good listener. You might need some time to process your feelings first, but when the time's right, tell them about your disability or health condition and how it's affecting you. Communicating about it will help you feel that you're not alone and will assist in gaining a sense of connection to others.

Online or in-person support groups

Both online and in person support groups offer support and knowledge about managing your specific condition. Many of the popular social media channels have support groups you can join. These enable you to meet virtually with people who are dealing with similar health conditions and write and respond to blogs. There is also a plethora of in-person support groups for specific conditions which are located in your local area. Some offer transportation to enable you to access their services.

Talk to a counselor

Talk to a counsellor about how you feel. Friends or family might not be able to put themselves in your shoes or may react to issues differently than you would. That doesn't mean they don't care about you or don't want to help. A counselor or therapist is trained to help you talk about your feelings, and they'll listen to you without judging you. They're able to see things more objectively than friends and family can.

Different options are available for counseling. You can see a counselor on a one-on-one basis or in a group. You can visit face to face, by telephone, or online. You can have a one-off session or a series of sessions, usually on a weekly basis. If you decide to opt for counseling, ask your doctor or medical practitioner to refer you to specialist counseling support for your disability or condition. Alternatively, you can look online at the options available and select one that you feel most comfortable with. Some of the main health conditions or disability charities offer specialist counseling support, where they can discuss how your life is being affected by the illness.

Exercise

Exercise is important, especially when you have a health condition or disability. It improves your sense of well-being, gets you out of the house, and introduces you to other people, all of which will help you feel less lonely. However, if you're undergoing intensive treatment, are homebound, or perhaps rely on a wheelchair, you may not always feel like or be able to engage in intensive exercise. Take it steady. Gentle exercise is as useful as vigorous exercise. Some medical centers and charities offer specialist exercise classes for people with health conditions and disabilities. These are ideal because they help you meet other people who are experiencing similar things. In addition, the classes are designed for your particular condition.

Engaging in meaningful activities

Carrying out activities that have a purpose and that you enjoy can distract you from your illness or disability, improve your well-being, and bring you in contact with others. A range of activities are available. You might want to select ones that are specifically designed for people with your health condition or disability, or you might prefer to select those that are available for the general public. Activities that can be particularly beneficial include art and music therapy. If you're not the arty type, think about activities that you enjoy, and look for an appropriate class. If your condition, disability, or treatment is making you feel tired and ill, you might not always be able to attend, but attending when you feel able to is sure to help you feel less lonely.

Write a diary or journal of your experience

Sometimes writing about how you feel can help you feel better. Write on a daily basis, but try to make sure you write down some positives each day, as well as negatives. It's helpful to put in writing at least one thing to be thankful for at the end of each day before you go to bed.

Create a bucket list

Write a bucket list of all the things you'd like to do, and check them off as you do them. Include a range of things on the list. They can be simple things you've always wanted to do but haven't managed to. For example, your list could include things such as making fresh bread, playing the drums, or visiting a particular place you've always wanted to go. Fill your time with activities that you enjoy doing.

Explore YouTube

YouTube is a free site you can use to listen to music, watch videos, and view how-to guides for any topic you might be interested in. It, along with many other social media platforms, is increasing measures to protect vulnerable persons, including individuals with disabilities. YouTube's services can keep you busy and help you learn new skills and knowledge at the same time.

Accept yourself and your condition

To reduce your feelings of loneliness, it's important to be able to feel comfortable with yourself, regardless of any health condition or disability you may have. By being comfortable with who you are, you'll be more confident and gain more self-esteem. This will help you engage in meaningful activities that you enjoy, visit places where you have a sense of belonging, and interact socially with others. Accepting yourself can take a bit of work. I've provided tips on different techniques you can try in Chapter 13. Some of these require the assistance of a therapist, and some you can do yourself.

Discovering ways to socialize

It may often feel as though your health condition or disability is restricting your ability to socialize. However, there are various different ways to meet new people which you can take advantage of. Here are a few examples.

Online coffee lounges

If you're finding it difficult to get out of your own home to socialize, online coffee lounges can be a great way to connect with others. Some of them have support for people with disabilities or specific health conditions. They enable you to discuss issues linked to your condition with others who have similar issues.

Friendship and dating apps

These can be helpful if you're homebound or find it difficult to connect with people face to face. A number of friendship apps are available, some offering connections with people generally and some targeting specific groups. If you prefer to meet and interact with other people who don't necessarily have a disability or health condition, you might want to try the more general kinds of friendship or dating apps. Some also offer online events. Do an internet search and find a friendship or dating app that suits your needs. If the first one you try isn't for you, attempt a few more because they all operate slightly differently.

Gaining paid or voluntary employment

If you feel lonely and disconnected, obtaining paid employment or voluntary work can help you enormously. Your health condition or disability way well inhibit you from intensive full-time work, but you may be able to work on a part-time basis, or for a small number of hours each week. Voluntary work can be helpful if you need more flexibility and often charities supporting your health condition or disability have such opportunities available. Paid employment and voluntary work can help you engage in meaningful activities, give you a sense of purpose, and connect you with work colleagues, allowing you to meet and interact with others. Some specific organizations dedicate themselves to helping people with disabilities gain paid employment. If you're not sure what assistance is available for finding work in your local community, ask your doctor, medical practitioner, or local job center.

Join social media groups

Social media allows you to make social connections and friends without having to meet people face-to-face. This can be an easier way for many people to meet others. Meeting and interacting with people online can be a good way to practice and implement your social skills and will give you confidence in communicating with others. It's important to select your social media platform carefully and to ensure that it has appropriate safeguarding measures in place so you're not exploited.

Peer Support

Some support groups for disabilities or specific health conditions offer peer support. This usually involves connecting you with other people who have a similar disability or condition. These sessions are often available one-on-one or in a group setting; you can choose the option that's most appropriate and preferable. To find your local peer support group, ask your doctor or medical practitioner, or do an internet search. Most support groups offer helplines where you can find out what services are offered in your area.

Get a buddy or befriender

In some countries there are various projects and initiatives which provide buddies or befrienders so that you can lead a fulfilling and happy life without your health condition or disability being a barrier. These initiatives pair you with a person who's not only a source of companionship and support but can go out with you for walks in the countryside, engage in exercise with you, help you with different kinds of skills, go shopping with you, and even accompany you to festivals or other places.

Loneliness and Disabilities

Disability affects one in seven people globally, with over a billion people estimated to be disabled. What's more, due to an aging population and a rise in chronic health conditions, the number of people living with disabilities appears to be increasing.

A person is considered to have a disability if they have a long-term illness, condition, or impairment that causes difficulty with day-to-day activities. Symptoms of disabilities can be unpredictable; they can vary from day to day, week to week, and month to month. A disability isn't always obvious to other people, and you may well be living with symptoms that are invisible to people you know.

Having a disability is a risk factor and potential trigger for loneliness. This can be made worse if others don't know you have a disability. Indeed, research indicates that people with disabilities experience loneliness to a greater extent than people without disabilities. Young adults with developmental disabilities, autistic adults, and individuals with intellectual and development disabilities are particularly vulnerable to loneliness.

Physical immobility

Physical immobility occurs when a person has a limitation in the independent and purposeful physical movement of their body. Immobility can mean that aids are required for movement. This might include a cane, a walker, or a wheelchair.

Physical immobility can emerge for a variety of reasons and can be triggered by psychological or physical conditions. Examples of triggers for physical immobility include aging and associated conditions, amputations, life-threatening illnesses, obesity, depression and anxiety, and neurological conditions. Immobility can lead to a variety of additional health conditions, such as cardiovascular disease and deep vein thrombosis. It can also lead to a poorer quality of life, social isolation, and loneliness.

People with mobility issues often face barriers in their daily life that make them more likely to be lonely than those who are able bodied. What's more, they're more likely to experience *chronic loneliness*, which is when your feelings of loneliness occur often and last a long time.

If you're living with a physical mobility issue and feel lonely, a number of factors are likely to be contributing to it. If you can identify the main causes, you can decide which solutions to try. Several factors can lead you to being isolated and feeling lonely.

>> Immobility can impair your ability to perform everyday living activities, such as walking, bathing, going to the toilet, getting up and down stairs, and preparing meals. You may not be able to get out of the house to interact with other people, and you may not feel comfortable inviting people over. Both of these can limit your social interactions with others.

>> Immobility can be a barrier to your connections with family and friends and can create difficulties in sustaining intimacy with a romantic partner.

>> Both public and private transport can be difficult to use or might be inaccessible. Even if public transport is available and accessible, you might fear using it because of hate crimes or harassment.

>> You can face actual or perceived barriers around access to buildings and other venues. Barriers can include steps and narrow corridors, absence of handrails and ramps, and a lack of nearby parking.

>> You can feel as though you're not part of your local community and don't have a sense of belonging to the place where you live. This means that even if you manage to get out and about in your local neighborhood, you might not feel a sense of connection to it.

>> Physical immobility can make it difficult for you to undertake paid employment. This can exclude you from a source of meaningful activities and meaningful relationships with work colleagues.

>> Inappropriate housing and living conditions, with a lack of appropriate adaptations, can mean that you feel trapped. One man who we visited and interviewed for a research project reported needing to leave his wheelchair outside his front door because it wouldn't fit in his apartment. He was unable to leave his property without assistance.

REAL WORLD EXAMPLE

Fatima, an older Arabic woman, is a good example of someone who used to be socially connected. When she was fit and well, she entertained and cooked meals for guests at her house.

Unfortunately, she has been living with a long-term health condition for a number of years that has severely affected her mobility and her ability to interact with others. With her physical mobility issues, she can no longer cook for herself, let alone for others. She is no longer able to invite guests over for dinner. She has become immobile and lonely.

TIP

Chair-based exercise classes can keep you physically fit even if you're unable to stand for long or are confined to a wheelchair. Ask your doctor to refer you to a local chair-based exercise class.

Alternatively, do an internet search or contact your local disability support group and ask for local chair-based exercise classes. Many options are available, including chair-based Pilates and yoga. Exercise classes like these improve your physical fitness and well-being, get you out of the house, and connect you with others.

See the Appendix for some helpful links and hotlines.

Intellectual/developmental disabilities

An intellectual and development disability is usually present at birth and affects your physical, intellectual, or emotional development. An intellectual disability can affect your intellectual functioning or intelligence, including your ability to learn, problem-solve, and reason. It can also affect your everyday social and life skills. A developmental disability, on the other hand, can be intellectual, physical, or both and often leads to a series of challenges over your lifetime.

If you have an intellectual or developmental disability, you might have experienced some or all of these:

» During your life you may have fewer social opportunities than your non-disabled peers, which can adversely affect your ability to develop social skills around social interaction. This can mean you find friendship development more difficult.

» If you have had a developmental disability from early childhood, you might have fewer friends and might find it more difficult to make and maintain meaningful relationships than others do.

» You can find yourself spending more time alone than those without a disability.

» If you have an intellectual disability, it can be difficult to differentiate between a genuine friend and someone who could take advantage of you. This can lead you to befriend people who are potentially damaging, or you might avoid having friends for fear of them taking advantage of you. In both cases, a lack of positive meaningful relationships can lead to chronic loneliness.

» In adolescence and adulthood, you may find that your relationships are limited to family and care staff. This can restrict your ability to gain the kinds of meaningful relationships that are required to sidestep loneliness.

» An intellectual and developmental disability can be seen as a stigmatized condition, perhaps even by you. This can make it difficult for you to discuss your condition, go out in public, and interact with others.

» You might be subject to abuse and hate crime by others in society and feel unsafe in your own home, fear going out, and avoid interacting with others. This can restrict your movements and contribute to your feeling trapped in your own home.

TIP

If you have an intellectual or a developmental disability you can contact your local support group and take advantage of the range of services available to help you feel less lonely, They often offer one-to one peer support services, advice about relationships, and help you to gain social skills so that you can more easily form and maintain social relationships. Or you might be able participate in paid or voluntary employment, depending on your condition. In some countries and localities employment support projects help people with intellectual and developmental disabilities gain employment, for example. Listening to music and YouTube videos can also be a helpful distraction. YouTube's services can help keep you busy and learn new skills and knowledge at the same time.

See the Appendix for some helpful links and hotlines.

Sensory impairment

Sensory impairment includes hearing impairment, vision impairment, and *dual sensory impairment*, which is defined as the coexistence of both hearing and visual impairment. *Visual impairment* refers to poor vision, and its severity can be moderate, severe, or total blindness. *Hearing impairment* is when you lose your ability to hear sound either partially or entirely. Hearing impairment is sometimes referred to as hearing loss. The severity of hearing loss is measured in degrees, ranging from mild, moderate, and severe to profound.

Billions of people across the world have a sensory impairment, and given that the population is aging, this number is likely to increase in the future. Indeed, it's estimated that around one in every ten people globally will have a hearing impairment by 2050. Hearing and sight loss can affect your mobility as well as your ability to communicate, and these in turn can affect the social environment you live in and your social connections. It's hardly surprising then that sensory impairment is associated with an increased risk of loneliness, and that it feels more intense.

You might be experiencing loneliness for a number of reasons if you have a sensory impairment:

>> **Social skills:** If you have sensory impairment, in particular severe visual impairment, it can lead to fewer opportunities to gain appropriate social skills, which can make creating and maintaining meaningful relationships with others more difficult. You may also feel less able to attend and engage in events that might enable you to meet others and form meaningful relationships.

>> **Reduced social participation:** Vision loss, hearing loss, and dual sensory loss can limit your ability for social participation. The impairments can make communication more difficult and lead you to engage in social interactions less frequently due to the challenges of communication with others.

>> **Lack of understanding by others:** Other people around you may not fully appreciate the communication implications of your impairment, which can lead them to either underestimate or overestimate what you can or can't see, hear, or do. This can make social interaction and engaging in social activities with others a challenge.

>> **Self-isolation:** To cope with these challenges of social participation, you might isolate yourself. You might feel that it's easier to avoid or miss social events because you fear that you won't be able to participate in conversations. Large groups or events with lots of background noise can be particularly difficult if you have hearing loss. You might feel frustrated and embarrassed by your difficulty communicating and tend to avoid situations like this.

>> **Communication:** Communication can pose a challenge if you're experiencing any combinations of sensory impairment. If you have vision loss, you may find that interpersonal communication is restricted by loss of nonverbal cues, including facial expressions, body language, and lip movement. If you're dealing with hearing loss, you might struggle to listen for missing words and meaning during conversations, which can lead to frustration, stress, anger, tiredness, or resentment in your social relationships.

>> **Inaccessible environments and activities:** Buildings and public places and spaces can be designed in a way that makes them inaccessible if you have sensory impairments. You might find it more difficult to visit places, engage in social activities, interact with others socially, and gain a sense of belonging to your community. All these factors can make you feel more isolated and lonelier.

>> **Self-acceptance and self-identify:** Sensory impairments can negatively affect how you perceive yourself and how you believe that others perceive you. This can contribute further to self-isolation and loneliness.

>> **Depression:** Dual sensory impairment, in particular, can lead to difficulties carrying out everyday life activities, increasing your dependence on others, and seemingly diminishing your decision-making abilities and sense of control. All this can combine to a greater risk of depression and anxiety, which can make socializing with others even more challenging. (See Chapter 10 for further details on depression and loneliness.)

TIP

It might feel obvious to you, but if you have a sensory impairment, chances are other people won't fully grasp the full implications for you. Unless they can understand, they won't know how to help. So try to explain how people can best help you communicate with them. If you have hearing loss, for example, ask people to face you when they talk. If you're in a group, ask people to take turns talking. Request that external noises such as the TV and radio are muted while you're having a conversation. My grandmother had hearing loss for as long as I knew her, and she would always tell me how best to communicate so that she could understand me.

Sensory walks allow you to use your senses to connect with your surroundings while you stay active. These walks are generally designed for people with complex disabilities, but anyone can enjoy them. You can go for a walk of any length either alone or in a group. These walks are designed for people who are able to walk, but you can also go if you're a wheelchair user or use a walker to aid your movement. Sensory walks connect you with other people, improve your self-esteem and confidence, and give you a greater sense of well-being. All of these help you feel more connected and less lonely. Sensory walks are available through various organizations.

See the Appendix for some helpful links and hotlines.

Inhibiting Disorders

Some health conditions can make you feel self-conscious and unable to act in a relaxed and natural way. Being diagnosed and living with these conditions can make it difficult to have a positive meaningful relationship with yourself and with others. Such disorders can also prevent you from going to places where you might have, or gain, a sense of belonging. They may also thwart you from engaging in meaningful activities. The cumulative effect of this is that you can isolate yourself and become lonely. A number of inhibiting disorders can affect you in this way, but I focus here on two: skin conditions and urinary incontinence. If you have other inhibiting health conditions, you might find some similarity here with your experience. Some of the tips offered here to help you feel less lonely will undoubtedly be useful too.

Skin conditions

REMEMBER

Many types of skin conditions can affect your self-confidence and your ability to interact positively with others. Three well-known skin conditions are acne, atopic dermatitis, and psoriasis.

>> **Acne** is perhaps one of the most common skin conditions. It causes red bumps and oily skin, and your skin can be hot and painful to touch. The bumps appear on your face but can also emerge on your back and, less often, on your chest. Linked to the changes in hormone levels during puberty, acne is believed to affect up to 80 percent of young people between the ages of 12 and 18. Acne often disappears as you get older, but for some people it can continue into adulthood.

>> **Atopic dermatitis** is a chronic inflammatory disorder. It's a type of eczema that triggers itchy, dry, and inflamed skin that often manifests itself in the form of a rash. The rash can appear anywhere on your body, but especially on your hands, elbows, backs of your knees, face, and scalp. It can affect

people of all ages but is most frequently reported in children. Atopic dermatitis is thought to be caused by a combination of genetic and environmental factors.

>> **Psoriasis** is a chronic immune disease that involves chronic inflammation of the skin. It's a long-lasting autoimmune disease that presents itself in the form of patches of abnormal skin. The patches can vary in color and are dry, itchy, and scaly. Psoriasis varies in severity from small, localized patches to partial or complete body coverage. Psoriasis is believed to be a genetic disease that's triggered by environmental factors. It can affect you at any age, but typically it emerges in adulthood.

Like so many health conditions, there can be a two-way relationship between skin conditions, such as these, and loneliness. Feeling lonely can trigger a stress response that can affect your immune system, and this can affect all parts of your body, including your skin, and thus trigger various skin conditions. On the other hand, skin conditions themselves can adversely affect your quality of life, reducing your confidence and self-esteem, your perception of yourself, and others' perception of you.

REMEMBER

Skin conditions can lead to feelings of loneliness in several ways:

>> **Negative comments by others:** Skin conditions that are easily visible to other people, such as those on your face, arms, hands, and legs, can lead to negative reactions by other people. You might get stares from strangers, hear people making upsetting comments, or see people keeping a distance for fear that your rash is contagious. This can reduce your self-confidence and make you feel uncomfortable and reluctant to engage with them.

>> **Stigmatization:** There can be a societal stigmatization of skin conditions. If you have a skin condition, especially if you're a teenager or young adult, you might experience bullying, teasing, and taunting, which can adversely affect your self-image and self-esteem. Peers can sometimes avoid interacting with you, thinking your rash is contagious. You can start to internalize these negative messages and feel a dislike or hatred of your skin and a need to cover it so others can't see it. This can affect the way you present yourself to other people and make it difficult to form relationships.

>> **Poor self-image:** Skin conditions that are visible, particularly on your face, can affect your self-image. This can be especially difficult if you're an adolescent because body image is perceived to be so important then. Poor body or self-image can negatively affect your ability to form and maintain social relationships with peers.

- >> **Low self-esteem:** Reactions of others and poor self-image can lead to low self-esteem and confidence, which in turn can lead to anxiety and depression. Collectively, these can cause you to withdraw from connections with others, feeling that you're unworthy of relationships.

- >> **Sexual intimacy:** You may worry about what a romantic partner thinks about your skin condition and try to conceal it. This can affect intimacy with a romantic partner.

- >> **Avoidance of activities:** In an attempt to avoid others knowing about your skin condition or to side-step the negative consequences that might arise when people do, you might avoid certain activities that expose your skin to others, such as sporting events. Such avoidance means you can miss out on activities that give you a sense of belonging, but also being in touch with other people.

TIP

Regardless of whether you have a skin condition yourself or a member of your family does, it can help if your whole family gets educated about the impact of the skin condition, how to manage it, and how to develop healthy coping skills. Sometimes siblings and parents might joke about your skin condition without realizing the full impact of their actions and how they're hurting you. Ask your doctor or healthcare practitioner for any information you can bring home. Then sit down with your family, either one on one or as a group, and discuss your skin condition and how it's making you feel. Start by talking to a person in your family whom you know will be empathetic and understanding.

PREVENTING BULLYING

If you're a parent of a child who has a skin condition and they're feeling lonely and isolated at school, perhaps because they're being bullied about the condition or because people are making hurtful remarks, it's important to bring this to the attention of their teacher as soon as possible. Teachers need to understand skin conditions and the implications they can have on a young person. They need to deal with the bullying behavior that can lead to loneliness among those who have skin conditions. The National Education Association (NEA) in the US has provided a Tools for School Kit designed for teachers, parents, and students to learn more about Atopic Dermatitis. The National Psoriasis Foundation has produced a similar kit for children with psoriasis.

See the Appendix for some helpful links and hotlines.

Urinary incontinence

Urinary incontinence is the involuntary leakage of urine. This can be associated with sneezing, coughing, or a greater sense of urgency to empty your bladder. It's a common condition that affects more than 200 million people across the globe. Anyone can experience urinary incontinence, but it tends to be more common in women than men, and you're more likely to experience it in later life. There are different types of urinary incontinence, all of which have quite specific symptoms and causes. Urinary incontinence can affect your quality of life, your ability to engage in daily activities, and your susceptibility to feeling lonely. The good news is that there are ways to deal with your condition so you can avoid or reduce your feelings of loneliness.

Urinary incontinence can trigger feelings of loneliness:

» **Disruption to daily life:** If you have urinary incontinence, it can affect your everyday life activities. In more severe cases, activities of daily life can be a challenge to sustain because they can be continually interrupted by a need to visit the bathroom. The need for, or worry about the need for, frequent visits to the bathroom can mean that you feel less comfortable leaving the home and therefore become isolated and feel lonely. In some cases, people with urinary incontinence can almost feel homebound.

» **Avoidance of physical activity:** In an attempt to manage or control your condition, you might avoid physical activity that can trigger leakage or put additional pressure on your bladder. This can mean that you're less likely to engage in activities that keep you fit and healthy, which can directly affect your overall health. Feeling a need to avoid such activities can also contribute to loneliness, especially if you're no longer able to make social connections through activities that you liked doing in the past.

» **Avoidance of social activities:** You may be less likely to engage in activities outside of your home, such as meeting friends and relatives, shopping, working out at the gym, attending sporting events, going to bars, eating out, and riding public transportation. This may be because you feel discomfort from feeling smelly or wet and prefer to restrict your social activities. Or it might be because you're embarrassed about your condition and fear it becoming apparent to others.

» **Safety-seeking behaviors:** To manage your condition, you might avoid contact with others or avoid intimacy with a partner. You might also seek constant reassurance by asking people around you if you smell. These kinds of behaviors can lead you to feel rejected and depressed and can further trigger loneliness.

- **Depression and anxiety:** Urinary incontinence is also associated with poorer mental health, including anxiety disorders and depression. You can experience low self-esteem, low physical attractiveness, and a negative body image. Together these can lead to self-isolation, feelings of inadequacy, depression, and loneliness.

- **Stigma, embarrassment, and shame:** Incontinence can lead to feelings of frustration, embarrassment, and shame. As a result, you might reduce or avoid social contact and activities, which may lead to increased social isolation and feelings of loneliness.

- **Intimacy:** Urinary incontinence can have a negative impact on your privacy, dignity, and sexuality. You may find it difficult to have intimate relationships, which can affect your well-being as well as the intensity of the loneliness you may feel.

TIP

Here are some tips to keep you connected and active, which will help tackle your feelings of loneliness.

Take control through planning ahead

You can sometimes feel that your condition is controlling you. The best way to deal with that is to take back control. Planning your trips out of the house can reclaim control of your life and enable you to remain active and connected to others. If you're going out, use a toilet-finding app so you can decide where the best toilets are in relation to you. Some options include Flush, SitOrSquat, and Bathroom Scout. Make sure that you check that the app covers the location you're traveling in.

If you're traveling by car, scope out the route in advance, and identify where service stations or public toilets are located enroute. When traveling by public transport, check out which bus stations have toilets available. And when you can, select aisle seats on buses, trains and planes that are close to the bathroom. If you have to pay extra, it's worth doing so for that extra piece of mind. Similarly, if you're planning to go to the movies or the theater, select seats that are on an aisle and close to the bathroom or exit. Planning in this way will give you the confidence you need to start venturing out again.

Being prepared for accidents

Before leaving the house, make sure you have all the supplies you need. Create a list of essentials on a small card that you can keep in your bag, or use the Notes page on your smart phone. Items to add to the list might include incontinence pads, spare underwear, plastic bags, wipes, and a small towel. Vacations and overnight stays can be particularly challenging, but avoiding breaks away can affect relationships and your well-being.

New products are emerging all the time. You can buy a whole range of disposable underpads to use for bedding, chairs, wheelchairs, car seats, bus seats, and more. For extra reassurance, you can take a portable urinal with you. These are available for both women and men and offer dignity and discretion. You might feel embarrassed carrying and using such equipment, but young people are increasingly using them at pop concerts and festivals. If they can use them, so can you! The better prepared you are, the more confidence you'll gain in leaving the house and conducting everyday activities.

TIP

If you're worried about the smell associated with your condition, meet outdoors. Spending time in green spaces can improve your well-being anyway, so you have a double benefit of meeting friends of family members there. For more information on the benefits of green spaces, see Chapters 5 and 15.

Regaining intimacy

If you're feeling lonely because of the challenges that your condition is creating for your intimate relationships, you can use a number of different strategies. Regular pelvic floor exercises can be especially helpful for women living with incontinence issues. Experiment with different sexual positions, and identify ones that put less pressure on your bladder. Limit your fluid intake prior to sex, and go to the bathroom immediately prior to sex. Try *double voiding*, whereby you empty your bladder, wait a few minutes, and then try again to empty any residual urine that may still be present. If you're able to and feel your partner will understand, talk to them about your condition and the challenges it presents.

See the Appendix for some helpful links and helplines.

Serious Conditions

A *serious illness* is a medical term that refers to a condition that has a high risk of mortality, negatively affects everyday activities and quality of life, or is onerous in terms of its symptoms, treatments, or requirements for care. Examples of serious illnesses include cancer, stroke, heart attack, and major debilitating injuries. Because of the life-disrupting effects of many serious illnesses, loneliness can also be an undesirable outcome. Some reasons why you can feel lonely due to a serious illness are as follows:

>> **Changed behavior of your social network:** A serious illness doesn't just hit the person with the diagnosis hard. Friends and family can also have difficulty coming to terms with the diagnosis. They may not know how to behave

around you, know what to say, or be overly critical of your choices. Some friends and family may avoid calling or visiting or avoid talking about it when they do see you, which can make you feel even lonelier, particularly if you want to open up and discuss how you're feeling.

» **Mismatch of support you need and that offered:** Quite often, if you have a serious illness there can be a mismatch between the support you desire and need and that which is offered by friends and family. You may have expectations regarding the type of support that others should be offering. If they don't provide it, you might feel that no one cares. You might want friends and family to treat you as they did before your diagnosis, but they may be overprotective, which can make you feel overwhelmed and misunderstood. Your family and friends might not realize that you're lonely and might think that you want time to yourself, but you might want them to be around more.

» **Changing emotions:** A serious illness can lead to a wide range of changing emotions that you may not be used to dealing with. These may change throughout the day, week, month, or year. Such emotional changes can take place throughout the journey of your illness, from the initial diagnosis, when in treatment, and after. Having a serious illness can make any existing emotions or tendencies feel more intense. So if you particularly struggled with loneliness prior to a serious illness diagnosis, it can become much more intense and chronic.

» **The implications of treatment:** Treatment options for each serious condition can vary. Each can have side effects that can influence your ability to interact socially. Your susceptibility to loneliness can increase as a result. Your treatment may mean you experience illness and feel exhausted, your mobility might be affected, you can be in pain, or you might experience changes in your physical appearance. All these side effects can make you feel disconnected from your everyday life and the people around you. You may feel too ill or sick to take part in the hobbies and activities you used to enjoy or go to places where you feel a sense of belonging.

» **Depression, anxiety, and confidence:** Many serious illnesses can lead you to feel depressed and anxious. This can arise because of the diagnosis itself and worries about what it might mean for your future health and mortality. There can also be long-term physical effects to your appearance, such as scars from surgery. These can reduce your self-confidence and quality of life and may mean that you might not feel like connecting with others or even leaving your home.

» **Loss of health care and support services:** Even the completion of treatment can be a particularly lonely time. You may have enjoyed the support and social relationships of your health care team. This kind of social support is referred to as *Therapeutic alliance*. Once your treatment stops, you may feel as though the network of support around you has been taken away and experience a sense of loss or grief.

I discuss a few serious illnesses here. You'll find the tips in the earlier section "Preventing Loneliness Due to a Physical Illness or Disability" particularly useful if you have any of these serious conditions. If you need further help and support, see the Appendix for useful links and helplines.

Cancer

Cancer is arguably the most feared health condition; therefore, it's an emotive illness. Suspecting you may have cancer, being diagnosed with cancer, being treated for cancer, living with cancer, surviving cancer, or being told you're going to die from cancer all generate emotional highs and lows both for the person with cancer but also for people who know and love them. Some of the emotions you can experience during the cancer journey include fear, shock, anxiety, depression, grief, loss, uncertainty, denial, anger, and loneliness. Loneliness can be experienced by the person who has cancer and by their family and friends.

Experiencing loneliness with a cancer diagnosis is significant not just because of the unpleasant feeling it brings or because of the wider well-being and mental health issues. Loneliness also can affect the outcome of your treatment. If you're lonely, you're more likely to experience greater pain perception. Further, your recovery can be slower or delayed, and your immune function can be compromised. But remember, if you have cancer, you can adopt strategies to avoid feeling lonely or to reduce your feelings of loneliness.

Cancer can lead to loneliness for a number of interlinked and complex reasons. In particular, you can have feelings of aloneness and that no one else understands. The cancer diagnosis itself can trigger feelings of loneliness. The uncertainty surrounding your diagnosis, and the accompanying fear of the implications on your health and mortality, can make you feel like you're all alone and that other people don't understand what you're experiencing or don't share your concerns. You can feel like this even if you have close family and friends around you. If you don't want to upset your family and friends by talking about how you feel, and you believe you have to be brave for them, you can feel even more alone and lonely. You may also experience loneliness even when the treatment is over. Family and friends may not understand this and may assume that everything is back to normal.

TIP

If you have cancer or have had cancer and are now in remission, you'll find the tips in the earlier section "Preventing Loneliness Due to a Physical Illness or Disability" particularly useful. In addition you can call a helpline when you're feeling lonely. Do a search online for helplines in your country. There are some helpful links and resources in the Appendix too.

HIV

It's estimated that around 38 million people globally are living with HIV. If you have HIV and are lonely, it can be due to a number of factors:

>> **Stigmatization:** HIV is one of the world's most stigmatized health conditions. This is primarily due to the fear of contracting it and the lack of education, understanding, and accurate information about it. You can experience stigma from the day you're diagnosed. You might face rejection from friends, work colleagues, and even family members and staff in health care systems. As a direct consequence, you can find it difficult to retain social relationships and develop new social contacts.

>> **Self-stigma:** The societal stigma of HIV can lead you to internalize the stigma. This can in turn make you feel unworthy of interpersonal relationships, thus intensifying the loneliness.

>> **Intimate and interpersonal relationships:** HIV can make it difficult to find a life partner who can understand and live with your health condition. You may be reluctant to pursue a sexual or romantic relationship for fear of rejection. The wider societal lack of knowledge about the illness and stigmatization exacerbates this. This can mean that your HIV status negatively affects your interpersonal and intimate relationships, and you can find yourself living alone. In fact, older people with HIV appear to be more likely to be living alone and have limited and inadequate social networks.

TIP

Several dating services are designed specifically for people living with HIV. So if you don't have a partner, are feeling lonely, and would like to make a romantic connection, try one of the online dating apps.

>> **Friendships and family networks:** Being diagnosed with HIV can destabilize relationships with family, friends, and support networks. You might also fear disclosing your HIV status to new friends and acquaintances, or fear of them finding out, and this can make it challenging for you to form meaningful relationships with new people.

>> **Discrimination and hate crime:** If you're living with HIV, you can face both discrimination and hate crime. This can range from verbal abuse to physical harassment to pressure to disclose your HIV status. These factors can make you fear for your safety and cause you to withdraw and isolate from society and social connections.

>> **Stress, depression, and anxiety:** The stigmatization and discrimination you face can lead to stress, anxiety, and depression. These conditions can make it difficult for you to get out and about and interact socially or even do activities or go places that you used to enjoy.

>> **Substance abuse and other complex issues:** Some people living with HIV are users of drugs and illicit substances. Both HIV and substance misuse are triggers for loneliness. If you're dealing with both, you might be even more suspectable to loneliness, depression, and other mental health issues.

TIP

If you're living with HIV, self-acceptance is an important concept to embrace. Accept yourself for who you are, for your HIV status, and for any other characteristics that make you the person you are. Accepting yourself can help you counter the stigma associated with the illness, overcome any negative judgments and attitudes of others, and avoid internalizing the stigma. Accepting yourself can often be a first step to feeling less lonely because it means feeling happy in your own skin. I devote all of Chapter 13 to practicing self-acceptance.

You can achieve self-acceptance in a range of different ways, but it can require the assistance of qualified therapists. Depending on where you live, your health care practitioner will be able to refer you to psychological and therapy support.

If you're living with HIV you'll also find the tips in the earlier section "Preventing Loneliness Due to a Physical Illness or Disability" particularly useful. If you need further help and support, see the Appendix for useful links and helplines.

THERAPEUTIC ALLIANCE

Although you can feel lonely when diagnosed with a serious illness, you will inevitably find yourself surrounded by health care professionals and therapists who, because of the person-centered nature of their support, can provide you with an alternative series of relationships called *therapeutic alliance*. These are also referred to as *therapeutic relationships*.

A therapeutic alliance, or a therapeutic relationship, is how you and a therapist connect, behave, and engage with each other to achieve a goal or objective. The concept of therapeutic alliance dates back to Sigmund Freud. But the concept has evolved over time and can describe a wider relationship between therapists, healthcare professionals, social care staff, physiotherapists, nutritionists, and other professions and their clients.

These kinds of relationships can be invaluable if you have a health condition and don't have many or any family and friends you can talk to. Therapeutic relationships can be experienced by people with all kinds of health conditions and offer support to reduce or avoid loneliness. Although these are professional relationships, they're just as valuable as social connections.

Chapter 10

Understanding the Interplay between Mental Health and Loneliness

Although loneliness can lead to a range of mental health conditions (see Chapter 3), mental ill health itself can also lead to loneliness. Indeed, mental health illness can be a particular trigger point for loneliness. However, as with physical health conditions, it's not always easy to detect which came first: the mental ill health or the loneliness. Poor mental health can lead to difficulties connecting with others. You may start to isolate yourself from other people and places, and withdraw from social settings. Research shows that mental health distress can be a key contributor to the commencement and continuation of chronic loneliness. Chronic loneliness, which is explained in more detail in Chapter 1, is loneliness that occurs often and can last for a long period of time. If you're a caregiver for someone with a mental health illness, you can also be affected by loneliness. I provide some useful information and guidance for you in Chapter 11.

In this chapter I explore a range of mental health conditions that can lead to loneliness. I first explore the loneliness impact of some common mental health disorders, including anxiety and depression. I then discuss cognitive impairment issues — in particular, dementia. Following this, I discuss how addiction and eating disorders can lead to loneliness. Tips for avoiding or reducing loneliness, despite these mental health challenges, are discussed throughout the chapter.

WARNING

I can't cover in this chapter the whole magnitude of mental health conditions that can lead to loneliness, but you can use or adapt many of the tips I provide for other conditions. If you're in any doubt, check with your health care practitioner.

Common Mental Health Conditions

Loneliness isn't a mental health problem itself. But it's interlinked with poor mental health. Chronic loneliness (see Chapter 1 for more details) can play a significant role in the onset and continuation of mental health distress. Likewise, poor mental health can lead to loneliness. And social connectedness leads to greater well-being and better mental health.

Here are some of the ways that mental health can make you feel lonely:

>> **Stigma:** The stigma of mental health conditions can mean that it's difficult to talk to family and friends about your condition.

>> **Withdrawal:** You might find it difficult to make or sustain social connections and isolate yourself from others.

>> **Difficulties getting out of bed/leaving the house:** Some days you might find it difficult to leave the house or even climb out of bed, meaning that making connections with others or places is a challenge.

>> **Avoidance of gatherings:** You may well feel overwhelmed in busy, public places or at work events and parties and try to avoid them. Yet these are the very places where you can meet people.

>> **Worry:** You might worry about engaging with others for a whole variety of reasons. Maybe you don't feel as if you have anything interesting to say, you might not like the attention, or you may feel that you're a burden.

It's easy to see, then, how mental health can lead you to feeling lonely and how it can worsen your mental health even further.

The precise way in which different forms of mental ill health trigger loneliness and the strategies you can use to keep loneliness at bay vary depending on the mental health condition you're battling. Nevertheless, solutions are available.

Depression

REMEMBER

Depression is a complex mental health condition that can be caused by multiple factors. When you experience depression, you generally have a low mood that can affect your daily thoughts, feelings, and behavior. If you're depressed, you'll quite often have a loss of interest or reduced enjoyment from activities and experiences that would normally bring you joy or pleasure. You might feel a whole range of negative and unpleasant emotions and symptoms, such as these:

» Sadness

» Difficulty getting out of bed or leaving the house

» Difficulty doing everyday activities

» Difficulty concentrating or keeping focused

» Heightened anxiety and worry

» Negative thoughts you can't get rid of

Depression can lead to feelings of hopelessness, and for some people, suicidal thoughts. Millions of people globally are affected by depression. It can be triggered by specific life events, such as bereavement, specific illness, and medication. Also, certain personality types may be more prone to depression.

Feelings of depression and loneliness can be present at the same time and tend to reinforce one another. Depression can lead you to isolating yourself and feeling lonely, which can make your depression even worse.

Depression can lead to loneliness for a range of reasons. To start, if you can't get out of the house, you're unlikely to meet people who might be a source of companionship. Losing interest in activities or going to places outside of the home can cost you opportunities to interact socially.

If your depression causes negative thinking, you might feel that other people have negative attitudes towards you or are judging you for your depressive symptoms, which may make you feel less able to reach out to others.

And with depression can come physical symptoms such as headaches, heart palpitations, and fatigue, and these can make it difficult for you to carry on your everyday activities and social interactions. You might not have the energy to talk to people.

When you're depressed, it can quite often seem as though there's no escape. The more depressed you are, the more lonely you can feel, and you can easily get caught in a vicious downward spiral. However, it doesn't have to be like that forever, and you *can* break out. Here are some tips on how.

Talk to your family and friends and ask for help

Depression and loneliness can be taboo topics, so people don't always like to talk about them. Sometimes that's because there's a perceived stigma, and other times it's because they feel awkward and uncomfortable, or just don't know what to say. If you're feeling depressed and lonely and have close friends or family, try opening up to them about how you feel. Sometimes just talking about how you feel can make you less lonely. Share with your family and friends some ways they might be able to help you. You might find it useful to chat with them regularly daily or weekly. You can also arrange to meet up with them, which might be enough to force you out of the house. If you have difficulty getting out of bed and you live with others, you could ask them to make sure you get up and get dressed. During a period I was feeling particularly depressed, I asked my husband to force me out of bed because I knew I wouldn't be able to otherwise.

Join a peer support group

You may not have family or friends to turn to. Or they may not understand or be able to help you. In these cases, you can turn to peer support groups. They're run by staff or volunteers who have been trained to help. By attending these groups, you get to meet and chat with others who are experiencing similar feelings to you. And you can learn about ways others have broken out of the cycle of depression and loneliness and try those techniques out for yourself. Pop into your local library or do an internet search to find your local support group. Sometimes you'll find ads or posters in your local shop or medical center.

Identify enjoyable activities

Write a list of all the activities or places you've enjoyed visiting in the past. Are there activities you've always wanted to try but haven't? Or places you've always wanted to visit? If your answer is yes, add them to the list too. Once you have a list, select an activity or a place to visit and make a point of going there. The first step can feel a bit daunting, but once you arrive, you'll feel a lot better. You'll also be more likely to have opportunities for social interaction while you're out, which will help with your loneliness.

Engage in physical activity

Try going for a walk or a run, visiting your local gym, taking a swim, or joining an exercise class like Zumba, Pilates, or Yoga. Physical exercise releases feel-good endorphins, which can enhance your sense of well-being. And, again, while you're there, you're more likely to find opportunities to chat with others.

Talk to a therapist

If you're feeling depressed and lonely, it can help to talk to a qualified therapist. You can get different types of therapy, ranging from counseling to Cognitive Behavioral Therapy (CBT). I provide details about the different types of therapies and techniques in Chapter 13. Depending on where you live, you might be able to get a referral from your doctor or medical practitioner. If your doctor can't refer you or you'd prefer to find your own therapist, look for an appropriate therapist in your local area.

Visit your doctor

If you're still struggling with depression and loneliness and your feelings just won't go away, book an appointment to see your doctor. Be sure to mention that you're feeling depressed and lonely so they can offer you advice and options. They may refer you to a local social prescribing service, connecting you to local voluntary sector services (see Chapter 3 for more information). Or they may offer you anti-depressants. Be sure to discuss the benefits and drawbacks of any drugs you're offered. Taking antidepressants doesn't mean you've failed, and it doesn't mean you'll have to take them forever. Everyone needs a little help to get back on track from time to time.

WARNING

Be sure to check the qualifications of any therapists to ensure they're properly qualified and registered to be legally allowed to practice. If you're feeling particularly depressed or are having suicidal thoughts see the Appendix for some helplines you can contact.

Managing anxiety

Anxiety is an emotion characterized by feelings of worry and tension that can interfere with your daily life. If you have an anxiety disorder, you can experience recurring, intrusive thoughts. You can also have physical symptoms, such as a rapid heartbeat, sweating, trembling, or dizziness.

REMEMBER

Like depression, anxiety is both a cause and a symptom of loneliness. If you experience anxiety, you may worry about certain situations or people and avoid them. You can then isolate yourself, which makes you feel worse. This can make you feel lonely, and can make you even more anxious. The more anxious you feel, the lonelier you become; likewise, the lonelier you feel, the more anxious you become. Anxiety and loneliness feed off each other.

Some people are more likely to experience anxiety than others. These include people with disabilities, those with long-term health conditions, and single parents.

Anxiety can make you feel lonely in a number of ways:

» **Avoiding people and uncomfortable situations that make you anxious:** Although this makes you feel less anxious because you don't have to see people or put yourself in situations that make you feel anxious, it can mean that you avoid people and places, in turn isolating yourself and leading to feelings of loneliness.

» **Feeling that aloneness will help:** Sometimes if you're experiencing anxiety you can believe that being alone will help you feel better and reduce your anxiety. But this isn't necessarily true and can actually make you feel more anxious and lonely.

» **Feeling you're a burden:** Because of your anxiety, you may feel that you shouldn't go out and socialize with other people. You're afraid you'll spoil their fun, you'll be a burden on them, or they won't want to know you. These feelings are often spurred by irrational thoughts and can cause you to distance yourself from family, friends, and loved ones.

» **Catastrophizing:** If you're experiencing anxiety, you might imagine a worst-case scenario. Your thought processes tend to become skewed. This can lead you to overestimate the negative aspects of socializing. It can prevent you from leaving the house, going to particular places, or doing certain activities for fear of what might happen. This can make you feel lonely and isolated.

TIP

If you're experiencing anxiety and loneliness, it can feel all encompassing, like there's no escape. But there is. The trick is to take small steps at a time. Here are some useful ideas to get connected again. You can also find some suggestions in the previous section on depression.

» **Talk to your family and friends and ask for help.** Explain how your feelings of anxiety are making you feel and what impact they're having on your ability to get out and about, and connect with people. Try telling just one person to start with, and explain to them how they can help you. If you don't have anyone you can talk to, don't worry. Just move onto the next tip.

» **(Re)connect with one person.** This could be anyone you know or are acquainted with. It might be a neighbor, a family member, a friend, a work colleague, or maybe just someone you pass in the street or at the bus stop. Start by making eye contact or saying hello. Try striking up a short conversation. The next time you see them try to prolong the conversation a bit more. Chapters 5 and 14 have some useful tips on how to create meaningful connections and relationships with people. To avoid feeling overwhelmed, focus on getting to know this one person before adding more people into your network. In any case, a small number of quality relationships is more helpful to reduce your feelings of loneliness.

>> **Plan a trip or an activity that you've enjoyed in the past.** You might feel anxious leaving the house or going somewhere that's busy, so think carefully about where you want to try first. Start small and build up. Some people feel more anxious in a large crowd, but others can find a one-on-one situation more stressful. Decide on an activity or place you'd like to attend, and allow yourself a set amount of time to be there. It could be just 30 minutes. Give yourself permission to leave if you feel uncomfortable. Once you've been, try to go again and see if you can stay for a little longer. Chapter 15 has some ideas of places to try.

>> **Join a local support group.** Find a local support group for people who have anxiety disorders. They often offer clubs and activities that are designed to help you feel less anxious. They're also an opportunity to meet other people who are feeling anxious and lonely. You won't be pressured to stay too long, and you'll be surrounded by people who understand.

>> **Exercise.** Physical exercise is beneficial if you feel anxious. It can help you experience a greater sense of well-being and calm. You could try walking, going for a jog or a run, or swimming. If you feel able to, you could try an exercise class.

>> **Visit your doctor or healthcare practitioner.** If your anxiety is particularly severe, is preventing you from doing the things that you would like, and doesn't seem to be improving despite trying some of the techniques listed here, it might be worth visiting your doctor. Explain your symptoms and how your anxiety is preventing you from doing things you enjoy, and making you feel lonely. Your doctor might suggest medication or therapy (see Chapter 13 for details of different therapies you can try), or might refer you to a service in your local community that's designed to help people experiencing anxiety and loneliness.

Cognitive Impairment

REMEMBER

Cognitive impairment, or cognitive disorder as it's commonly known, falls in a specific category of mental health disorders. Cognitive disorders mainly affect your cognitive powers, which can include your capacity for learning, perception, problem-solving, and remembering. Cognitive disorders come in different types and are classified as minor or major according to their symptoms. Most of them involve damage to the memory part of the brain.

Dementia

REMEMBER

Dementia is a collection of symptoms that emerges due to damage to the brain. This damage can be caused by different diseases, including Alzheimer's. The symptoms you experience with dementia vary according to the part of your brain that's damaged. Symptoms can include loss of memory, mood changes, communication difficulties, difficulty with abilities to reason and make decisions, and difficulties carrying out everyday tasks and activities. Dementia is a progressive disease, which means that if you have dementia you have to deal with changing and worsening symptoms and abilities over time.

If you have dementia, you can feel lonely for a number of reasons:

>> **Loss of confidence to go out:** This can be due to fear of getting confused or lost. It means you might not be able to do the activities you enjoy.

>> **Mobility difficulties:** It can be hard to get out and about alone, without help.

>> **Residential care:** In the later stages, many people with dementia live in residential care, which, despite the proximity of other people, can be a lonely experience.

>> **Deteriorating social skills and personality changes:** This can make social relationships difficult.

>> **Loss of memory:** Even though you may have visitors, you may not remember seeing them.

>> **Anxiety and depression:** This might mean you don't always feel able to, or want to, see people or do things.

>> **Stigma:** If you have dementia, you may feel worried that other people will find out and consequently avoid social interaction. If you know someone who has dementia, you may not understand how to handle it and avoid them as a result. If you have a family member with dementia, you might avoid inviting people over because you're embarrassed.

TIP

Given the changing, progressive, and individualized nature of dementia, it's important to personalize care and support to the individual. This includes any strategies or tips to reduce feelings of loneliness. Here are some examples of the techniques that can help you feel less lonely, if you have dementia.

Attending dementia cafés

These are held by a community group or charity in your local area, often in libraries, cafés, community centers, or museums. They provide information about dementia and other support, and enable you to meet others in a similar situation.

They're an opportunity to talk to others who understand what you're going through, and can help combat loneliness if you have dementia, or you're a caregiver or relative of someone with dementia.

If you'd like to find out where your local dementia café is, ask your doctor or healthcare practitioner, perform an internet search, or do research at your local library.

Leaning on your family, friends, neighbors, and local community

Although it can be difficult due to the stigma of dementia, telling others about your dementia diagnosis early on can be helpful. That way you can discuss what support you might need in the future and how others might be able to help, so you feel less lonely. You might even inform your local store owner, post office staff, and pharmacist. If you don't feel comfortable telling people about the dementia, you could always just say that you might need help from time to time.

Using technology for connection and safety

If you live alone and have a computer, smart phone, or tablet, you might want to consider video calls with friends and family so that if you can't get out or don't feel confident leaving the house, you can see and chat with them in other ways. If you don't have, or feel confident using, this kind of technology, you can try a simple phone call.

Tracking devices can help you feel more confident going out, especially if you're alone. Different types of technology are available, including GPS (global positioning system) devices, which track you in case you get lost. Ask your health practitioner or local social services if they can refer you to appropriate technology. Or you can buy a tracking device online. Be sure to check the reviews to make sure it's suitable for your specific condition. Some people don't like to be tracked in this way. If that's true for you, you can also try helpcards; these explain that you have dementia and that you might need more time or support. They're simple to use and can help you feel confident when out and about.

Reaching out to local dementia support groups, advisors, and "friends"

Charitable organizations in your local area often support those who are lonely and have dementia. Online communities or forums can also be a good way to meet and chat with others who have dementia. Alternatively, you can try joining support groups for people with dementia through your favorite social media platform. I would recommend checking the authenticity and safeguarding measures of any online forums with your health practitioner or local dementia charity before using them.

Depending on where you live, you might be able to get access to a dementia advisor. This is a dedicated support worker who can provide you and your caregiver with one-on-one personalized support. You can ask your doctor to refer you, or you can refer yourself. A dementia adviser can help you access the support you need for the symptoms relating to your illness, including loneliness.

Again, depending on where you live, you might be able to get support from a "dementia friend." This is usually a volunteer who learns about dementia so they can help their community. If you're feeling lonely and have dementia, you can request a dementia friend to visit you. They can offer help, advice, and, most important of all, a bit of companionship.

Dementia-friendly communities

You might be able to find a dementia-friendly community. The Alzheimer's Society established these communities so that people with dementia are understood, respected, and supported. They're designed to ensure that people living there are aware of and understand dementia, feel included, and have choice and control over their everyday lives. Dementia-friendly communities offer an important route to reducing social isolation and loneliness for people with dementia and their caregivers.

The activities in your local dementia-friendly community can give you a sense of purpose and introduce you to other like-minded people who are facing similar issues.

If there isn't a dementia-friendly community near you, you can start one yourself. In the US, you can find useful information on how to do that here: https://www.dfamerica.org/toolkit-getting-started/ or in the U, here: https://www.alzheimers.org.uk/get-involved/dementia-friendly-communities/how-to-become-dementia-friendly-community.

Addiction and Eating Disorders

Like the other health conditions discussed in this chapter, weight-related challenges and alcohol and substance misuse can represent a two-way relationship with loneliness. Addictions and eating disorders can emerge in an attempt to escape from feelings of loneliness. At the same time, addictions and eating disorders can, themselves, lead to loneliness.

Alcoholism and substance misuse

Alcohol, substance misuse, and loneliness can have a two-way relationship. When people are feeling lonely, they may turn to drugs or alcohol to numb their feelings. They may feel that it's the only way they can get through the day or improve their mood. On the other hand, addiction can be lonely. When people are addicted to alcohol and drugs, they can become isolated from family and friends and feel lonelier than ever. What's more, loneliness can be a relapse trigger for those in recovery. This means you need to avoid feeling lonely when you're trying to break free of substance abuse. This is a frequently mentioned challenge to recovery for people. That's why it's important to find ways to reduce loneliness alongside breaking free from your addiction.

REMEMBER

Drugs and alcohol use are never a good way to solve your problems. Besides leading to loneliness, they can lead to wider health issues, such as kidney and liver damage. Here are some of the ways that drug and alcohol addiction can make you feel lonely:

>> **Damage to relationships:** The addiction and its accompanying side effects, which can include financial, legal, and personal challenges, can lead to distrust in relationships you have with family and friends. You may find your social circle diminishing as people start feeling resentment towards you and fear for what you might do when you're under the influence.

>> **Stigma:** Both illicit drug use and alcohol dependence are seen as highly stigmatized health conditions across the world. Therefore, understandably, people who are addicted feel unable to open up about their condition and may isolate themselves.

>> **Changing social needs:** When addicted to alcohol or other substances, people may engage with others who enable their habit, such as drug dealers and other users. However, when in recovery they'll likely need to avoid these social contacts to maintain their abstinence, thus exacerbating their loneliness.

>> **Wider related health conditions:** These can arise from alcohol and substance misuse and during the recovery period. These can include factors that can give rise to further loneliness, such as poor sleep, depression, low self-esteem, poorer well-being and quality of life, and suicidal tendencies.

TIP

If you're dealing with alcohol and substance misuse issues and are feeling lonely, you can try a number of potential solutions, as detailed next.

Joining a Recovery Fellowship

Numerous recovery fellowships worldwide are designed to helping you give up your addiction. One of the most well-known recovery fellowships is AA, or Alcoholics Anonymous. Joining such fellowships not only helps you on the road to recovery; it brings you in contact with individuals who are facing similar challenges. And you'll have a common goal, which can create a collective bond between you. These groups provide a supportive and nonjudgmental environment and often include social gatherings, which can relieve your loneliness and give you a renewed sense of purpose.

Spending quality time with family and friends

If alcohol and drugs have become your most important friends over the years, try spending some quality time with your wider social network. Time outdoors is always a good option because it can have a positive effect on your well-being. If you find that your relationships have been damaged, try opening up to your family and friends and explain how and why you've behaved in the way you have. The more they understand, the easier it will be to repair any damaged relationships.

Joining a local community group, club, or activity

Search for local groups in your area and join one that interests you. You'll find that the activities on offer keep you busy but also help you meet new people. This can be especially helpful if your addiction has damaged your relationships.

Physical exercise can be a key ingredient on your road to recovery, helping you gain a greater sense of well-being and meet new people. One option is walking, jogging, or running a 5k as part of a park run. Park runs are friendly and welcoming events that can assist you in meeting a range of new people. Alternatively, you might want to try some other form of exercise, such as working out at a local gym, taking an exercise class, rock climbing, or bike riding.

Seeking professional help

If you're feeling particularly lonely, are having difficulties kicking the habit, and feel that your mental health is suffering, you might want to seek help from a trained mental health professional. Your first point of call for this will usually be your doctor, who can refer you to a trained mental health professional with expert knowledge in alcohol and substance abuse and addiction.

A range of alternative therapies and techniques can help you deal with your addiction and your feelings of loneliness. Self-hypnosis is one such option that can have positive outcomes (see Chapter 13 for more details). Others that can help you in the recovery phase include mindfulness and meditation.

Eating disorders

Eating disorders can be a serious mental health issue. They particularly affect young people, especially young women. They can damage your physical health and well-being, besides making you feel isolated and lonely.

REMEMBER

Although, on the surface, an eating disorder is assumed to be about food or weight gain, the cause is often more deep rooted. It usually arises from psychological disturbances, emotional distress, lack of confidence, low self-esteem, or relationship difficulties.

Eating disorders come in many varieties, all of which can be triggers for loneliness. Three of the most common eating disorders are as follows:

>> **Anorexia nervosa:** This is characterized by a very low body weight, where you restrict your food intake or undertake excessive exercise in an attempt to lose weight.

>> **Bulimia nervosa:** This involves cycles of binge eating, followed by purging behaviors such as vomiting or taking laxatives.

>> **Binge eating disorder:** This is where you frequently consume unusually large amounts of food and feel unable to stop eating. You may experience a loss of control when eating.

People may turn to eating — or not eating — food as a way to cope with feelings of loneliness, but just like the consumption of excessive alcohol or substance use, these strategies are unlikely to overcome feelings of loneliness in the longer term. Instead, what often happens is that the eating disorder itself starts to cause you to become isolated and feel even lonelier.

Eating disorders can make you feel lonely for a variety of interconnected reasons:

>> **Shame and disgust:** You may feel embarrassed, shameful, or even disgusted about your eating disorder and hide away from people who are close to you so they don't find out about it.

>> **Hiding and avoiding:** You may avoid socializing with friends or family to disguise your eating disorder. This can be particularly difficult if you're in recovery. You might start avoiding social events such as birthday parties, family gatherings, or work socials.

>> **Fatigue and irritability:** If you're not eating enough or purging the food that you do eat, you may feel lethargic and apathetic and believe it's too much trouble to interact with those around you.

>> **Low self-esteem:** You may have a low sense of self-worth and feel that others won't want to know you or that you can't have a positive relationship with them.

>> **Loneliness spreads:** Family and friends of a person with an eating disorder can feel lonely themselves because they struggle to connect with their loved one, whom they can sometimes quite literally see slipping away.

TIP

I share tips on how to deal with loneliness when you have an eating disorder later in this chapter.

Loneliness can cause you to put on weight. When you're lonely, you might start eating more than usual or eating unhealthy foods such as chocolate, cake, and other carbs — so called comfort foods — in an attempt to make yourself feel better for a short while. You might also stop exercising. Both excessive eating of unhealthy food and a lack of exercise will inevitably lead you to put on weight. Even if you don't eat any more than you did previously, loneliness can lead to weight gain because it can trigger inflammation, which contributes to weight gain.

Conversely, weight gain and obesity can lead to greater loneliness. This can occur for a number of reasons:

>> **Stigmatization of larger people, and social norms of body shape and size:** This can cause you to isolate yourself and avoid being seen in public. It's often more severe for women and is exacerbated by media (including social media) representations of the perceived "ideal" body shape.

>> **Rejection and discrimination:** Obese people often feel discriminated against and rejected. They can be assumed to be lazy or incompetent just because of their size, which can heighten their sense of isolation and loneliness.

>> **Peer victimization and bullying:** This can take place at any age but appears to be particularly problematic in childhood and adolescence. Such negative social connections can lead to further social withdrawal and more intense loneliness.

>> **Self-blame:** If you're overweight you can start to blame yourself for your condition. You might internalize the stigma, which can lead to symptoms such as depression, anxiety, and other psychological conditions. These, in turn, can lead to loneliness.

>> **Lack of trust:** Obesity can lead you to feel a lack of emotional trust in friends and family. As a result you might feel less likely to share or disclose information with them and thus feel detached from your social network and feel lonely.

>> **Threatening social situations:** Obese individuals can perceive social situations as threatening and avoid certain public places, including healthcare settings, which can make them feel lonelier.

TIP

Whether you're overweight or underweight, have a diagnosed eating disorder, or simply have difficult relationships with food, you can start to connect with others again and feel less lonely. I provide some tips for you here.

Building confidence in yourself and your body

Having a healthier relationship with your body can help you be happier and more likely to want to interact with other people and with places where you have a sense of belonging. Instead of focusing on what you don't like about your body and what it can't do, think about all the amazing things your body *can* do. You could try repeating some positive affirmations about what your body can do. For example:

"My body is strong and powerful and gets me through each day."

"I appreciate my body every minute of every day."

"I appreciate the unique features of my body."

Write down some positive body affirmations of your own and repeat them daily. Even if you don't believe what you're saying, just saying the phrase can help you feel better. The more you repeat positive messages about yourself, the more you start to believe them.

Setting yourself a goal or challenge to achieve

This can help with your loneliness in a number of ways. Achieving objectives can build your self-esteem, which will make you feel better about yourself. You're likely to meet other people in the process and gain more social connections. The process of achieving an objective, or carrying out a challenge, can distract you from your weight issues and loneliness. Write a list of anything you'd like to achieve, and set out a plan for how you're going to achieve it.

Set yourself a date for when you're going to achieve the objective, and then set some milestones along the way. You can put these on a chart and check off each milestone as you complete it. Give yourself a small reward every time you meet one of the milestones. The end goal can be anything, but it might be a good idea to set something that's health related.

As an example, Ian was overweight, and his wife had recently left him. He was feeling desperately lonely and was suffering from depression. He decided that he was going to do a 5k run for charity. He set a goal of walking 10,000 steps a day for a month as his first milestone. At first walking this many steps was hard work and took a while. But after a few weeks it started to get easier.

Then he set another milestone: to eat five portions of fruit and vegetables a day for the next month, besides walking 10,000 steps a day. In the third month, he added some short jogs to his daily step counts. Two months later he was able to run the 5k he'd planned. Ian not only lost weight and felt healthier and better about himself, but met other people as he was doing his initial daily walks. He also really enjoyed the community spirit of the 5k run. Following that, he joined a running group, where he has made lots of new friends.

Your goal doesn't have to be exercise related. It could be focused on learning a new skill, growing some fruit and vegetables, or anything else you want.

Joining a local body-positive support group

A body-positive support group can offer a range of services that you might find useful. You can take advantage of peer support and meet others who are dealing with similar issues. The group might offer activities you can get involved in, or you can offer your services as a volunteer, which will introduce you to other people and improve your feelings of self-worth and sense of purpose. See Chapter 14 for more details on volunteering.

Doing activities that you enjoy

Go to a particular place that makes you feel good and where you feel a sense of belonging, or indulge in an activity you like doing. You can also join or organize a group activity. You'll meet like-minded people with similar interests, which is likely to reduce the focus you're putting on your weight or appearance, at least while you're there. Once you've found somewhere that takes the emphasis off your weight, keep returning, and gradually you'll start to focus less on your weight and more on the relationships you're making with others.

Seeing a therapist

Consider this step to discuss any negative thoughts about your body or unhealthy eating habits. I present details about different types of therapy that might help you in Chapter 13. You might want to read through these before deciding which therapy to opt for. Depending on where you live, you can ask your doctor or health care practitioner for a referral, or you can arrange to pay for a therapist yourself. Make sure that you select a trained and qualified therapist. Ideally, it should be someone who has treated loneliness and weight-related issues before.

REMEMBER

Regular conversations with your therapist can reduce your loneliness. This is called *therapeutic alliance*, which means that you have a meaningful connection with a health care practitioner or therapist.

WARNING

If you're living with an eating disorder, it's important that you receive professional support as soon as possible. If you haven't already, talk to your doctor or health care practitioner and explain the challenges you're facing. They'll be able to talk through the range of treatments available and sign you up for local services in your community.

Chapter **11**

Becoming a Caregiver

You usually have some idea of the kind of caregiving that's required when you become a parent, even if it's not always exactly as expected. However, sometimes you find yourself providing unpaid care for other people around you: for parents, spouses, or other loved ones. And you may not have prior knowledge of the kind of care that's required or know how long it'll be necessary.

The care might be needed because loved ones fall ill or are diagnosed with a long-term health condition, such as dementia. They might rely on the care you provide to enable them to continue living independently in the community. Sometimes you get some warning that you're going to be required to take on a caregiving role, particularly if a loved one's health condition is deteriorating slowly over time. However, at other times, a caregiving role is thrust upon you without warning, such as if a loved one has a sudden and unexpected stroke and is left unable to look after themselves.

Regardless of how you end up in your caregiving role, who you're caregiving for, or what their health condition is, becoming a caregiver is a key life transition point that can trigger loneliness. Providing unpaid care is tiring and time consuming and affects your social relationships. It can change your relationship with the person you're caregiving for, as well as your relationships with other family members and friends. As a caregiver, you might find that you have little time for yourself. Consequently, you can become socially isolated and feel lonely.

In this chapter I discuss the impact of becoming a caregiver on your social relationships. I walk through the implications of caregiving for different loved ones: adult and disabled children, your spouse, and your parents. I then discuss what happens when the caregiving role changes and how you can adapt to that. I offer some tips throughout the chapter on how to be less isolated and feel less lonely while continuing your caregiving role. I don't discuss mainstream caregiving for children in this chapter, but if you want some ideas on how to feel less lonely as a parent, you can find some useful advice in Chapter 4.

Knowing What to Expect as a Caregiver

REMEMBER

Every year millions of people across the globe take on caregiving responsibilities. At the same time, millions of others cease becoming a caregiver. The transition point of experiencing a change in your caregiving role — whether it's becoming a caregiver, taking on more caregiving responsibilities, or stopping caregiving — can trigger feelings of loneliness. This transition into and out of a caregiving role is something you might experience.

Adapting to a caregiving role

Sometimes a caregiving role will creep up over time. You may start helping an elderly parent with the odd bit of shopping, for example, and over time need to offer more and more support until you're supplying daily care. Other times you may be thrown into your caregiving role suddenly when a loved one becomes unexpectedly ill, is diagnosed with a long-term health condition, or has an accident. It can be an isolating and lonely experience regardless of whether you gradually become a caregiver or your caregiving role is thrust upon you overnight.

TIP

Here are some simple steps to take to help you adjust to your changing role and feel less lonely.

Acknowledge that you're a caregiver

You might not always see yourself as a caregiver. Many caregivers don't. It takes an average of two years to accept that you're a caregiver. If you're wondering if you are, ask yourself the following questions:

1. Do you spend some time each week caring for someone?

2. Is the person you care for unable to care for themselves because of an illness, disability, mental health issue, or frailty?

3. Does the care involve assisting the person do one or more everyday essential tasks, such as shopping, preparing and cooking meals, or keeping up with personal hygiene?

4. Is the care you provide unpaid?

If your answers are yes to all of these, you may well want to identify as a caregiver.

REMEMBER

You can be a caregiver at any age, and you don't have to live with the person you're caregiving for to be able to get help and support.

Get as much information as possible

As soon as you realize that you're becoming — or have become — a caregiver, get as much information as possible about your caregiving role and the health condition and needs of the person you're caring for. Ask their doctor what care support might be needed. Contact your local caregivers center and social care support services and ask what support is available for you as a caregiver. Find out if financial support or respite care are available. Do an internet search on your loved one's health condition. Discuss with your employer whether they offer support or flexible working conditions to help you balance your caregiving role and paid work.

Make a plan so that you're fully prepared for your caregiving role

It's never too late to make a plan, but the sooner you do, the better. If you've been a caregiver for a number of years and have only just realized that you're a caregiver, it's still useful to prepare a plan. Plan out what care is going to be needed, on which days, and how much time you're going to allocate to each task. Identify where you can get additional help in caring for your loved one. Be sure to build in time for yourself and keeping in touch with your other family and friends.

Be open with the person you're caregiving for about your needs

Quite often caregiving becomes an activity you take on for a loved one without ever discussing it with them. As soon as you realize that you're becoming a caregiver for a family member or friend, be sure to start a conversation about their caregiving requirements. Discuss how it might affect your relationship, and together think about ways in which you can build in some quality time to spend with each other outside of your caregiving relationship.

Talk to other family and friends about your caregiving role

As soon as you realize and acknowledge that you're a caregiver, it's useful to talk about your caregiving responsibilities with family and friends. This will help them understand why you might not be as easily available as you were in the past and offer you a source of emotional support. Discuss with them ways in which you can continue to keep in touch even though you're busy with your caregiving responsibilities, and, if it's appropriate, ask them to help you with your caregiving.

Identify other caregivers like yourself whom you can confide in

Discussing your caregiving role and feelings of loneliness with fellow caregivers can help you realize that you're not the only person experiencing these feelings and can be a great source of support and comfort. You can find other caregivers through your local caregivers center, through social media caregivers groups, through word of mouth, or through your local library, community center, or health center.

Managing changing relationships

REMEMBER

Becoming a caregiver can have a big impact on your life. It affects your relationship with the person you're caring for and with others. The time you're spending with the loved one you're caring for can be dominated by caring tasks, thus deflecting from any meaningful interaction. You might notice more stress and tension in your relationship as you try to fit caregiving tasks into your busy schedule. Meanwhile, the person you're caring for can become frustrated, having to rely on you and others for tasks they used to be able to do themselves.

If you're caring for a parent, you may experience role reversal, which can be difficult to adjust to for both you and them. (See "Caregiving for your parents," later in this chapter, for more information.) If you're caregiving for a spouse or partner, you might feel as though you've lost the intimacy of your relationship. (See "Looking after your spouse," later in this chapter, for more details.)

Whoever you're caregiving for, you may miss the relationship that you used to have with that person. You may also have very little time to maintain meaningful relationships with your wider social network of family and friends. This can be especially true if you're holding down a job too. When relationships change like this, you can feel lonely, bereft of meaningful social contact, and with few opportunities to engage in activities you enjoy or visit places where you feel a sense of belonging.

TIP

If you're a caregiver and you've noticed that your relationships with either the person you provide care for or others has changed since you started caregiving, you're not alone. In fact, around half of caregivers report difficulties in their relationships because of their caring responsibilities. However, you can manage your changing relationships so that you feel less lonely and isolated. Depending on your circumstances, this chapter offers tips for how to maintain relationships both with the person for whom you're caregiving and for those in your life you may feel less connected to now that you are a caregiver.

Understanding the Caregiving Role

Millions of unpaid caregivers across the world are looking after adults or children with disabilities. In the US, UK, Canada, and Australia alone, the number of caregivers who are identified number at least 60 million. And because people often don't identify as caregivers, there are likely to be many more people who are providing care for a loved one.

A caregiver is anyone who provides unpaid care for a friend or family member. Often the person in receipt of the care can't cope without the care provided.

REMEMBER

It's important not to confuse between an unpaid caregiver and a paid care worker. An unpaid caregiver supports someone they know, usually without financial reward. In contrast, paid care workers are employed. They can be domiciliary care workers providing care in a person's own home. Or they might be aides responsible for looking after people who live in residential care.

The amount of care that caregivers provide varies tremendously. It can range from just a few hours per week to 24/7 care. The care can be provided for others in your own home or in the cared-for person's home. Caregivers can be any age and gender. Even some younger children find themselves in the caregiving role, often for one of their parents.

If you're a caregiver or become one in the future, you might find yourself providing a whole range of care for your loved one. Responsibilities could include:

>> Keeping a watchful eye on the cared-for person

>> Preparing and cooking meals, washing clothes, shopping for groceries, and administering medication

>> Providing companionship

>> Accompanying the cared-for person on shopping trips and to medical appointments, social visits, and leisure activities

>> Paying bills and other financial matters

>> Facilitating personal care, such as bathing, supporting visits to the bathroom, and dressing

Given the range of tasks that unpaid caregivers can carry out, it's hardly surprising that many have little time to themselves and worry about the impact of caregiving on their relationships with friends and family. Research suggests that caregivers are seven times more likely to say they're always or often lonely compared with the general population. And their likelihood of feeling lonely increases as their number of hours spent caregiving each week rises.

TIP

If you're an unpaid caregiver, no matter who you're caregiving for or how many hours a week you provide the care for, make sure you take care of yourself and maintain social contact with friends and family. By looking after yourself and maintaining a support network, you'll not only protect your own health and well-being but be able to provide quality care for your loved one for longer.

Caregiving for disabled and adult children

If you're providing care for a child with a disability or an adult child due to a disability or a long-term health condition, your caregiving responsibilities are likely to go above and beyond what's usually expected from a parent. What's more, you're likely to be carrying out these tasks for a lot longer than the average parent. You'll probably find yourself carrying out a whole range of caregiving duties on a daily basis. These will vary significantly depending on the individual circumstances and needs of your child, but they can include:

>> Helping with eating and feeding

>> Attending to them in the night, especially if they have difficulties sleeping

>> Helping them with personal hygiene, which might include washing, bathing, and visits to the bathroom

>> Supporting them with their mobility, which might include some lifting

>> Accompanying them on visits outside the house, such as for medical appointments, shopping, and support groups

Carrying out these caregiving tasks while continuing your everyday life can be exhausting. You might be balancing work alongside these caregiving responsibilities, as well as looking after other children and sometimes an elderly parent. You might have very little, if any, time for yourself and can feel extremely lonely. If this resonates with you and, like many parents of disabled and adult children, you're feeling overwhelmed, exhausted, and lonely, you're in good company.

There are many reasons you might be feeling lonely as the caregiver of a disabled or adult child. You may not feel able to talk to friends, family, or work colleagues about your caregiving responsibilities for a range of reasons. You might feel self-conscious that your child has a disability or might feel that there's a stigma. You might feel others don't understand. Or you may believe that talking about your caregiving is a sign of weakness, that you're not doing a good enough job. Any of these can lead to a rift between you and your network of family and friends.

In addition, you're likely to lack time and energy to get out of the house and socialize with friends and family. And even if you can muster up some power to get out, it might be difficult to leave your child without alternative care support. Furthermore, you may worry about leaving your child in the hands of someone else, which can prevent you from socializing. Or when you do go out, you might find it difficult to relax and enjoy yourself. Guilt can play a role also. You may feel guilty about leaving your child to go out and enjoy yourself without them.

Your relationships with your immediate family or close friends might come under strain because your caregiving responsibilities occupy your time and energy. Your spouse and other siblings can feel neglected, and the tiredness and stress of caregiving can lead to tensions in relationships.

If you're managing to work alongside caregiving for your child, you may find yourself unable to attend work social events and feel disconnected from your colleagues.

You may not have time or energy to participate in social activities or hobbies that you used to enjoy or to visit places where you feel a sense of belonging, such as a favorite beach or lake. And if you do manage to engage in such activities or get to these places, you might not be able to relax and fully appreciate them. You may be on caregiving duty if your child is with you, or you may feel guilty or worried if you've left your child behind.

You may not be able to afford to participate in social activities. This might especially be the case if you've had to give up work to undertake your caregiving role or you've had to spend money on expensive aids and equipment.

If this resonates with you and you're feeling lonely or socially isolated, you might feel unsure what to do or where to turn. Here are some useful suggestions for you to try.

>> **Seek assistance from your local caregivers center.** You can find a caregivers center in most towns and cities. These centers can inform you of all the support you can get for your loved one and for yourself to help you feel less lonely. This support might include respite care so that you can have some time off from caregiving or ways to connect with other caregivers.

>> **Access specialized peer support for caregivers.** This can be group peer support or one-on-one provision. Because other trained caregivers who understand how you feel offer the peer support, you may feel like someone is there solely for you. Peer support can be offered in person or online.

>> **Seek music or art therapy.** Music and art therapy are specifically designed to reduce loneliness among caregivers and the person they care for. They provide a stimulus for interaction between you and your child and can help you reconnect beyond your caregiver/cared-for relationship.

>> **Practice mindfulness meditation.** Ten minutes of daily meditation can help you feel more calm and relaxed and improve your sense of well-being, especially if you do it before you start your caregiving or other daily tasks. You can practice meditation in your own home using an online app, or you can attend a group meditation session.

>> **Exercise regularly.** Endorphins from exercise improve your mood and protect you from loneliness. If you're able to leave your child or arrange for someone else to look after them for a short while, try to get out by yourself. Otherwise, incorporate exercise activities that you can do with your child.

>> **Take advantage of caregivers support groups at work.** If your employer has a support group for working caregivers, join it. It's a good way to meet and chat with other caregivers. You'll learn how to balance work and caregiving for your child and how to find time for yourself and other relationships so that you feel less lonely.

>> **Allocate time to reconnect with your friends and other family members.** Spending even just a few minutes of quality time each week with people other than your child is important. You'll feel less lonely, which will improve your health and well-being and make you better equipped to care for your child. If you can't meet in person, try a regular phone call, text, or video chat or even a letter or a postcard to let them know you're thinking about them.

>> **Seek psychological support.** If you're struggling to come to terms with your child's care needs and are particularly lonely, it might be worth trying psychological therapies. You could try self-hypnosis or other techniques that are known to help. I provide details about the different possibilities and help you select the best option in Chapter 13.

>> **Talk to your doctor or health practitioner.** If you're particularly struggling as a caregiver, it might be a good idea to chat with your doctor and ask them to refer you for additional support.

Looking after your spouse

Paul is a retired schoolteacher and the primary caregiver for his wife, Gillian, who was diagnosed with dementia a few years ago. When Gillian was first diagnosed, her symptoms were fairly mild, so Paul was able to continue working while providing care. However, as Gillian's condition worsened, she required more intense caregiving. Paul was forced to give up work and retire early.

When Paul first started caregiving for his wife, he managed to maintain a social life. He met up with his work colleagues and invited friends over to play cards. However, as Gillian's condition worsened, Paul became unable to leave her alone. He also stopped inviting friends over to play cards because he felt awkward that Gillian couldn't engage. Paul began to feel extremely lonely. He felt as though he'd lost his intimate connection with his wife and lost his social connections with his friends and work colleagues.

Paul's case isn't unusual. Many unpaid caregivers find themselves caring for their spouse or their partner, often in their own home. When you embark upon life with your partner, it might seem unimaginable that you could become their main caregiver. But various circumstances can result in this outcome. A classic example involves a couple gradually growing older together until one becomes more frail or ill and requires care from the other. In other cases, an individual may be diagnosed with a long-term health condition, such as heart disease, cancer, or dementia, or be involved in a life-changing accident that requires care at home.

Sometimes the requirement for caregiving develops over a long period. But in other cases, the need to care for a spouse can emerge without warning. No matter how the care needs arise or for what reasons, caregiving for a spouse can have an impact on both partners, their relationship with each other, and their relationships with others.

REMEMBER

Caregiving for your spouse can feel more intensely lonely than when caregiving for other family members. Quite often people rely on their spouse for their main form of social interaction. This relationship can protect you from emotional loneliness that arises when you lack an intimate relationship. When you're caring for a spouse, however, it can feel as though your relationship with them has changed. You can feel as though you've lost that intimate relationship. Your caregiving role can also take a lot of time and energy, and you can find it difficult to maintain relationships with other family and friends. This can mean that you feel socially lonely because you lack a wider network.

TIP

If you're a caregiver for your spouse, you may find yourself feeling lonely for a whole host of reasons. If this sounds like you, it's important to take action. Here are some tips on how to do this.

» **Maintain regular communication with your spouse.** Explain how you're feeling and allow your spouse to express how they're feeling. Ask them what kind of support they want and need from you, and explain to them what support you need as a caregiver. Some health conditions such as dementia can make communication more difficult as the symptoms progress, so you may need to seek help from expert medical practitioners for the best ways to maintain lines of communication.

» **Consider how to retain intimacy.** Your spouse's health condition may mean that the nature of intimacy between you has changed. Discuss this with your spouse, and try different means of retaining your intimacy so that you can still share an emotional connection. Touch and massage are great ways to preserve or spark an emotional connection, which can help stave off loneliness in your relationship.

» **Keep contact with friends and family.** Even though you may feel too tired or busy to maintain your wider social network, prioritize some time for this each week even if it's only for a few minutes. If you can't leave your spouse alone, invite people to the house. If you don't feel comfortable doing that, have a chat on the phone or send a text, or do a live video call.

» **Ask family for help.** If you feel able to, explain to your family what's going on in your life and how the caregiving is affecting you. If you have a son or daughter nearby, ask if they can spend short regular slots of time with their parent. This will give you a break but will also help them retain a bond with their parent.

» **Engage in activities with your spouse.** Make some time on a regular weekly basis — daily if possible — doing an activity together. It could just be for 30 minutes or so and could involve listening to music together, playing a game, or looking through old photographs. Anything that takes the focus away from caregiving will work.

» **Seek support from your local caregivers center.** The center can offer advice on your caregiving role and provide information on respite care so that you can spend some time with friends and family or visit places that will help you feel less lonely. The center will most likely have support groups and activities for caregivers so you can get to know other people in a similar situation.

» **Join social media caregiver support groups.** Log in to your favorite social media app and look for caregivers support groups. You'll find a whole range of tips and advice and will be able to connect with other caregivers who'll understand what you're going through.

» **Consider marriage therapy.** It's worth exploring marriage therapy or counseling. Becoming a caregiver for your spouse can change your relationship, and a specialist marriage counselor can help you both come to terms with your new relationship. You can get things back on track, even if they're in a slightly different direction than they were before.

Caregiving for a parent

Caregiving for a parent is the most common type of caregiving after mainstream childcare. Parents are thought of as strong authoritative role models who care for their kids as they grow up and who continue to offer a helping hand into adulthood. But as parents age and become frailer or perhaps are hit by a long-term health condition, they can need help and support so that they can continue living in their own home. One or more of their offspring often take on the caregiving role, whether it's a few hours a week or several hours a day.

REMEMBER

Caregiving for a parent can involve different tasks and activities, depending on what their care needs are. It can involve keeping the garden under control, shopping for their weekly groceries, sorting out their finances and making sure bills are paid on time, preparing and cooking meals for them, accompanying them on social trips or to medical appointments, or helping with bathing. The caregiving can entail lengthy journeys back and forth between your home and theirs. Some find that they need to stay over at a parent's house for one or more nights a week.

If you're caregiving for a parent, you might be feeling lonely for a whole variety of reasons. Perhaps you're balancing caregiving while holding down a job. People caregiving for a parent are more likely to still be working than people caregiving for any other type of person. This can mean that you have little, if any, time for the kinds of things that can prevent you from feeling lonely, such as relationships with other family and friends, hobbies or social activities, and visits to places where you feel a meaningful connection.

As you're caregiving for a parent, you might notice that the roles have been reversed. Instead of them taking care of you, you're now looking after them. This can sometimes create a sense of unease for both you and your parent. You can feel as though you've lost that special person who was always there to offer you advice and support.

Likewise, your parent can find the adjustment to needing care difficult. They may not want to ask for, or accept, help and may feel a loss of autonomy and dignity. This can put a strain on your relationship, and you might start to feel loss, grief, and loneliness.

Caregiving for a parent can also create tension among siblings, even those who were previously very close. It can lead to feelings of guilt by the siblings who aren't providing the bulk of the care and resentment from those who are. You might find that your sister or brother, whom you've always felt really close to, suddenly feels more like a stranger.

This kind of caregiving role can also create difficulties with other family members. You might feel too tired to spend quality time with the rest of your family. Your spouse and own children can start to feel neglected and feel that you're prioritizing your parents over them. You may also find that your spouse and kids are spending more quality time together without you, which can make you feel excluded, lonely, and isolated.

Here's an example from my work. Keira, 49, has three children and has become the main caregiver for her 81-year-old mother, Sheena, whom she's always been close to. Sheena has been living on her own since her husband passed away four years ago. She fell a couple of years ago and dislocated her shoulder. She also had a bout of pneumonia last year and was hospitalized for a few weeks. Sheena's sight and hearing are deteriorating, and she's progressively finding it more difficult to look after herself. Keira has gradually been providing more care for Sheena. Kiera works full-time in a high-pressure job and is finding that she's spending most of her time working at her job or caregiving for her mother and her own three kids. She has very little time for herself and is becoming increasingly lonely. She's lost touch with many of her friends because she can't easily find time to meet with them. Her relationship with her mother and her three kids and husband are suffering because she's too busy and stressed to enjoy their company.

TIP

If you're caregiving for one or more parents and are feeling lonely, I'm here to help. Lots of people who provide care for a parent are experiencing similar feelings to you. And although no caregiving situation is the same, you can try some things to alleviate your loneliness.

>> **Spend quality time connecting with your parent.** As a caregiver, you can find that the relationship with your parent doesn't feel quite the same, especially amid the pressures of balancing caregiving with work and other responsibilities. Try to carve out some time to really connect with them rather than focusing solely on their care needs because it will help both of you reconnect and feel less lonely. This might simply involve having a cup of tea and talking. Whichever way you decide to spend the time, be sure to give your parent your full attention. Don't get distracted by things such as your mobile phone, emails, and washing machine cycles.

>> **Learn as much as you can about your parent's condition.** Find out what your parent can and can't do and how you can best help. You can often get such advice from your local caregivers center, their doctor, or medical practitioner. The more you know about your parent's condition, the better because you'll have more confidence to make decisions that are beneficial for all of you. You might find out that you're doing too much for your parent or that you can seek support for some tasks from elsewhere. Both of these will free you up for spending time with other friends and family.

>> **Identify and connect with others who are caregiving for parents.** It's often beneficial to discuss how you feel with others who are in a similar position to

you. Just talking about your respective caregiving roles can make you feel less lonely. You may form friendships and meaningful connections with other caregivers. You can find other caregivers through local caregivers centers, through social media groups, or through work. Some employers provide caregiver support groups, which tend to be run by Human Resources or fellow working caregivers.

>> **Make use of services for caregivers in your community.** Take advantage of services such as adult day care centers, home-delivered meals, respite care, transportation services, and domiciliary care workers. That way you'll free up some time to engage in meaningful connections beyond your caregiving role.

>> **Ask family and friends for support.** If you're the main caregiver for your parent, talk to other family members about your caregiving and how it's affecting you. Don't be afraid to ask them for help. You could agree on a shared caregiving schedule that divides some of the tasks so that no one becomes overburdened. This should free up some time that you can spend on your own interests or with your friends

>> **Have regular breaks from your caring role.** Ask other family members to take over for a day or a week so you can get a full break and use this time to spend time with your family, friends, or just to look after yourself. If you can't get other family members to help out, or don't have any, find out about options for respite care. This is alternative care which is provided for short periods of time to give you a break from your caring role.

>> **Find time to spend with your family and friends.** Let them know you still care about them. If you're a full-time caregiver for your parent and their health condition means that you can't leave them or arrange respite care, use technology to connect with your family and friends. You can find some useful tips on how to do this in Chapter 7.

Adjusting To Life When Your Caregiving Role Ceases

REMEMBER

Your caregiving role can cease for a variety of reasons. The person you're caregiving for can recover, they might move into residential care, or they might pass away. It can be a shock when caregiving ceases. Even though you'll have more time for yourself and for relationships with other people, you might feel lonely — sometimes lonelier than when you were caregiving. You can feel a loss of purpose, especially if your loved one has passed away or gone into residential care.

TIP

Here are some tips to help you feel less lonely after your caregiving role has ceased:

» If your loved one has recovered and no longer needs your care or support, it's common to feel a loss of purpose for a while. Be sure to continue your relationship as they regain their autonomy and independence. Use your time to engage in activities that you missed while caring for them.

» If your loved one has moved into residential care, find ways to maintain regular contact with them. Visit them regularly if you live close enough. If you live too far away for regular face-to-face visits, keep in contact by writing, by video chats, or by telephone chats. Ask the care home staff to help you arrange these. Be sure to use these valuable times to engage in meaningful interaction. Talk about things that you both find interesting and engaging. Carry out simple activities together like drawing, painting, or playing games together. Reminisce about memories from your shared past.

» If your loved one has moved into residential care and you would like to continue some involvement in their care, discuss with the staff how you can do that. You can also get involved in the care home's relatives and caregivers group if they have one. By maintaining a role in your loved one's care, you can retain a sense of purpose.

» It's natural to feel sad after a loved one has died, and if you've had a close bond through a caregiving role, it can be a particularly lonely time. But time is a healer. If the person you cared for has passed away, talk to others who knew them. This will help you share your grief and support each other. You'll find some specific tips for dealing with grief and bereavement in Chapter 8, but if you're finding your loss particularly difficult and things aren't getting easier, it might be worth contacting a bereavement support group or bereavement counselor.

» Caregiving may have been a big part of your life. Whatever the reason you've ceased your caregiving role, it can take some time to adjust. You may find that you have a lot of spare time, don't quite know what to do with yourself, and feel lonely. When you feel ready, reconnect with friends and family you haven't had time for, find new people to connect with (see Chapters 5 and 14 for more details), or put your caregiving knowledge to good use by volunteering at your local caregivers center. (See Chapter 14 for more info on volunteering.)

There are also some useful helplines and resources listed in the Appendix.

Chapter **12**

Making an Education or Employment Change

Outside of the home, it's common to spend most of your young life in educational settings and most of your adult life in a work environment. These are places where you're likely to engage in meaningful relationships, form friendships, and develop a sense of belonging.

A change in either of these settings can disrupt those relationships and has the potential to trigger loneliness. This is a perfectly understandable and normal reaction to change.

In this chapter I explore the key transition points involved in education and employment changes that have the potential to trigger loneliness. I examine how a new educational setting can cause you to feel lonely. If you're a parent or guardian helping your child navigate a new school experience that's creating loneliness and other challenges, I offer some tips for you as well.

Later in this chapter I explore how a new employment situation can lead to loneliness, whether the change involves starting or changing employment, finding yourself unemployed, or retiring.

This chapter covers ways to help you deal with and overcome the loneliness that's triggered by these types of transitions. These suggestions are useful whether you're a student or employee who's struggling with loneliness or a parent, teacher, or employer who wants to help others experiencing loneliness.

Facing New Educational Situations

Starting a new educational institution can be exciting, but it can also be challenging. Children and adolescents spend a large portion of their daily lives in school and place a lot of emphasis on having friends there. Indeed, the number of friends a young person has is often seen as an indicator of the level of acceptance by their peers.

If you feel a connection with your peers, make friends with your classmates, and engage in meaningful relationships with teachers and support staff, you're less likely to feel lonely and more likely to enjoy your learning experience. These, in turn, lead to a greater sense of belonging, increased well-being, and a better chance of successful educational achievement.

Parents, teachers, and young people often assume that making friends in an educational setting is simply a matter of course. It is thought that because young people are surrounded by others, they'll inevitably have lots of social connections. However, just like in the adult population, young people can be surrounded by others and still feel lonely. They may actually feel lonelier when they're surrounded by others if they see their peers connecting with friends, while they themselves feel excluded. There's also an assumption that young people will find it easy to make friends, but that's not always the case.

Given the amount of time young people spend each day in a school setting, if they don't have friends or meaningful relationships with their classmates and aren't comfortable there, they can feel lonely, which can negatively affect other aspects of their lives.

Research has shown that an increasing number of young people feel lonely at school. This can affect their well-being and self-esteem. Fortunately, this loneliness is often only temporary, triggered by a change. Once they adapt to that change, they can start to feel socially connected again. Some might feel lonelier for longer than others, and some might need a bit of assistance to help them feel more connected.

Helping a child who's starting school

Starting school for the first time is a big step for a child. The first day at school is often a day you can remember for the rest of your life. It can be new and exciting but also a bit scary.

Even once a child has adapted to school, they may need to change schools. Moving to a new school can bring about feelings of loneliness.

I remember well my first day at school. I really enjoyed it and couldn't wait to return the next day. But after that initial euphoria I was unhappy and lonely there for a number of years, which adversely affected my confidence as a young person. Had someone seen the signs and helped me make friends and integrate, things could have been different.

REMEMBER

A child might feel lonely when starting school for several reasons. Maybe they have separation anxiety, discomfort interacting in group settings, or unease about adapting to different ages and maturation levels. Perhaps they're missing an established peer group from a previous school. The key is to understand the triggers so that you can try to prevent or mitigate their impact.

TIP

If your child finds it difficult to talk to new people in general, it can be worthwhile to support the development of their social skills in other contexts outside of school. Encourage them to communicate with others in various settings. For example, have them ask for items when they accompany you to stores. This will build their confidence when talking to people.

If you're a parent, guardian, or teacher, you can take some steps to help your child feel less lonely when they start school or switch schools.

Explain what to expect

Before your child starts school, explain in a straightforward way what to expect from school so they feel comfortable when they arrive. Explain the structure of the day, the rules, and the expectations. Keep upbeat and positive about school, even if you had a particularly bad experience.

Take your child along to any settling-in sessions so that they can get used to the building and become familiar with it before the official start day. That will put them at ease in their new surroundings.

If your child's loneliness is triggered by separation anxiety, speak to your child's teacher so they're aware of it and plan ways to help your child manage their feelings. Ask if the teacher can greet your child in the morning so there's a smooth transition from leaving you, or inquire whether they can bring a familiar item with them into school, such as their favorite teddy bear.

Acknowledge how your child feels, reassure them that it's normal, and don't show signs of being upset yourself. Make a proper exit when you drop them off; say goodbye, give them a kiss, and leave. Don't linger or hesitate because that will make them feel worse.

Help your child connect

Connect with other parents whose children are going to be starting that school, and invite the kids over to play. Begin this process a few months before your child starts school to allow your child sufficient time to make friends with other new starters. Remember that just because you get along with a particular parent doesn't mean that your child will get along with their child!

Once your child has started school, arrange playdates with other children, or invite them over to play or have a sleepover.

REMEMBER

Check with your child about who they like and don't like before organizing this. I remember very well my mother arranging for me to go to another girl's house after school without consulting me. Little did she know that the girl had been bullying me for weeks and making my life hell!

If your child is finding it difficult to make friends at school, they might benefit from joining a club or a team so they can participate in activities outside of the school day. They'll interact with other kids who have similar interests to them, which can stave off loneliness.

Communicate with your child regularly

Regularly talk to you child about how they're feeling, and encourage them to draw pictures of it. Remind them how much you love them and that you're still there for them. If you discover that they're feeling lonely, focus on implementing some of the tips here and try not to worry. Their feelings of loneliness can be quelled when they make friends and connect with others.

Talk to your child's teacher

If the loneliness goes on for a few weeks, doesn't show any signs of diminishing, or is particularly severe and is adversely affecting their mental and physical health, it's worth booking an appointment with their teacher and explaining the situation. The teacher might be able to pair them up with another child for specific activities or connect them with others for group activities.

Navigating a change of school

Even when you're older, starting at a new school can bring about feelings you've perhaps not felt in many years. You may feel like you're the only one who doesn't already have a group of friends or that you don't have anyone to really click with. Adapting to a new, unfamiliar environment can add to feelings of isolation and uncertainty, which contribute to loneliness.

TIP

All of these feelings are completely normal and are usually only temporary. However, to get rid of them and to stop the loneliness from lingering for longer than it needs to, this section has some suggestions for you to try. If you're a parent or a teacher, you can think about how to incorporate these ideas so your own child, or children in your class, adapt to their new school and feel less lonely.

Seeking out like-minded people

Try to find like-minded fellow students who have similar interests to you. Most friendships are initiated through a common interest. Look out for other students who share your interests and start a conversation with them. Make small talk by asking about their favorite music or movies or why they're interested in a particular class. Consider joining a club either connected to your school or outside of it to find people with parallel passions to your own.

REMEMBER

It can take time to find other people with similar interests, so don't expect to click with someone right away. When I was 11, my family moved, which meant I had to switch schools. My teacher asked another girl to spend the day with me, but we had absolutely nothing in common and, in fact, I don't think we had another conversation after that. I did feel lonely at first, but it wasn't long before I found peers with similar interests whom I could connect with.

If somebody is friendly toward you, be friendly back and start a conversation. Following my school move, I was feeling particularly lonely and sitting on my own during a lunch break. A girl in my class came up to me and started talking, and from then on, we became best friends. I still don't know what made her approach me, but it didn't really matter.

TIP

Displaying positive body language can be helpful when you're trying to make new friends and acquaintances. When you approach fellow classmates, smile, look them in the eyes, and speak clearly and confidently. Avoid looking down at your feet because that will give them the impression that you're not interested in them. If you're particularly shy or find it difficult to approach people to start a conversation, practice by approaching an imaginary person at home.

TIP

If you're a teacher or a student and suspect that someone is lonely, find out what that person is interested in and introduce them to others with similar interests.

Retaining links with old friends

Just because you've moved schools doesn't mean you need to abandon your old friends. Make efforts to keep in touch, and try to arrange a regular timeslot to meet up with them after school or on weekends. If you've moved far away, you could arrange a video chat or phone call with your old friends once a week to keep your connection going. Chances are, they'll be missing your friendship and may feel lonely too.

Talking about your experiences

No matter your age, if you feel lonely and are struggling to connect with others, it's always helpful to talk about how you feel with people close to you. You could discuss your loneliness with a parent, a sibling, a grandparent, or a friend from your previous school. Sometimes just articulating your feelings can make you feel better. Also, others have undoubtedly felt lonely at some point in their lives and should be able to offer some good advice. If you're a teacher or parent, look for signs that children and young people are feeling lonely and not engaging with their peers at school, and offer to chat with them.

If you don't have anyone to share your feeling with or prefer not to talk to them about it, you can contact a specialized counselor.

WARNING

If you're feeling particularly lonely on a regular basis, it's been going on for some time, and you've tried the tips in this chapter and elsewhere in the book, it might be worth talking to your doctor or medical practitioner and asking them to refer you for therapy.

Going to college or university

College life can be a particularly exciting time for young people. For many it involves living away from home, usually for the first time. This, along with factors such as unfamiliar surroundings, new classmates, and perhaps the first experience of roommates or housemates, makes college a challenge for some. Research suggests that loneliness among college students is commonplace, particularly for first-year students.

I came across Coen a few years ago when he was feeling lonely during his first year of college in London. He was from a small rural town and wasn't used to city life. When he moved to London, he felt lost in the big city. He didn't know how to connect with all the new people he was surrounded by. Those he'd come across so far were from different backgrounds and didn't seem to have anything in common with him. Coen would sit on his bedroom floor each evening and call his mother in tears because he felt so lonely.

His mother advised him to join a club so that he could meet people. He decided to take her advice and join the badminton club that met twice a week. There he met other students he had some things in common with. He even made friends with some students who happened to be from a nearby village to his hometown. Coen felt much more positive after he joined the badminton club because he was establishing a life outside of his studies that included meeting up with these new friends in his spare time. Joining a sports club also meant that he kept physically active, releasing endorphins that improved his well-being.

There are many ways to feel less lonely when you're at college.

Socialize with your housemates

Suggest to your housemates that you all cook a meal and share it. It's a good way to bond while learning or practicing your cooking skills. Food is always effective in bringing people together and often facilitates social connections. If you want to make it even more interesting, each of you could invite someone. For more on how to connect at home through food, see Chapter 4.

Join a club

Colleges usually offer clubs for an array of activities and hobbies, from political parties to lobbyist groups, choirs, art, and drama. Look at the range of clubs available at your college and try out a few. Clubs create opportunities to make social connections, meet like-minded people, gain new skills, and engage in meaningful, enjoyable activities.

Attend your classes in person

Loneliness can lead to anxiety and depression. You may not feel like leaving your bedroom, let alone going to lectures and classes. However, it's important to attend your classes. Attend them in person, even if you have options to join online. Since the Covid-19 pandemic, hybrid and online options have become more popular, but attending in person really helps you connect to other students as well as to lecturing staff. You can find yourself discussing aspects of the lecture or even last night's football results with your peers. Before you know it, you'll find yourself down at the student bar or café for a sociable drink together.

Get out and explore

If you're in a new city or town, find out what the key attractions are, and visit them in turn. Perhaps visit one per week to start with. This will familiarize you with your new surroundings but also create a bond with your new environment and enable you to come into contact with other people.

Chapter 5 discusses the well-being benefits of visiting green spaces and spending time there. It's helpful to spend a small amount of time each day in green spaces, whether they're parks, trails, canal paths, sports fields, or even tree-lined streets.

Volunteer or get a part-time job

Both volunteering and participating in paid employment can enable you to help others and can bring you in contact with other people. It shouldn't be hard to find a range of volunteering and paid employment positions available. You can start by talking to someone at your college's career development center.

Join social media groups

Use your favorite social media platform to identify groups that will enable you to connect with like-minded people. This avenue should bring you in contact with a wider, non-student population to add some diversity to your current contacts.

Make video calls to friends and family

Even though you've moved away, you can still keep in contact with your family and friends back home. Arrange for regular catch-up calls. Plan for some of your friends back home to visit you if you don't live too far away, or plan your next trip back home so that you have something to focus on and look forward to.

Talk to a counselor

If you're feeling particularly lonely, it's persisting for a while, and it's not getting any better, you may want to talk to a college counselor. They have expertise in dealing with all kinds of mental health issues among students, including loneliness, and will be able to direct you to other resources and activities that will be able to help you.

My colleague set up a successful therapeutic running program for college students called Mindfit. It was based on walking, jogging, or running in small groups, followed by a hot drink, chat, and mindfulness activities. It had a positive effect on tackling loneliness and connecting students who felt lonely. If you want to know more about mindfulness and meditation techniques, you can find some useful information in Chapter 13.

TIP

If you're feel particularly lonely, it's leading to depression, anxiety, or a lack of self-esteem, and your loneliness doesn't seem to be improving, seek advice and support from your doctor or healthcare practitioner. They can find you support services in your local area.

Starting Work or Changing Jobs

The workplace is a place of productivity, but it's also a place of social interaction. It's where you interact with coworkers to complete jobs, work in teams to solve problems and reach solutions, take instructions from your boss, and report back to them. It's where you form friendships and a sense of connection and belonging to the building or venue, and it's sometimes where you meet that special person you want to spend the rest of your life with.

Starting work for the first time can be exciting. You're likely to have spent most of your life up to that point in school, so the workplace is a new phase that will undoubtedly bring with it unique challenges and opportunities. Changing jobs can likewise bring with it uncertainty, which is true whether you're changing your job role for the same employer, changing employers but have the same job title, or venturing into something completely new, such as self-employment or establishing a new business.

A change in your employment situation can be a daunting and isolating experience that can trigger loneliness. The loneliness can occur regardless of whether you're starting work for the first time, switching employers, or retiring. The good news is that this loneliness is often only temporary as you experience a disruption to your daily routine.

REMEMBER

The anticipation of the change is often much worse than the reality of your new employment situation. What's more, if you can prepare yourself for the change and arm yourself with strategies to tackle loneliness, you can adapt more easily.

You can feel like an outsider when you start a new job. That feeling is amplified when you see your coworkers spending time together and talking about shared experiences. Because you don't know anyone yet, it can feel difficult to engage in conversations. To help you on your way, here are some techniques and strategies to assist you in settling into your new employment situation, feeling more at ease, and avoiding or reducing those feelings of loneliness.

Adapting to workplace culture

Each workplace has a distinct set of norms and cultures, and it can take some time to understand them. This, together with the fact that you're working with a new set of people you barely know, can leave you unsure of what to say, how to say it, and when. These uncertainties can sometimes mean that you remain silent for fear of saying the wrong thing.

You'll also encounter acronyms or terms that are commonly used for departments, people, places, and processes. You'll hear a whole set of jargon that your new coworkers use but you're unfamiliar with. This can especially be the case when you're changing employment sectors. The use of jargon can feel like your coworkers are talking a foreign language. You might feel a sense of exclusion initially.

TIP

Create a list of words and terms that are commonly used in your new place of employment, that are specific to the organization, or that you haven't come across before. This will help you feel more confident in following conversations at work.

Facing imposter syndrome

When you start a new role, you can sometimes feel as though you're not good enough to be in the job. This can particularly affect women, who can lack confidence in the workplace, and people who are starting their first job or who have recently been promoted. This can lead you to fear being "found out" and make you feel out of place.

If you encounter these feelings, remind yourself that you have been selected for the job based on your skills and qualities. If you're particularly lacking in confidence or self-esteem there are some useful strategies to try in Chapter 13.

Making conversation with colleagues

You don't need to wait for your new colleagues to start talking to you. Take the initiative and make conversation with them. Start by getting to know just a few people.

REMEMBER

If you were close to your coworkers in your previous job, you can yearn for them in your new job, which can trigger loneliness.

Select your timing when initiating conversations with your new coworkers. You don't want to suddenly initiate a conversation if they're in full workflow and require quiet or need to concentrate particularly hard. If you're an employer or an existing worker and have a new starter, you can help them feel less lonely by introducing them to other workers and bringing them into your conversations.

A particularly effective way to get to know coworkers and find out more about the structure of the organization is to meet individually with your coworkers and have conversations about their roles. This will help you understand more about the everyday working practices and learn more about the workplace cultures. It will also help you get to know your work colleagues a bit better. You'll find that they'll generally be pleased that you're taking an interest in them and their job.

Initiating meetups outside the office

Having a conversation over a drink or food can aid social interaction. If your work colleagues don't have a regular lunch or coffee break where you can have informal conversations, suggest to one or two of them that it would be nice to meet up over lunch or after work. This will help you find out more about your work colleagues and get to know them better. You won't necessarily click with all of them, so try meeting a few different people. You'll find out fairly quickly who you're most likely to get along with.

Large companies often have clubs or groups you can join. These can range from book clubs, workout buddies, and sports clubs, to groups that support diverse types of employees, such as LGBTQIA+, working caregivers, and ethnic minority workers. By joining these groups and clubs, you're likely to meet like-minded coworkers with whom you can connect.

If you're feeling particularly lonely at work or are an employer who's concerned about loneliness in your workplace, you can find more information in Chapter 6.

Finding Yourself Out of Work

People can find themselves out of work for myriad reasons. Whether you're looking for your first job, you've been laid off, or you left your job to seek something better, it can bring about uncertainty and worry for practical reasons, as well as isolation and loneliness caused by a break in routine and built-in social interaction.

According to research, people who aren't working are more likely to say they feel lonely than people who are in employment. However, the link between unemployment and loneliness isn't one way; it's a bidirectional relationship. Job loss can lead to higher levels of loneliness, yet people who are lonely can be more likely to be unemployed. Research suggests that the latter is because loneliness can lead to reduced motivation, performance, productivity, and poorer health.

When you become unemployed, your social network tends to shrink. This doesn't happen right away for everyone, but quite often, over time you lose contact with work colleagues. You may not be invited to after-work events that you were once involved in. A reduction in salary might mean that you can't afford to go to the same places that your previous work colleagues frequent. Or you might have less in common with them now that you're not working. You can quickly find yourself out of the loop and have difficulty engaging in conversations about work experiences you're no longer part of.

Losing your job can make you feel that you lack a sense of purpose. You may start to wonder what your role in life is, why you matter in the world, and what difference you make. This can make you feel isolated and lonely and lead you to question your self-worth. Losing your job can result in depression and demoralization, and it can damage your self-esteem and confidence. This can be particularly true if you're nearing retirement or if your career has played a particularly important role in your life. Once these feelings set in, you can find yourself avoiding social interaction. See Chapter 10 for more information on depression, anxiety, and loneliness.

If you felt a strong sense of belonging to your company and you're no longer able to be part of that venue, you can be left with a sense of emptiness and loneliness. This won't necessarily apply to everyone who's made unemployed. Some people don't feel a sense of connection to their place of work. However, even if you didn't connect to the physical workplace, you may feel a loss of belonging to your place in the workforce more generally.

Many forms of social participation and interaction require an income, and if you become unemployed you can find that the activities and places you used to go are no longer affordable. This may mean that you're forced to stop frequenting places where you're able to interact with friends and family and feel a sense of belonging.

One of my friends, Graham, was a big fan of Sheffield Wednesday, and I used to see him every week when Wednesday were playing. When he was let go from his job, he suddenly had to stop watching his team play because he could no longer afford it. This led to him feeling extremely lonely, first because he couldn't participate in an activity that brought him joy on a regular basis, but also because he lost contact with many of his friends and acquaintances whom he only saw at the matches.

Being unemployed can be stigmatized. People's perceptions of you can change, and your perception of yourself can change. This can be especially true in modern western societies where there's a strong work ethic and people can be quick to apportion blame on the individual for unemployment — until it's their turn! Stigma can adversely affect your self-esteem and confidence and can mean that you avoid social interactions and places where you might bump into or meet other people. You can find yourself avoiding eye contact or walking the opposite way or across the street to avoid talking to people you know, especially if you think they're going to ask you about your employment status.

WARNING

Losing your job can adversely affect your family relationships. Tensions can emerge between spouses especially as household finances become constrained. What's more, the longer you're unemployed, the more likely it is that household relationships will become frayed. Such tensions can trigger loneliness at home. See Chapter 4 for more information on loneliness in the home and how to deal with it.

Whatever the reason you've become unemployed and however lonely it has made you feel, you can find silver linings in your unemployment, overcome your loneliness, and regain your confidence and ability to engage in social interaction again.

Finding good uses for your time

If you're unemployed, you probably have lots of time on your hands. Use it wisely. Once you've completed any job search and domestic activities, get yourself out of the house. Visit local green spaces where you have a sense of belonging and can improve your well-being (see Chapter 5). Use every opportunity to chat with passersby and ask how they're doing. If you feel comfortable and it's appropriate mention to people that you're seeking work. You never know they might know of a suitable job going! Visit local community facilities such as libraries and community centers. Join in local activities that are free of charge, such as parkrun, or a hiking group. By engaging in these ways, you'll connect with others in your local community whom you may not have had an opportunity to before. Some of them may be unemployed also. You can make a whole set of new friends and acquaintances and will have more opportunities to form meaningful relationships outside of the workplace.

TIP

Once you no longer have to be up and out of bed by a certain time to start work each day, it can be easy to lose a daily routine and structure. Before you know it, the day can have passed you by. Try having a set time to get out of bed so you can make the most of your time but also make your return to the labor market much easier when it occurs.

Keeping up your existing connections

When you're employed, sometimes it's hard to have enough time to meet friends and family. Take the opportunity now to connect with people whom you don't normally get to spend time with. You don't need to participate in anything that will cost you money. You can arrange to go to their house for coffee or invite them over to your house for a simple lunch. Go for a walk together in the local park or visit the local community center.

If all your friends and family are at work during business hours, ask if there are any activities you can help them with while they're at work. You could volunteer to walk their dog, plant or harvest their garden, do a house project they haven't had time for, or maybe do some cleaning. They're likely to be thankful of the help, and the activities will keep your mind occupied. They might even offer to pay you!

Keeping your mind and body active

Ensure that you fill your time with activities so that you're not dwelling on your employment situation or your loneliness. Keep your mind active by reading or watching educational YouTube videos. Alternatively, you can learn a new skill, such as a foreign language.

Engage in regular physical activity. Go for a walk, a run, or a bike ride. Get outside in the open air and in green spaces. This will improve your well-being as well as your physical health, and you'll find that you're more motivated. You're also more likely to meet other people while you're outdoors.

If you're struggling to regain employment, use the opportunity to volunteer. It won't ease your financial situation in the short term, but it will help you gain a sense of self-purpose and self-worth. It will ensure that you continue to use your skills and exercise your mind, will bring you in contact with others, and will give you the opportunity to do a social good: helping someone else. You may learn new skills along the way too, and the volunteer work will be a positive addition to your resume.

Accepting yourself and your situation

Without a job, you can start to blame yourself and feel demoralized. Make sure that you spend some time looking after yourself and engaging in self-compassion. Take up yoga or meditation; you can follow a range of different classes free of charge on YouTube or elsewhere on the internet. You can also find local classes in your community for a small charge.

You might want to try some techniques and therapies to help you accept yourself. I provide more information on various options in Chapter 13. Some of these you can practice alone, and some require the help of a therapist or counselor. If you feel you need the latter, contact your doctor and explain how your employment situation is making you feel. They should be able to refer you to a therapist or counselor.

Facing Loneliness in Retirement

When you end a lifetime of employment, you can be susceptible to loneliness.

Retirement from paid work often marks the end of a lifetime of employment, or for some, the end of a career. The average age of retirement across the world is 64, but generally people retire between the ages of 55 and 68. The retirement age has been increasing in many countries. Retirement is understandably a major life transition. It marks the end of one life chapter and the beginning of a new one.

Retirement has many positives. Finally, you can feel free from the burden of work and have more time to enjoy yourself, carrying out activities that you enjoy and haven't had time for while in paid employment. It also gives you more time to spend with friends and family. However, retirement does have some challenges. It involves a big and sudden change in your lifestyle that can lead to temporary loneliness as you adjust to it.

Regardless of how much you're looking forward to retirement, the change can come as quite a shock. But the more knowledge you have in advance, the better. That way you can anticipate any potential challenges and be equipped to deal with them as they emerge.

There are a number of reasons you can feel lonely following retirement. They can emerge quite unexpectedly, even if you've been looking forward to and planning for this point in your life for many years.

>> **Loss of social connections with coworkers:** The most immediate and obvious change that can trigger loneliness is that you no longer spend each and every day with your work colleagues. When you're working every day, most of your social interactions take place in the workplace. The degree of interaction you have with your coworkers varies depending on where you work, the type of employment, and the type of employment contract you are on. Work colleagues often form friendships that go beyond the workplace, and meaningful relationships can be created through places of employment that last for a lifetime. However, once you're out of the workplace loop, you might find that you miss the office banter and that you're no longer invited to after-work events. You can also find that without work to talk about, your relationships with coworkers change.

>> **Changed household relationships:** Following retirement, relationships between those in your household can change. You may be spending much more time in the house, which might mean that you're suddenly home alone much more. You might have been looking forward to spending more time with your partner and family, but if they're still working, the reality of retirement can

be that you're on your own all day until household members return from work, and by then they might feel too tired to engage in activities you've planned.

>> **Loss of sense of purpose:** Regardless of what you've achieved in your working life, and even if you've been looking forward to retirement, you can suddenly find yourself questioning your purpose in life and the meaning that your life has in retirement. You can experience a sense of unfulfillment and a loss of self-worth, which can lead to a lack of self-esteem and a loss of confidence.

>> **Loss of identity:** Retirement from paid work can be accompanied by a feeling that you've lost your identity. If you're no longer a teacher, a lawyer, an actor, an athlete, an artist, a police officer, or a bartender, who are you? So much of adult life is spent working that when that role is suddenly taken away, you question who you are, which can lead to feelings of loneliness.

>> **Too much spare time:** When you retire, you can suddenly find yourself with too much time on your hands. When you were in employment you might have looked forward to retirement, but now that the time is here, it can feel as though you have too much time and not enough to do. This can particularly affect those who have placed a high priority on paid work and their career.

>> **Reduction in disposable income:** Depending on your pension package, savings, and monthly expenses, you might have less disposable income in retirement. It might be more difficult to afford some of the activities, vacations, or outings that you enjoyed when you were working. If you have to give up activities that added meaning to your life and that you enjoyed, you can feel lonely.

>> **Bereavement:** As you get older, unfortunately, so do your family and friends. And the older you get, the more of your family and friends sadly pass away. Unfortunately, as you retire, you're more likely to experience bereavement. Your social network can diminish just at the time you might most need it.

TIP

Although I have outlined many reasons why retirement can lead to loneliness, it's important to remember that for many, loneliness is just a transitory phase. Moreover, if you follow some of the suggestions I provide here, you can prevent loneliness from setting in or reduce the length of time it stays with you.

Plan for retirement

If you can, plan for your retirement. Consider what the reality of retirement will mean for you on a daily basis. Who will be at home in the day, how much money will you have, what will you do, who will you interact with, and where will you go? How will this differ from your everyday life when you were employed?

By preparing your mind for the changes, you won't be in for a shock. In your planning process, if you think that you're likely to feel lonely, create a plan of things to do to avoid loneliness setting in. Even if you don't expect to feel lonely, it's worth having a plan ready, just in case.

Move closer to family

Spending more time with family can combat loneliness in retirement. You might find that you've dispersed as a family unit over time as people have moved for employment, relationships, and other reasons. Once you've retired, you might want to consider moving closer to family members. You may feel that you can help your children out by looking after your grandchildren, for example. If you're considering moving closer to family members, discuss it with them first so that you can agree on an arrangement that works for everyone.

Bonding with grandkids

Now that you're retired, you're free to spend more time bonding with any grandchildren you may have. Young people are increasingly facing loneliness themselves, so by spending more time with your grandchildren, you're likely to be helping them as much as yourself. Plan a trip to the movies, play in the local park, or go out for a milkshake after school. If you're not very tech savvy, ask your grandkids to teach you some IT skills, like using social media, gaming, or accessing YouTube videos. If you live far from your grandchildren, use technology to keep in contact with them. FaceTime them, or carry out video calls. If you don't have the technology or don't know how to do this, ask them to help or inquire at your local library.

Maintain and expand your social connections

Keep in contact with work colleagues, friends, and neighbors. Now that you have more time on your hands, you can prepare a meal and invite people over for dinner or host a games night. Alternatively, arrange a drink or a meal out, or go for a hike together on a weekend. Consciously make an effort to remain connected with friends. If you've lost contact over the years, now is a good time to reconnect. Chapter 14 has some useful tips on how to maintain and expand your social relationships.

TIP

A pet can be especially useful in retirement to help you expand your social connections. Pets can provide companionship and a dog, in particular, can help you meet other dog walkers as you take it on walks. Pets can also ensure that you make time for exercise and access frequent green spaces, which can improve your well-being and make you feel less lonely. In Chapter 4, I discuss the usefulness of pets in reducing loneliness, suggest how to select the right pet for you, and offer some tips.

Pick up a hobby, skill, or good cause

Now that you have lots of spare time on your hands, you can start a new hobby or resume one that you've had in the past but haven't had sufficient time to continue with. This could be anything at all. You could learn a foreign language, learn to play a musical instrument, take up a sport, learn some DIY skills, do arts and crafts, sew, cook — the options are endless. Some of these activities you can do on your own, and some involve joining a group. Joining a local group has the added advantage of bringing you in contact with other people.

If you find that you're particularly missing the sense of purpose that paid work brings, consider volunteering for a local or national charity. A range of options are available for different charities of your choice. Choose one that resonates with you, and you'll find yourself meeting new people, learning new skills, and helping others.

Challenge yourself to learn something new. This could be something you've always wanted to develop but haven't had time to try before. A friend of mine did a car mechanics course when she retired. This was something she'd wanted to do when she was working, but she never had time to fit in. If you're not sure what new skill(s) you'd like to learn, try an organization such as a lifelong learning institute. It's a way for those over 50 to get together for college-level study.

TIP

Exercise maintains your physical health, improves your well-being, and connects you with others. You could go for a walk; try a Tai Chi, Yoga, or Pilates class; join a running group; play badminton; or anything else that takes your fancy. Look for details of local groups in your local community center, library, or online. Some groups will be designed specifically for older people and those in retirement.

4
Beating Loneliness

Chapter **13**

Overcoming Loneliness Through Therapy or Healing Practices

lthough it's common to experience loneliness at some point in your life, the feeling is usually temporary, and is often caused by circumstances such as a loss of a relationship or a relocation to a new city. The loneliness usually goes as you adjust to the changed circumstances. But sometimes the loneliness can linger for a while longer.

Many people worldwide feel lonely often or all the time and when loneliness like this lasts for a long time, it is referred to as *chronic loneliness*. Although chronic loneliness is an uncomfortable state at best, don't lose heart if you're experiencing it. Numerous approaches can help you if you're chronically lonely, beginning with techniques to help you feel better about yourself and accept yourself for who you are.

Sometimes when you've been lonely for a long time, you start to have negative feelings about yourself. You might feel that other people dislike you or don't want to know you. This can make it difficult to reach out to people to connect with, and then you feel even lonelier. The downward spiral of negativity can make your loneliness worse. You might also start to feel sad, anxious, or depressed, or maybe all three.

If you've been lonely for a long time and you've tried some of the techniques in this book but the feelings of loneliness just won't go away, you may be chronically lonely and need a different kind of support.

TIP

If you think you might be chronically lonely, you can explore this topic further by completing the loneliness scale exercises in Chapter 2.

Although these feeling are unpleasant, the good news is that many solutions are available, and once you've found the right remedy for you, the negative spiral of thoughts will quite quickly turn into a positive upward spiral. You'll feel more positive about yourself, gain more energy, and want to meet new people. You'll also start believing that people want to meet you too, and you'll stop seeing their gestures towards you in a negative way. You might even start to enjoy the time and space of being alone, known as *solitude*.

This chapter focuses on providing solutions if you're chronically lonely and haven't had luck with the techniques elsewhere in the book. I provide details of some of the main kinds of therapies that can help you feel better about yourself and become less lonely. I also show you some simple self-help healing techniques you can try without the need for a therapist.

Getting Therapeutic Support

If you're chronically lonely, you might experience other symptoms, such as depression, insomnia, extreme worry, anxiety, and stress. These symptoms can sometimes perpetuate each other, so the lonelier you are, the more depressed and anxious you feel. And the more depressed and anxious you feel, the lonelier you become.

You can also start to dislike your life and yourself and feel that other people dislike you too. You might start to experience a heightened sense of social threat and become more sensitive to rejection. This might mean that you fear trying to connect to people, to ask a friend if they want to meet up, or to say hello to a passerby because you believe they won't want to know you. In these circumstances it can be helpful to try one of the many available therapies.

Therapeutic support can help you change your perception of yourself and alter how you feel other people view you. It can help you accept yourself for who you are, feel better about yourself, and have the confidence you need to start interacting or socializing. It can even help you feel comfortable being alone so that you can enjoy solitude rather than perceiving being alone as being lonely.

Therapeutic support can supply the tools to help you change your thoughts, your feelings, and your actions. You can choose from a number of different therapies. It's usually best to seek a qualified therapist to help you. Make sure you check the qualifications of any therapists to ensure they're properly qualified and registered to be legally allowed to practice. I provide a step-by-step guide to some of the different therapies that are available and present information to help you decide which therapy is best for you.

Cognitive Behavioral Therapy (CBT)

When you feel lonely, it's easy to get trapped into the habit of thinking negatively. You might think negatively about yourself and about how others see you. If you walk down the street and someone smiles or looks at you, you might question their motives, or you might interpret their smile as them laughing at you.

If this sounds like you, you might benefit from CBT. A key aim of this kind of therapy is to help you change your thought processes. It focuses on how your thoughts, beliefs, and attitudes affect your feelings and behavior, and it helps you develop coping strategies for situations that you find difficult. It's also effective in treating depression and anxiety. So if your loneliness is accompanied by these symptoms, it may well be a good therapy for you to try.

REMEMBER

Cognitive Behavioral Therapy is based on the idea that how you think about situations can affect the way you feel and behave. It brings together two types of therapy to deal with negative thoughts and behaviors: Cognitive Therapy which examines the things you think, and Behavior Therapy which examines the things you do.

CBT is based on the notion that your thoughts, feelings, and actions are interconnected. So negative thoughts and feelings can trap you in a negative cycle. It's often referred to as a *talking therapy*, which can help you change the way you think and behave. It helps you stop a cycle of negative thinking. It shows you how to change negative patterns so that you can feel better.

Sometimes the negative thoughts you feel seem overwhelming. CBT breaks them down into four main areas: thoughts, emotions, physical feelings, and actions.

Some other talking therapies, such as counseling, can focus on issues from your past, but CBT usually deals with your current problems and looks for practical ways to improve your state of mind on a daily basis.

CBT can also help with a range of mental and physical health conditions. So if you have other symptoms alongside loneliness, it might just be the therapy for you. Other health conditions that it can help with include panic disorder, phobias, post-traumatic stress disorder (PTSD), psychosis, schizophrenia, sleep problems, alcohol or drug misuse, irritable bowel syndrome, chronic fatigue syndrome, fibromyalgia, and chronic pain.

REAL WORLD EXAMPLE

Joan, age 55, used CBT successfully following her divorce. She and her husband of 30 years, Simon, divorced five years ago after he left her for another woman he met at work. Joan was feeling as though she would never be able to have another romantic relationship again. She was lonely and depressed. She started to feel bad about the way she looked and began eating lots of junk food. This made her put on weight, which made her feel even worse about her appearance. She became trapped in a negative cycle of sitting at home alone and feeling bad about herself. Joan found that CBT helped her analyze how her marriage had ended in a more objective way. She started to feel more positive and optimistic about future relationships. She decided to start learning Italian in the evenings, which introduced her to new people. Joan is now much more positive about herself and her interactions with other people. She's even actively looking for another romantic partner.

How CBT works

Cognitive Behavioral Therapy is usually a short-term treatment with a set number of sessions, from 6 to 20. You will probably have a session with an expert therapist once a week or once every two weeks. Sessions typically last between 30 minutes and 1 hour. They often take place in a clinic and are usually one on one, but they can also take place in groups with others who are facing similar challenges to you. You can also benefit from CBT without contact with a therapist, through a growing number of interactive online tools. This could be useful to test out the therapy to see if it's for you, or to try if you're waiting for a therapist to become available.

If you elect to have a therapist, they'll work with you to identify and challenge any negative thought patterns and behaviors you're exhibiting. You'll work with your therapist to break down your problems. Your therapist is likely to focus on what's going on in your life right now, but it might be helpful for them to talk to you about how your past experiences have affected you. Your therapist will then be able to help you work out how to change negative thoughts and behaviors.

Once you've agreed with your therapist what to work on, they'll ask you to practice those things in your daily life, and you'll discuss how you got along during the next session. So you might need to commit some additional time beyond the sessions for activities the therapist suggests. By the end of the treatment, you should be able to apply the skills you've learned during the sessions to your everyday life.

Evaluating whether CBT is right for you

Consider CBT if:

>> You're chronically lonely (see the tools in Chapter 2).

>> You feel as though you're consumed with negative thoughts and emotions, or you're feeling depressed or anxious.

>> You've tried other techniques in this book to reduce your feelings of loneliness and they haven't worked for you.

>> You're happy to have a structured discussion where you discuss specific problems and set goals rather than talking more freely about your life and your feelings.

>> You're keen to focus on your current problems and how you think and act now, rather than attempting to resolve issues from your past.

>> You like working collaboratively. In general, a cognitive behavioral therapist won't tell you what to do but will work with you to find a way forward to solve your current issues.

REMEMBER

If you decide to try CBT, you might want to use the helpful guide later in this chapter that has advice on selecting a therapist who's right for you. Also, see the Appendix for links on more useful information about CBT.

Interpersonal and Relationship Therapy

Interpersonal and Relationship Therapy is designed to help you feel less depressed by improving your relationships with other people. Because it's designed to give you the tools and skills you need to improve and maintain relationships, which will then improve your mood and make you feel less depressed, it can be especially helpful if you're chronically lonely and have started to view your relationships with other people more negatively. It's particularly useful if you're having difficulties in your relationships with a romantic partner, family, or friend.

This kind of therapy works on your communication skills, your ability to connect to people emotionally, and your problem-solving techniques. So if you have relationship difficulties and you're feeling depressed and lonely, this therapy may be ideal for you.

The relationship difficulties you're encountering could be due to conflict with another person or a life change such as an illness that has affected how you feel about yourself or how you feel about others. Or it might have arisen due to grief and loss, or perhaps because you have difficulties getting a relationship started or keeping one going.

This type of therapy can also help if you have relationship difficulties and depression alongside other conditions, such as anxiety, bipolar disorder, borderline personality disorder, eating disorders, perinatal and postpartum depression, post-traumatic stress disorder, social anxiety disorders, and substance and alcohol use disorders.

Two of the main types of Interpersonal and Relationship Therapy are Dynamic Interpersonal Therapy (DIT) and Metacognitive Interpersonal Therapy (MIT). DIT is designed to improve your understanding of your own thoughts and feelings as well as understanding the thoughts and feelings of others. MIT is designed to address your relationship difficulties if they arise because you're holding back your emotions or avoiding relationships.

REAL WORLD EXAMPLE

Paula is married to Kevin, and they have a 19-year-old daughter, Kelly. They live in the UK, but about a year ago, Kelly went to the US on a sports scholarship, which triggered Paula to feel lonely and depressed. Paula felt that she'd lost her daughter and was struggling to deal with the life change this precipitated. She was also having difficulties adjusting to living alone with Kevin. She started to feel more and more depressed and lonely, which was making her relationship with both Kevin and Kelly worse. Because the depression was linked to Paula's relationships, Interpersonal and Relationship Therapy was just the support she needed.

How Interpersonal and Relationship Therapy works

Interpersonal and Relationship Therapy is a short-term therapy that's time-limited and focuses on enhancing your relationships to treat depression. You'll need to get a therapist who can guide you through the therapy, which will likely be 12–16 sessions. Sessions are usually structured and involve the therapist talking to you and setting you tasks between sessions. These might involve practicing new techniques for interacting with other people. The therapy is usually offered as an individual session, but you can also access it through a group activity.

When you first see your therapist, they'll help you work out why you're having difficulties with your relationships, and then they'll design the therapy to focus on that specific interpersonal and relationship issue.

Sessions are most commonly done face to face, but they're becoming increasingly available online. The therapy is done in slightly different ways based on the therapist you decide to work with and the specific relationship difficulties you have. The therapist will help you work out what's best in your case.

The therapist will conduct a detailed review of your significant relationships. It will cover your current relationships and any you've had in the past. This will be similar to the sociogram or timeline activities in Chapter 14. It might be helpful for you perform the activities in Chapter 14 before you see your therapist so you know what to expect. The therapist will guide you through the process. It's quite straightforward.

Your therapist will then help you categorize the relationships you have into four main problem areas, as summarized in Table 13-1.

TABLE 13-1   **Relationship Problem Areas**

Problem Area	How It Presents
Grief	Someone you know has died or you no longer have contact with them.
Role dispute	You have different expectations about your role in the relationship than another person does. Maybe you'd like your husband to show you more affection than he currently does.
Role transition	You have difficulties adapting to changes in relationships, such as after marrying, getting divorced, or becoming a parent.
Interpersonal deficits	You find it difficult getting relationships started, keeping the relationships going, or both.

The therapist might use a number of different techniques to help you. Some examples are spelled out in Table 13-2.

TABLE 13-2   **Techniques for Dealing with Relationship Issues**

Technique	What It Entails
Guided imagery and rescripting	You go over a difficult relationship issue and imagine how you could approach it differently.
Drama techniques	You role-play a tricky relationship issue to help you understand how other people might interpret a situation.
Bodily work	You use activities and exercises that are based on grounding, breath regulation, and physical training. These might help you improve your emotional regulation.
Mindfulness techniques	You practice meditation to become more self-aware of your mind and retain your focus on the present moment.
Restructuring attention	You focus your attention on your body's internal signals so you're more aware of why your emotions are like they are.

Evaluating if Interpersonal and Relationship Therapy is right for you

Select Interpersonal and Relationship Therapy if:

» You're chronically lonely (see the tools in Chapter 2).

» You've tried other techniques in this book to reduce your feelings of loneliness, and they haven't worked for you.

» You're feeling lonely and depressed and having difficulties with your relationships.

» You feel depressed or have other mental health conditions that might be linked to your relationships or your lack of relationships.

» You have relationship difficulties that are linked to grief, life adjustments and transitions, differing expectations, relationship conflicts, or attachment issues.

» You're willing to invest some time and effort talking to a therapist in detail about your relationships.

» You're motivated to do some work on your own, while being guided by the therapist.

REMEMBER

If you decide to try Interpersonal and Relationship Therapy, you might want to use the helpful guide later in this chapter that has advice on how to select the best therapist. The appendix has some key links to useful websites.

WARNING

Make sure you check the qualifications of therapists you're considering to ensure they're properly qualified and registered to be legally allowed to practice.

Eye Movement Desensitization and Reprocessing (EMDR)

Eye Movement Desensitization and Reprocessing is a relatively new therapy that involves you recalling traumatic memories while doing two-sided stimulation, such as eye movements or tapping, under the guidance of a therapist.

Many clinical trials have shown this technique to be an effective and relatively quick treatment. It can reduce any distress and negative thoughts associated with past memories, especially traumatic events. So if your loneliness has been triggered by, or resulted from, a trauma in the past, or you're suffering from post-traumatic stress disorder, this is a good option to try. It can also be helpful if you're suffering from other conditions, such as anxiety, depression, addictions, behavioral difficulties, relationship issues, psychosis, and personality disorders.

EMDR is based on a theory about how your brain stores "normal" and traumatic memories differently. During everyday life events, it's believed that your brain stores memories and connects the memories in a smooth and easy way. But when it's dealing with distressing or disturbing memories, there can be a disconnect, and your brain can store and connect memories differently.

This disconnection doesn't allow your brain to heal from the trauma, and because it doesn't heal, your brain might not receive a message that the danger is over. When you experience new things, your brain links them to the past trauma experience, which can reinforce the negative experience over and over again. This can happen with events that have been suppressed and that you're not necessarily aware of, as well as traumas you can remember.

Your different senses can trigger these memories that haven't been stored properly. So, for example, your brain might connect things you see, hear, or smell to a trauma of the past, even though the threat has passed. This in turn can trigger those improperly stored memories and cause you to feel overwhelmed with fear or panic.

REAL WORLD EXAMPLE

Josh is 22 years old. He's a keen cricket player who was abused by his coach when he was younger. He's still playing cricket, but the trauma of his abuse means that he finds it difficult to form a relationship with other people and especially with his new coach and teammates. He's frequently reminded of the past trauma when he's practicing and playing cricket, and that causes him to panic and feel anxious. His peers and coach don't know about his past trauma and perceive his behavior as unusual. They feel that he doesn't want to connect with them. Josh has tried a number of different therapies with no success, but once he had Eye Movement Desensitization and Reprocessing, he was able to connect with other people without reliving his past trauma.

How EMDR works

This therapy involves moving your eyes a specific way while you process traumatic memories. This helps you heal from trauma or other distressing experiences. Unlike some of the other therapies discussed in this chapter, EMDR therapy doesn't require talking in detail about the issue that's causing your feelings or behavior.

Your therapist will ask you to identify any negative beliefs about how the trauma has made you feel, as well as positive beliefs that you would like to feel about yourself going forward. The therapist will then stimulate a sense — usually your vision — on both sides of your body. The therapist might hold their hand up with two fingers extended and have you follow their finger from side to side with your eyes. Or they might use a specialized light device for you to follow. They can also use sounds by placing speakers that play tunes on either side of your body; alternatively, the therapist might tap on either side of your body.

By these movements and guided instruction from the therapist, you can access memories of a past trauma in a specific way. This helps you reprocess what you remember from a traumatic event. It repairs the injury of that memory to your brain, and then when you remember what happened to you in the past, the related feelings will be much more manageable. It focuses on changing the emotions, thoughts, or behaviors that emerge from the distressing experience. By working in this way, the therapy can heal your brain.

The therapy usually requires weekly sessions that can last between 50 and 90 minutes. You might need between 4 and 12 sessions, depending on the number of traumas you've experienced, their complexity, and how you respond to the treatment.

Evaluating if EMDR is right for you

Select EMDR therapy if:

>> You're lonely (see the tools in Chapter 2) and you've experienced trauma in the past that might be contributing to your loneliness.

>> You've tried other techniques in this book to reduce your feelings of loneliness and they haven't worked for you.

>> You're looking for a therapy that can work relatively quickly. (Note: Major traumas may take a bit longer.)

>> You're happy to revisit your past trauma with a therapist but don't want to talk about it at length.

REMEMBER

If you decide to try EMDR, you might want to use the helpful guide later in this chapter that offers advice on how to locate the right therapist. The Appendix also includes some key links to useful websites. Try https://www.emdr.com/ if you're in the USA or https://emdrassociation.org.uk/ to find a EMDR therapist in the UK.

WARNING

This therapy only works with conditions related to traumatic experiences. If you have a mental health condition because of an inherited condition, an injury, or other physical effect on your brain, Eye Movement Desensitization and Reprocessing may not help.

TIPS FOR FINDING THE RIGHT THERAPY AND THERAPIST

If you opt for one of the therapies discussed in this chapter, it's usually best to get a therapist who's an expert in the therapy type you're looking for. Here are some tips for how to find the right person for your particular situation.

- Depending on what country you live in and its arrangements for health care, you might be able to get a referral from your doctor.

- If you can't get a referral from your doctor or you prefer not to, you can seek out an appropriate therapist yourself online or via word of mouth.

- It's often best to go to the relevant governing organization for each therapy you're interested in to get a list of approved therapists. I listed some relevant websites in the Appendix.

- Once you have a list of therapists, check out customer reviews to pin down the right person for you.

- If you can, arrange for a chat with the selected therapist before you commit to the sessions. This will help you assess whether you're going to be able to work with them.

- If you start sessions with a therapist and feel that the therapy or the therapist isn't right for you, discuss your concerns with your therapist before deciding to make a change. They'll understand and be able to offer you some advice. Don't blame yourself if a therapy doesn't work. Not all therapies work for everyone, and not all therapists suit everyone. There's usually a therapist and a therapy for everyone, but sometimes it might take a few rounds to find the best one for you.

Developing Healing Techniques

If you're lonely and want to feel better about yourself and the way you interact with other people, you can try these self-care techniques that don't require a health care practitioner or therapist. These are easy and simple to implement, and you can try them by yourself, right away, by using the step-by-step guide I provide later in this chapter.

TIP

These techniques can be especially helpful if you can't afford a therapist or you're on a waiting list to see one. Chances are that if you try these techniques, you might not have to see a therapist after all. Or they might make such a difference that you need fewer sessions.

Meditation

Meditation is a practice you can do yourself. It trains your mind to focus and to redirect your thoughts. You train your mind on a regular basis to achieve a mentally clear and calm emotional state. Meditation can be particularly helpful if your loneliness is accompanied by stress, anxiety, and depression.

You can use meditation to increase awareness of yourself and your surroundings. It can help you accept yourself and the situation you find yourself in, and put you at ease with yourself. As I mentioned earlier in this chapter and in Chapter 1, when you feel lonely you can start to develop a negative perception of yourself and how other people see you. Meditation is one way to improve your relationship with yourself. It helps you accept yourself for who you are, so that you can start enjoying time alone rather than fearing it.

Meditation can help you feel more comfortable going alone to places where you have a sense of belonging. As the perception of yourself and of how others view you becomes neutral or more positive, you're more inclined to reach out to other people and connect with them.

Exploring different types of meditation

Used for thousands of years, meditation helps you develop awareness of the present moment. Many spiritual traditions include meditation as part of their teachings and practices, with Buddhists most noted for their practice of the technique. However, you don't have to be a Buddhist or belong to any particular religion or faith to meditate. Cultures all over the world appreciate meditation's ability to create a sense of peace, calm, and inner harmony. There isn't really a right or wrong way to meditate, but there are some different types of meditation practice you can follow, as shown in Table 13-3.

TABLE 13-3   Meditation Practices

Type of Meditation	What It Involves
Loving-kindness meditation	Strengthens your feelings of kindness, compassion, and acceptance toward yourself and others. This often involves opening your mind to send and receive love. It can be particularly helpful if you're feeling lonely and disconnected from other people or you're retaining feelings of anger or resentment. It can increase your compassion towards yourself and other people, improve your positive emotions, and boost your interpersonal interactions.
Mindfulness meditation	Involves sitting in a quiet room or space and focusing on your breathing and awareness. You pay attention to your thoughts as they pass through your mind, but you don't judge them or become involved with them. You just observe them and let them pass by.

Type of Meditation	What It Involves
Focused meditation	Involves focusing on something to direct your attention and concentration. You could focus on something internal to you, such as your breath, or perhaps something external, such as an object in the room. If your mind wanders and you start thinking about things, simply refocus and start again.
Spiritual meditation	Focuses on developing a deeper understanding of spiritual and religious meaning and often aims to achieve a connection with a higher power. Used in many spiritual traditions and religions, it can be practiced at home or in a place of worship, such as a temple, synagogue, or church.
Movement meditation	Incorporates movement to guide you into a deeper connection between your body and the present moment. It can involve gentle movement such as walking or Tai Chi.
Mantra meditation	Involves making a repetitive sound, word, or phrase to clear your mind. Most commonly people use *om*, but you can select a word or phrase that suits you. You chant your mantra over and over again, either quietly or loudly.
Transcendental meditation	Uses a mantra that helps you induce a state of calm and peace. This specific practice is often taught by a practitioner in a group.
Progressive relaxation	Relaxes different parts of your body, one at a time, by doing what's often called a *body scan*. It's aimed at helping you relax and reduce tension in your body.
Visualization meditation	Involves visualizing positive scenes, images, or pictures to help you feel calm and relaxed or achieve a certain goal or objective. You'll need to imagine the scene or image in as much detail as possible, thinking about the smells, sounds, and tastes that the image emits.

Getting comfortable with meditation

The good thing about meditation is that there isn't a right or wrong way to do it. However, if you're new to meditation, you may feel unsure about how it's done, how effective it is, and whether you're going to be able to do it. As with anything you're trying for the first time, it's natural to feel a bit of beginner's resistance. But don't let these feelings put you off; meditation is a personal experience that can take some experimentation before you find a style that's right for you. Here are some guidelines to get you started.

1. Select a type of meditation from the list I provided in Table 13-3. Don't worry if you're not sure what will work for you. Try one that you like the look of, and if after a few attempts it doesn't work, try another. It's important to give meditation some time because it can take a while to get the hang of it.

2. If you're feeling lonely but aren't sure which type of meditation to use, try starting with the loving-kindness meditation because it's specifically geared toward helping with relationship issues.

3. Find a quiet space or place, where you're unlikely to be disturbed. This could be inside or outside. Just make it somewhere you feel comfortable and at ease.

4. When you're comfortable and centered, you can start meditating. Start by sitting quietly, and focus on your breath. If you prefer to lie down you can but sitting is a preferred option. With your eyes closed, simply breathe in and breathe out slowly. Don't rush your breathing.

5. Depending on the type of meditation you're going to try, use the next few minutes to focus on whatever it is, whether it's an object, a phrase, sending and receiving love to others, or one of the other options mentioned earlier.

6. Notice when you get distracted by a thought, and consciously bring your mind back to whatever you're focusing on.

7. When you're ready to finish your meditation, try not to stop suddenly. When you feel it's time to end, stop but stay in the same position with your eyes closed for a few minutes. Once you feel ready, gently open your eyes and stay seated (or lying down) for a little longer before getting up.

REMEMBER

There's no set amount of time that you can or should meditate for. It might be best to start with five or ten minutes and try to increase that duration over time. For the best results you should meditate often — on a daily basis if you can.

TIP

If you prefer to have some structure and guidance to your meditation, you can try one of the many apps that are available. Do a quick search for meditation apps and select one or two to try. Again, you might need to try a few to find one that works for you, but don't move onto another app until you've attempted a meditation technique a few times. You might try https://www.headspace.com/meditation/loneliness. YouTube also offers guided meditations. Search there to see which voices and styles you prefer.

Try to allocate a certain time each day to meditate so that you can develop a consistent daily habit. If you find it difficult to meditate alone, join a mediation class or group. Numerous classes are available to help you mediate regularly and be guided by a facilitator. You can find classes near you by doing an internet search or looking for ads in your local library or in shop windows. The classes are an opportunity to meet other people, which in itself will ease your feelings of loneliness.

Emotional Freedom Technique

The Emotional Freedom Technique is a method that can help you let go of negative thoughts, memories, and emotions. It involves stimulating specific pressure points on your body by tapping on them with your fingers while you're repeating a statement that relates to an upsetting or negative thought.

The technique can quickly diminish the impact of any negative emotional memories, incidents, or thoughts that can trigger distress and anxiety. Many clinical trials have been carried out on this technique and shown that it's effective for a range of issues that can be tied up with your feelings of loneliness, such as social anxiety, general anxiety, depression, trauma, pain, phobias, and some resulting physical health conditions such as fibromyalgia, migraines, and skin rashes. It's been found to be particularly effective in treating post-traumatic stress disorder. So if a trauma is the main cause of your loneliness, the Emotional Freedom Technique is a quick and easy technique to try.

The Emotional Freedom Technique involves focusing on distressing thoughts or emotions while tapping on certain places throughout your body. The spots you tap are points of energy, known as *meridians*. They're the same ones used in acupuncture. By tapping on these areas while bringing your awareness to negative emotions, you can let go of the negative emotional energy associated with the thoughts.

When you carry out the Emotional Freedom Technique, it allows you to release emotional memories. Once those memories don't hurt anymore, or they hurt less, the stress response in your body lessens, and your body is able to heal. You can use it to overcome any traumatic events that have led you to feel lonely. This reduces the potential physical health conditions that can arise if you feel lonely too (see Chapter 9).

You can use the technique to clear away the emotional impact of any past events that might be stopping you or holding you back from interacting with other people, going out, and socializing. You can guide yourself through the help of a worksheet or, if you prefer, you can get an Emotional Freedom Technique therapist to help you.

REAL LIFE EXAMPLE

Julian is a 38-year-old gay man. He was the victim of a hate crime a few years ago and was beaten up badly. He suffered numerous injuries and was admitted to the hospital for treatment. The incident left him badly scarred emotionally. He started to experience social anxiety, was worried about meeting new people, and felt like he didn't fit in. Julian tried the Emotional Freedom Technique after a work colleague recommended it. Julian's negative thoughts immediately lessened, and he began socializing again.

How EFT works

The Emotional Freedom Technique is a quick and easy-to-use tool that's an effective self-help method. Within a few minutes you can feel better, as the intensity of your upsetting or traumatic feelings diminish. Once you've mastered the technique, you can use it again and again to deal with a whole range of negative thoughts. You can do the technique yourself, or you can see an Emotional Freedom

Technique practitioner. I provide a simple step-by-step guide on how to perform the technique yourself and a link to a free online resource to download. There are five simple steps to doing EFT:

1. Assess how intensive your levels of distress are when you think about the issue or thought. Use a score of 0 to 10, where 10 is the highest level of distress and 0 is the lowest.

2. Think carefully about the nature of the issue or problem, and write it in this sentence "Even though I have *(insert the name of the problem)*, I deeply and completely accept myself."

3. Tap continuously on the Karate Chop point while repeating the sentence three times (see the sidebar).

4. While repeating the sentence again, tap about seven times on the other pressure points.

5. Assess how intense your levels of distress are when you think about the issue or problem again. It's likely that your distress levels will have fallen.

EFT PRESSURE POINTS

The nine meridian points (or "tapping points") most often used for EFT are the following:

1. The side of the hand, on the outer side of either palm below the little finger (Karate Chop Point)

2. Top of the head, at the center

3. The inner eyebrow, at the beginning point of the brow near the nose

4. Next to the outside edge of the eye, on the bone

5. Underneath the eye, at the top of the cheek bone

6. Under the nose, just above the upper lip

7. On the chin, halfway between the point of the chin and the lower lip

8. Beneath the collarbone, where it meets the sternum and ribs

9. On the side, several inches below the armpit

Evaluating whether EFT is right for you

TIP

Select EFT if:

>> You're lonely (see the tools in Chapter 2) and you've experienced trauma in the past, or you have specific negative thoughts or emotions that might be contributing to your loneliness.

>> You've tried other techniques in this book to reduce your feelings of loneliness, and they haven't worked for you.

>> You're looking for a therapy that can lessen your negative emotions almost immediately.

>> You want a therapy you can quickly and easily do on your own, without the necessity of having a therapist.

REMEMBER

To try EFT immediately, you can download a free starter pack at this link: https://eftuniverse.com/. This gives you all the information you need to try EFT on your own.

If you feel better after using the technique but feel you need more in-depth support, you can get help from an EFT practitioner or attend a dedicated EFT workshop. Go to https://eftuniverse.com/eftu-practitioners/ for an EFT practitioner. You might want to use a helpful guide earlier in this chapter for advice on finding a therapist that's right for you.

WARNING

If you have any underlying health conditions or have experienced a major trauma, consult a qualified health practitioner before trying a health procedure such as the Emotional Freedom Technique.

Self-hypnosis

Self-hypnosis is a technique you can use to change your state of awareness and focus on adjusting your subconscious mind. You can do self-hypnosis yourself or with the guidance of a registered hypnotherapist. Self-hypnosis can help you gain control over the way you think and behave. It's not like the images you sometimes see on TV or in the movies, where someone hypnotizes you and makes you do weird things or act in uncontrolled ways.

With self-hypnosis, you remain in control but can work on specific issues to change the way your subconscious mind perceives things. Hypnosis can help you change the way you feel about yourself, overcome fears about interacting with other people, help you overcome relationship traumas from the past, and improve current relationships. It can be useful if you're feeling lonely but can also alleviate a range of other conditions, such as addictions, phobias, weight loss, sexual dysfunction, depression, anxiety, pain relief, self-esteem issues, trauma, bad habits, and other conditions.

REMEMBER

All hypnosis is self-hypnosis. Self-hypnosis involves putting yourself in a trance-like state (with or without the help of a trained hypnotherapist) in which you have heightened focus and concentration. It's a state of mind in which suggestions are acted on much more powerfully than under normal conditions.

When you're in hypnosis, you suppress the power of conscious criticism and focus more intently on a particular issue or topic. During this heightened state of focus and awareness, you're able to make suggestions that can bypass your conscious mind and go into your subconscious mind. This means you've shifted your focus away from the conscious everyday world and towards your inward thoughts instead. Because you're not paying attention to the conscious world, your mind can drift off, and you're free to focus on the single topic you want to address. Being in a hypnotic trance feels pleasant and relaxing, like being in a place or situation where you're completely at ease.

How self-hypnosis works

If you've been feeling lonely for a long time, you might have started to make negative associations with being alone. This might then trigger other negative feelings, such as anxiety, worry, and unhappiness. Self-hypnosis can help you break the subconscious associations that trigger the unhappiness and anxiety you feel when you're alone.

If you're not sure why you're lonely, self-hypnosis can assist in identifying the underlying reasons. It can help you find creative new ways to connect with other people, feel more comfortable with yourself, and be confident visiting places where you have a sense of belonging, all of which can make you feel less lonely. It can help in coming to terms with relationship difficulties you've had in the past or particular triggers that have led you to feel lonely.

Self-hypnosis can help you reconnect with yourself more deeply, reflect on your thoughts, and feel more comfortable and accepting of yourself and who you are. This in itself can make you feel less lonely, but it can also give you the confidence to reach out to others.

Self-hypnosis can help you overcome shyness and social anxiety issues which make it difficult to connect with other people. By working on these barriers through self-hypnosis, you can find it easier to be around other people.

You can use self-hypnosis to rid yourself of behavioral patterns that are preventing you from feeling less lonely. For example, if you fear walking into a room full of strangers, you can use self-hypnosis to visualize yourself walking confidently into a room and talking to anyone and everyone.

You can also use it to learn to relax, stay calm, and feel comfortable in any social situation. Hypnosis can give you the tools you need to engage with people fearlessly and comfortably.

How hypnosis works with a hypnotherapist

If you're not sure about doing the hypnosis yourself, you can see a hypnotherapist. If you decide to choose a hypnotherapist, make sure you select one who's registered and certified. Do some research to find hypnotherapists near you, and read reviews. Some hypnotherapists specialize in different aspects of emotions and behavioral change, so make sure you select one who focuses on the particular aspects of your life that are making you feel lonely.

Each session will last for 60–90 minutes. When you attend the hypnosis sessions, wear comfortable clothing to help you relax, and make sure you've had some food and drink before you go so you're not hungry or thirsty in the sessions. Allow some time after the session to contemplate the experience before rushing to carry on with your everyday activities.

TIP

The benefit of seeing a qualified hypnotherapist is that they'll discuss the particular difficulties you're experiencing and tailor the session accordingly. Self-hypnosis using a qualified practitioner can start to work after the first session, although you'll usually need at least three sessions to see a big difference.

REAL WORLD
EXAMPLE

Jade was feeling lonely. She wasn't happy in her relationship with her partner and scheduled three sessions of self-hypnosis with a hypnotherapist. Through these sessions, it emerged that the main issue preventing Jade from feeling positive and happy in her relationship was the negative view she had of herself. This had come about because her mother had abandoned her when she was younger. Following the self-hypnosis sessions, Jade started to feel better about herself and was happier in her relationship with her partner. When she started the hypnosis she was thinking about leaving her partner, but six months after the sessions, she and her partner decided to get married.

Getting started with self-hypnosis

Try this simple step-by-step self-hypnosis exercise. You don't need a hypnotherapist for this:

1. Find a quiet room or place where you won't be disturbed.

2. Sit down and make sure you feel comfortable.

3. Close your eyes and rest your hands, palms upward, on your legs or on the arms of the chair.

4. Focus on your breath, taking slow, deep breaths in and out, trying to make your exhale longer than your inhale.

5. Begin to relax your body. Start with your head, and go around each body part telling yourself to relax that part of your body as you continue to breathe slowly. Focus on keeping your exhale longer than your inhale.

6. In your imaginary mind, picture yourself in a place that brings you peace. It could be a beach, a garden with lovely bright flowers, a lake, a mountain, or anywhere else you want.

7. While you're in this place, engage all your senses to ensure that you're fully immersed in your imaginary place. Think about the noises, the smells, and the tastes.

8. Once you've fully immersed in your special place, select an affirmation or statement that you feel you need at the moment. Examples might be, "I'm making meaningful connections with people," or "I'm confident and assertive when speaking to other people." Repeat the affirmation to yourself a few times.

9. Continue to focus on your breathing.

10. Count yourself out of the hypnotic state, counting backward slowly from 5 to 1. When you get to 1, say to yourself, "Now I'll open my eyes and feel wide awake."

TIP

You can download hypnosis apps to guide you through self-hypnosis. You can also try some of the guided hypnosis sessions at upnow.com. Finally, YouTube offers a wide range of guided self-hypnosis sessions. Here's a specific guided hypnosis session for if you're feeling lonely: https://upnow.com/self-hypnosis-downloads-for-loneliness/.

WARNING

Self-hypnosis done by a trained practitioner is safe for most people. However, it may not be safe for you if you have severe mental illness. If you're not sure, check with your doctor or health care practitioner before practicing self-hypnosis.

If you work through a stressful event from earlier in your life during the hypnosis, it may trigger a strong emotional reaction, which may make you feel upset or worse for a while.

Chapter **14**

Developing Meaningful Relationships

When you feel lonely, it's often because you don't have the kinds of meaningful relationships with people that you'd like. You might not have contact with other people at all. Perhaps you know lots of people, but your relationships with them are superficial. You might have some meaningful relationships but not with the right people. Or you may not have as many meaningful relationships as other people have. In all these cases, you may well feel lonely.

Being lonely when you lack meaningful relationships is a normal part of being a human being. Loneliness is simply a trigger for you to reach out and find people to connect with. When you're hungry, you need to find food to eat. When you're lonely, you need to find people to connect with.

Connecting with others might feel daunting, especially if you've felt lonely for a long time, or are a particularly shy person. Never fear. In this chapter I provide a step-by-step guide on how to develop the right kinds of meaningful relationships. I help you assess your relationships by using some easy-to-use tools called lifelines and sociograms. You can use these to check on your current relationships or to rekindle relationships that might have faded over time. By using these tools in conjunction with the loneliness scales in Chapter 2, you can monitor whether you have the right kinds of relationships.

I help you reconnect with people you may have known in the past and give you some tips on how to meet other like-minded people you're more likely to get along with. You might prefer to develop meaningful relationships by helping others. I offer some strategies on how to do that too.

Assessing Your Current and Past Relationships

A meaningful relationship enriches your life and supports your well-being. So what makes a relationship meaningful?

A meaningful relationship is one in which one or more of these factors are present:

>> You feel valued by the person.

>> You share a common goal or interest.

>> You have a positive relationship.

>> The relationship has depth and isn't superficial.

>> The relationship is sustainable in the long term.

The first step to developing meaningful relationships is to assess any relationships you currently have and any you might have had in the past. If you're feeling lonely, you might well be thinking that you don't have any relationships at all.

REMEMBER

If that's the case, you're not alone. Many of people around the world feel they don't have any meaningful relationships.

This section has two exercises to help you assess your relationships. Even if you feel you don't have any relationships or haven't had any in the past, you'll find value in these exercises. Sometimes when you start these tasks, you'll remember people from your past who you might be able to reconnect with.

Or you might find, after completing the tasks, that you actually know more people than you thought. When you feel lonely, especially if you've been lonely for a while, you can start to view social relationships in a negative way. Maybe you've forgotten about some people you enjoy spending time with.

If you complete the tasks to assess your relationships and find that you have no one to connect with or that you actually know fewer people than you thought, there's no need to worry. The information presented later in this chapter has all the tools you need to develop new, meaningful relationships that will help you feel less lonely and isolated. However, if completing the tasks triggers you to feel even lonelier or perhaps depressed or anxious, take a look at the useful helplines and resources in the Appendix where immediate help is at hand.

To start assessing your relationships, you can use a lifeline or a sociogram. Try both if you want and see which you prefer.

Looking at your relationships chronologically

Throughout your life, you're likely to have experienced relationships with various people, be they family members, school friends, or neighbors. When looking at current relationships or pursuing new connections, it can be helpful to look back on bonds you formed with others in your past. This will help you to assess the kinds of relationships that have made you feel more connected, and to identify any that you might be able to re-kindle.

A *lifeline* is a visual arts–based way of mapping your social relationships. It enables you to place your relationships in chronological order and map them against significant events that have taken place in your life, such as going to school and then graduating, starting work, getting married, getting divorced, and mourning the death of a loved one. By creating a lifeline of your relationships, you can see when you've had relationships, who they were with, and what kinds of events either triggered those relationships or caused them to fade. By completing the lifeline, you can identify people whom you might be able to reconnect with, or people you're already connected with but might want to try to spend more time with.

Take a look at Figure 14-1, a sample lifeline by Charlie, who's an extroverted 55-year-old. He likes interacting with others and being the center of attention. However, Charlie is currently feeling lonely following a sudden and unexpected layoff from his job.

You can see from Charlie's lifeline that when he was younger, he had an active social life, with lots of friends from school, his local neighborhood, and work.

Nevertheless, there have been times when Charlie has lost contact with people and felt lonely. These were mainly when he went away to college, when he got divorced and moved back to his hometown, and when he was recently laid off from work.

Charlie's Lifeline

Key Life Events		Key Relationships
	5	Mark Malcolm Brian
	10	Tony Clive John
	15	Gary Keith
Went to University	20	
Got Married	25	Sharron Silvia
	30	Chris Don Sean Sue
Divorced	35	
	40	(Gary) Clive Don
	45	
Made Redundant	50	
	55	

FIGURE 14-1: Sample lifeline map of social relationships.

After completing the lifeline, Charlie, initially felt a sense of loss as he thought about the many friends he'd had in the past. But once he worked through the exercises later in this chapter, he started to remember people from his past that he liked spending time with and wanted to try reconnecting with. He specifically selected Gary to try to reconnect with.

Charlie and Gary became acquainted at school but lost touch 15 years ago. Charlie decided to send Gary a postcard while he was on vacation (later in this chapter, read some tips on how to reconnect with people from the past). Charlie included his email address on the postcard, and Gary responded in turn. The two met for a drink and were reminded of how much they had in common. Charlie and Gary now spend every Saturday playing the guitar together and are planning to re-create a band they used to play in many years ago.

TIP

Completing your own lifeline like Charlie did can help you think about relationships you've had in the past so that you can identify friendships worth rekindling.

Here's how to create your own lifeline diagram. You can draw it on paper or use a laptop or tablet.

1. Draw a vertical line down the middle of a blank piece of paper or your screen.

2. Put horizontal lines on the vertical line, one for every five years of your life. Start with your birth at the top, and proceed down to your current age.

3. On the left side list any key life events that took place, and on the right side list any relationships you had at those times. If you're not sure how to do this, follow Charlie's example.

4. Once you've completed your lifeline, highlight, underline, or circle any relationships you'd like to rekindle — something I help with later in this chapter.

Understanding "meaningfulness" in relationships

All relationships are different and not every relationship is meaningful. Some are simply functional. You can sit next to a colleague for eight hours a day and never get to know much about them outside of their function at work. Similarly, you can form a warm, friendly bond with a barista you engage with daily. Understanding the different types of relationships you have and how meaningful they are to you can help you decide who it's best to spend more time with and what kinds of people you should seek out when developing new relationships.

Alongside the lifeline which I explained earlier, another way to assess your relationships is to do a sociogram. A sociogram is a visual depiction of the relationships between you and other people. It's a tool for charting your relationships and what they mean to you. Like a lifeline, a sociogram can help you map your relationships and think about which people on the map it might be worth reaching out to.

You can chart a sociogram in different ways, but one way is to use a series of concentric circles, with you in the middle circle and others you're connected with in the circles around you. The closer the other people are to you, the stronger and more significant the relationships are. The further away people are from your inner circle, the weaker and less significant the relationships are. Figure 14-2 shows an example.

Jordan is a 23-year-old young man who spent the early part of his life in foster care. As a result, he spent most of his childhood moving around, from one foster care home to another, to different foster parents, and eventually to his adopted parents. Jordan's sociogram illustrates few social relationships, and most aren't strong or significant to him. He has a strong and significant relationship with his biological sister and his adopted mother. He has a weak relationship with his adoptive father. He also has some relationships with service providers and counselors. On his sociogram are a couple of young men Jordan went to school with. He used to hang around with them, but they bullied him, so he placed them on the outer edges of the circles.

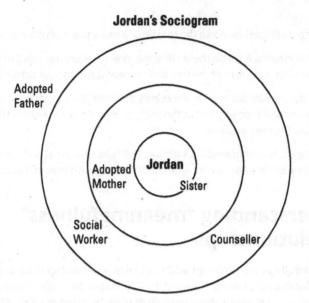

Jordan's Sociogram

Adopted Father

Adopted Mother

Jordan

Sister

Social Worker

Counseller

FIGURE 14-2:
Sample
sociogram.

Here are the simple steps to follow to create your own sociogram of relationships:

1. Draw three concentric circles, as shown in Figure 14-2.

2. Put yourself in the center circle of the diagram.

3. Plot your connections to other people in the circles.

TIP

Plot as many people as possible on the diagram. These might be relatives or friends, work colleagues, shop owners, library staff, those riding public transportation, hairdressers, or health practitioners such as physiotherapists or counselors. Plot anyone you can think of who you're connected to.

Start with your most significant social connections, which you'll plot closest to you on the diagram. The stronger the relationship is, the closer they should be to your name. Place the names of those you share weaker and less significant relationships with further away from you, in the outer circles.

As you're considering how meaningful each relationship is, think about the things that are important to you in that relationship. For example, Jordon placed his adopted mother on the inner circle because he trusts her, whereas he placed his adopted father farther away because he feels his father lacks respect for him. You can write the key words that have influenced where you place the people in your sociogram next to their name or on lines flowing into the center. Some important concepts to think about are: trust; mutual reciprocity; equal power relations; positivity; feeling valued; sharing common goals, interests or values; sustainability.

REMEMBER

You don't need to put people closer to you just because you're related or you feel that they *should* be closer to you. For example, on my sociogram, I placed my mother further away from me than anyone else because we have a poor, negative relationship. Those who are unrelated but have been supportive and positive, I placed much closer to me on my sociogram.

TIP

Once you've completed your sociogram, see if you can identify some people whom you'd like to develop a stronger relationship with. I provide some tips later to help you do this.

You can also use the sociogram to monitor your relationships and the way they change over time. You might want to return to your sociogram after doing the rest of the exercises in this chapter so that you can view your relationship progression.

Figure 14-3 shows how Jordan's sociogram changed as he carried out the activities in this chapter. In the first sociogram, he listed only a few people, and they were mainly in the outside circles, showing that they weren't significant relationships. However, after Jordan followed some of the tips in this chapter, he began volunteering at a local charity doing conservation work near a canal. The volunteering work involved picking up litter, lockkeeping, and doing wildlife conservation tasks. He always liked the outdoors, and the voluntary work connected him to other people with similar interests. He now has three additional people on his sociogram: two fellow volunteers and a charity staff member.

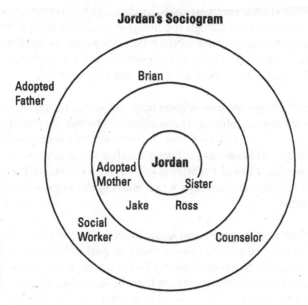

FIGURE 14-3: Changes to sociogram over time.

Connecting with Like-Minded People

If you feel lonely, connecting with others can be quite scary. You might feel all alone in the world, as though nobody understands you or you don't fit in. You may feel as though everyone else has lots of friends and relatives they have positive relationships with, which might leave you feeling left out and on your own. You may well be surrounded by other people at work, at home, or in your neighborhood and still feel lonely. If you've been lonely for a long time, you might have started to give up hope of finding people you can have a meaningful relationship with.

If you find yourself in this situation, you're not alone. Luckily, there are some quick and easy solutions.

One of the best ways to make meaningful ties with others and reduce your feelings of loneliness is to start connecting with like-minded people. The following sections include some pointers on identifying these people and connecting (or reconnecting) with them.

Identifying like-minded people

Think about all those you know now or have known in the past and ask yourself whether it's possible to develop a meaningful relationship with them. Are they like-minded? Being like-minded doesn't mean you have to be the same. It's more about having similar common goals, interests or similar values, and being able to find commonality even though you disagree on certain things. See Figure 14-1 on lifeline maps to help you map all the relationships you've had during your life. You can do this exercise for every year of your life or for a particular part of your life, such as from ages 30 to 50. It's a simple and easy exercise.

REMEMBER

Once you've completed your lifeline map, list all the people on there in table format (like the one in Table 14-1) and identify whether they're capable of having a meaningful relationship with you. Include all the people you've known in the past and may still know now. It doesn't matter if you never see these people anymore. Likewise, it doesn't matter if you've never spoken to these people but you see them occasionally, perhaps when walking the dog or shopping at the local grocery store.

Include their names, where you know them from, and when you last connected. Then put a tick mark if you share a common goal or interest, and state what that goal or interest is. In the end column decide which, if any, of the people you want to: a) reconnect with (mark with an R in the last column), or b) strengthen connections with (put SC in the end column). It doesn't matter how long ago it was that you last saw them, or if you see them but never or hardly ever speak.

Here's the example in Table 14-1. Jeanette is 62, and she's been lonely for around nine years. She first felt lonely when she split up from her husband, which was just after their two boys had grown up and left home. Most of Jeanette's friends were also her husband's friends, and since they split up, she hasn't seen them. She had some friends from work, but following the marital breakup, she lost contact with them. To avoid feeling lonely, Jeanette initially immersed herself in her work, but now she's really missing social interaction with others and wants to find some people she can chat with and go to social events with. Jeanette did the lifeline map earlier in this chapter and listed in Table 14-1 the people whom she has links with now or did in the past.

TABLE 14-1 **People from Jeanette's Lifeline Map**

Name	How I Know Them	Last Had Connect With	Share Common Interest or Goal	Description of Goal or Interest	R — Reconnect SC — Make a Stronger Connection
Jen	Past work colleague.	Nineteen years ago. Had an argument about work and fell out of touch.	Yes.	We both have similar aged children. Do similar work. Both like running.	R
Sharon	Sister.	Last week.	No.	Nothing in common.	
Man — don't know name	Walks dog past house in morning. Occasionally says hello.	This morning.	Don't know.		SC
Wayne	See him at football games.	Three weeks ago at football game.	Yes.	Don't know, but both like football.	
Emily	Neighbor in previous house.	Nine years ago.	Yes.	Member of same political party.	

Once you've completed the table, see if you can identify one or more people you might be able to reconnect with. Try also to see if there are any people listed who you could strengthen an existing connection with.

In Table 14-1 you can see that Jeanette has identified Jen, whom she's going to try to reconnect with. Jeanette and Jen had a work-related argument many years ago and haven't spoken since. Jeanette has identified Jen as the first person to try to reconnect with. This is because despite the argument, they used to have a lot in common. Jeanette has also identified a man whom she doesn't know to try to strengthen her connection with. He passes her house every day while walking his dog, and she quite often says hello to him as he passes by. Jeanette doesn't even know his name.

If you've identified one or more people to reconnect with, you'll find some simple tips in the next section on how to make those reconnections. If you've identified one or more people to try to make a stronger connection with, you'll see some tips on how to do this later in this chapter. Don't worry if you've completed the exercise and can't identify anyone. I've provided a simple step-by-step guide on how to make a fresh start on developing new meaningful connections later in this chapter.

Reconnecting with people from the past

TIP

You can try a number of ways to reconnect with someone:

>> **Send a text message or email:** Include a simple message such as "Hi there, Louise. It's Natasha. Long time, no see. I thought about you recently and wondered how you're getting along."

>> **Ring or send a voice message:** Say that you were reminded of them the other day and thought you'd make contact to see how they're doing and what they're up to now.

>> **Send a message via social media:** Use a platform where you know the person you're trying to reconnect with is active. Send them a personal message, perhaps with an old photo of the two of you on the post.

>> **Send a postcard:** Include a short note asking how they are. Make sure you include your contact details so they can get back in touch with you. If you happen to be going on vacation, use the opportunity to send a postcard from your holiday destination.

If you don't have contact details for the person you're trying to reconnect with, do some research and see if you can find them on social media, through their place of work, or in the last place you saw them. Don't worry if it takes a few attempts to reach the person. Try a few times, and hopefully they'll make contact, and that will spark a discussion. Because you're like-minded spirits, you'll soon start chatting again and eventually might get the opportunity to meet up.

This is exactly what Jeanette, whom I introduced in the previous section, did. She contacted Jen through the message function on a social media platform. Jen didn't reply the first time, but she did the second time Jeanette reached out. They started texting and eventually met up in person. Once they reconnected they realized how much they had in common. They agreed to put their past differences behind them, which Jeanette confessed to Jen were due to her marital difficulties at the time. Those in turn caused her to be stressed at work.

REMEMBER

Don't fret if you try to reconnect with a like-minded person and you can't find them or they're not interested. If there's no response after one or two times, move on quickly to the next step and try to make stronger connections with someone else you've identified in your table.

WARNING

Don't be tempted to reconnect with someone who's had a damaging influence on your life, such as an abusive partner. Negative relationships can be more damaging than not having any relationships and being alone. If you need help, there are some useful helplines listed for you in the Appendix. If you don't have a suitable past connection that you feel it's best to rekindle, it's fine and perfectly usual. In that case move onto the tips for making stronger connections or making new connections later in this chapter.

Strengthening existing connections

If you decide to try to make a stronger connection to someone, think about the best way to do this.

TIP

Here are some tips to get you on your way:

>> **Smile and make eye contact** the next time you pass them.

>> **Make small friendly gestures** like holding open a door or letting them pass first.

>> **Make small talk** about the weather.

>> **Tell them your name** and ask for theirs.

>> **Progress** to having longer conversations.

>> **Invite them** for a coffee, a chat, a walk, or a meal.

After a few chance meetings and positive gestures, you'll start chatting, and who knows where your new friendship could lead? Jeanette decided to make a stronger connection with the man who regularly passed her house while walking his dog. She decided to look at him the next time they passed each other and to smile.

After she did this a few times, she started to make small talk with him, such as, "Hello. Nice morning isn't it?" She then tried to coincide her walks with his so that they passed each other in the street more often. After a few weeks they started talking and then began walking together. Now they hike together every weekend.

Making new connections

REMEMBER

Don't give up if the lifeline task doesn't reveal anyone you can either reconnect with or build a stronger relationship with. Likewise, don't despair if you've identified people to build or rebuild relationships with but it hasn't worked, and you still feel lonely. In these cases, or if you've had some success but want to gain more relationships with like-minded people, the next step is to make new connections. Try not to feel anxious by this. Instead, view it as an exciting challenge. Who knows who you'll meet!

TIP

Follow these simple techniques to help you find like-minded people whom you can start to develop meaningful relationships with:

>> **Go somewhere that feels familiar,** where you experience a sense of belonging. If you're comfortable in your surroundings, you're more likely to feel happy and positive. While in such a place, smile at people and say hello to passersby. Try to visit the same place at the same time each day so you have better chances of meeting the same people. In no time you'll find yourself striking up conversations with people, and who knows where the relationship could take you. (Flip to Chapter 15 for more information on finding meaningful places.)

>> **Search your local area for groups** you might want to get involved in. Look online, in your local library, or for ads or posters displayed in your neighborhood. You can find plenty of groups for all tastes and preferences. These might include singing in a choir, building DIY projects, knitting, participating in sports, playing musical instruments, gardening, walking with others, creating arts and crafts, meditating and yoga, gaming, participating in martial arts, swimming, playing dominos — the list is endless.

>> **Write a list of your main interests** if you've looked at the groups in your area and you're not sure which ones to join. Think about the types of activities that make you feel happy, and then look for groups that do that. It's important that you enjoy attending any groups and care about the activities taking place.

>> **Join a political party or a lobbying group** that corresponds to your values and way of thinking. Search for groups of interest to you online, at your local library, or at local community venues. These groups tend to have regular meetings where your values will be welcomed and you'll be sure to meet

other like-minded people. This kind of activity is often helpful if you feel like you don't fit in or are having difficulty being yourself.

>> **Find out what events are happening in your local area** and pop in to any that take your fancy. If you don't know what kinds of events you're interested in, just go to a few and see if you enjoy them. If the first one isn't for you, don't give up. Try another. There's usually an event for everyone in your community. There may be a park run, a local band playing, a choir singing, or a play or musical. The main thing is to ensure that the event is something you enjoy and care about.

>> **Individual loneliness services** exist for connecting like-minded individuals. Search the loneliness services available in your local area. Various options are often available, such as peer support services, where you're connected to others like you in a group and you provide each other support. These are often facilitated by a trained worker or volunteer. Peer support groups are often designed for older people, those with specific health conditions, for young adults, and for caregivers. They're often run by local volunteer and community sector organizations.

>> **Friendship or dating apps** are designed to match you with like-minded people. These apps make the first steps in forming a new relationship a little bit easier. Dating apps have been around a while for those looking for a romantic relationship, but now numerous friendship apps are emerging worldwide. See Chapter 7 for details on connecting through technology.

>> **Exercising** is a great way to make meaningful connections with like-minded people. You can exercise individually, of course. But you're often exercising in a group setting, so you might encounter other people and start conversations with them. Gyms are good places to experience chance encounters with other like-minded people. If you attend the same gym, at the same time, on the same days of the week, you'll increase your chances of bumping into the same people and striking up a conversation. Participating in a park run is another good way to make connections. People of all abilities take part, as do dog walkers and stroller pushers. The positive atmosphere of the park runs fosters a community spirit. Increase your chances of meeting others by showing up at the park run on a weekly basis.

>> **Attending sporting events** is a great way to connect with like-minded people who have similar passions to you. If you support a local football, soccer, basketball, or other sporting team, get yourself to the next match. Sporting events are one of the easiest places to go to alone and one of the easiest places to strike up a conversation. Fans have a strong sense of identity and belonging and support each other. Drop in on your local team, and you'll soon find yourself discussing with a fellow fan the team's promotion or title chances, or maybe their likelihood of avoiding relegation. Sit or stand in the same place each game, and before you know it, you'll develop lifelong friendships.

>> **Get tickets for a pop concert or festival** and immerse yourself in the music. Singing and dancing to your favored tunes doesn't only provide a feel-good factor but connects you with fellow groupies. Try striking up a conversation between songs or at intermission. I've made several friends this way by watching my favorite band, Orchestral Manoeuvres in the Dark.

Helping Others

Alongside connecting with like-minded people in the ways I outlined earlier, helping other people can make you feel less lonely. You can do this through volunteering, offering peer support, or in some countries becoming a befriender. In all of these you're performing an act of altruism while developing meaningful relationships with the people you're helping. Don't worry if you don't know how to start helping other people or if you're unsure what terms like *peer support* or *befriender* mean. In this section I explain more about ways you can assist. Before long you'll be on your way to creating meaningful relationships as you do good in the world.

Volunteering

Volunteering involves spending time doing something to benefit another. Your time will be unpaid, although you might be able to get reimbursement for travel and subsistence. Volunteering is a great way to become involved in your community, make a difference, and meet new people. To gain the most of volunteering opportunities, it's best to do it regularly and often. So it's helpful to find volunteer opportunities you care about and enjoy, and which fit in with your weekly calendar and lifestyle. To see how volunteering might reduce your feelings of loneliness, read how George benefitted from helping other men.

REAL WORLD EXAMPLE

George is a 67-year-old man who lives alone and recently retired from his job. Since retirement, he has started to feel lonely and isolated. He decided to look for opportunities to meet new people in his community and saw a project that targeted lonely older men building furniture. George liked making things but wasn't keen on the idea of attending a group designed for lonely people. Although he was isolated, George didn't really want to admit to being lonely. That's why he went to the group as a volunteer instead. He began offering support to other lonely men by helping them make furniture. George no longer feels lonely and now has a renewed sense of purpose. The volunteering has rebuilt the self-esteem and confidence he lost upon retirement, and he has made meaningful relationships with the men he's helping. The men have started to meet socially outside of the project. They often go out for drinks together.

Volunteering can help you feel less lonely in several ways:

>> **Forming connections:** By engaging with others who share your interest for an activity or cause, you're more likely to meet like-minded people with whom you can build lasting, meaningful relationships.

>> **Building social skills:** Volunteering can do wonders for your social skills. It will inevitably push you a little beyond your comfort zone, helping you build social skills and improve your ability to talk to new people. This will boost your confidence and enable you to make new friends both within and outside the volunteer opportunity.

>> **Developing intergenerational friendships:** Volunteering can connect you with people whom you wouldn't normally interact with. It often facilitates intergenerational friendships by bringing people of all ages together who are volunteers, service users, or customers. By spending time with people of different generations, you'll gain a new perspective and source of energy that will reinvigorate your interest in life and leave you feeling less lonely.

>> **Feeling needed:** Being needed is one of human beings' fundamental desires. Volunteering will make you feel more significant in the eyes of others. By volunteering you're playing an important role in the life of another person, for an organization, or for a particular cause. In fulfilling this need, you're likely to feel a greater sense of purpose and well-being and boost your relationship with yourself. This can help you break any negative emotional loops, so you feel like engaging with other people again.

>> **Getting you out of the house:** Volunteering can take you out of the house and to places where you have a meaningful relationship and sense of belonging (see Chapter 15). This can attack loneliness in two ways: expanding your meaningful relationships with others, and improving your meaningful relationship with the places you identify with.

If you decide to give volunteering a try, this section explores a few different options.

Helping a neighbor or local resident

An older neighbor might need help putting the garbage out, shopping for groceries, or getting to medical appointments. A busy, younger neighbor might need help walking the dog or babysitting. Once you've identified someone in your community you can help, use the tips I provided earlier to strike up a conversation and ask them if they would like assistance. Don't worry if they refuse at first; people don't always like to admit they need help. You might need to ask on two or three different occasions over the course of a few weeks.

Contacting charities or voluntary organizations

Charities often display their volunteering roles on their websites, in their offices, or on posters in local community venues, like libraries, community centers, and shops. Charities offering volunteering roles are ubiquitous and cover a whole range of interest groups, from conservation, to animal welfare, to support for those with long-term health conditions, to help for children, older people, or immigrants. One is bound to catch your eye.

The Red Cross, Salvation Army, and Meals on Wheels are humanitarian charities you're likely to be familiar with. They're always in need of volunteers, and you can benefit from social interaction with those you meet. You can also support any specific projects they run. Regardless of the type of initiative you get involved in, you're bound to meet new people in your voluntary role. Before long, loneliness will become a thing of the past.

Volunteering in a healthcare or hospital setting

This can be a particularly rewarding form of volunteering, where you're helping people who have an illness or a certain health condition. Or maybe you're just helping relatives and friends who are visiting. Options can include serving tea or coffee to visitors, reading to hospital patients, providing administrative support, fundraising, becoming involved in patient participation groups, or gaining a position on the board of governors or trustees. Details of such opportunities are usually displayed on posters, on digital display boards in the healthcare settings, or on their websites.

Local conservation, gardening, or "friends of" groups

"Friends of" groups are volunteer groups based in your local community that improve, care for, and protect local outdoor spaces. They usually consist of volunteers who are passionate about looking after their local park, greenspace, or waterways. These groups can offer a whole range of activities for you to get involved in, including working with local authorities, designing spaces, gardening, picking up litter, building walls or fences, and planting trees.

Local grassroots sports club

Options are available for many different sports, with track and field athletics and football being particularly popular. These sports clubs often operate for young people, but they're available for all ages. If you're a big sports fan, visit your local sports venue and ask about volunteering opportunities. Quite often you can take advantage of coaching courses if you decide to commit to being involved on a longer-term basis. This can offer additional skills, as well as opportunities for social interaction.

Board of governors

These opportunities are available in a number of settings, such as schools, hospital trusts, and some of the larger charitable organizations. They often require you to attend and get involved in regular meetings and can be a good way of extending your work-based skills to another setting or developing new skills, while meeting other people.

Political party or lobby group

Select a group of your choice that supports a cause you're particularly passionate about and offer your services. You might find yourself canvassing, distributing leaflets, fundraising, or drumming up support for the group in question. Your offer of help will be greatly received.

Volunteering at places of worship

If you have a religious affinity, you can volunteer at your local church, Kingdom Hall, mosque, synagogue, or temple. Voluntary opportunities are often posted in the halls themselves, or you might want to ask the religious leader after a service.

Picking up litter

There are plenty of opportunities for litter picking in localities near to you. In a local park, countryside location, or hiking route. You can also volunteer in environmental cleanups of specific locations, or a good option if you have a favorite band, or just love music is to volunteer to pick up litter at a pop festival. This enables you to get into a festival for free, and while making the grounds cleaner, you'll meet other volunteers and festival goers. These opportunities are more frequently available at large outdoor venues where the gig organizers are keen on keeping the venue tidy to ensure people return.

Peer support

If you want a more hands-on role in creating meaningful relationships while helping others, you could try getting involved in peer support provision. This is a great way to immerse yourself in conversations that are designed to help other people, as you help yourself at the same time. If you feel lonely, peer support might just do the trick. This section looks in more detail at what peer support is.

REMEMBER

Peer support involves people who have similar personal lived experiences helping each other. People involved in peer support offer emotional, social, or practical support; knowledge; and advice to each other. The distinguishing factor of peer support is that the people giving and receiving the support are peers who have an equal relationship. They have similar life experiences, although they may have handled challenges in different ways, and had different outcomes.

Peer support schemes often involve regular weekly sessions between the peers, with the ultimate aim of providing reassurance to each other and seeking solutions together that can be tested between sessions. Peer support sessions are usually time bound, so they might operate for a three- or six-month period. But quite often peers continue to meet after the formal sessions have ceased, which is important in helping you maintain the meaningful relationships you've gained and keeping loneliness at bay.

Peer support groups vary, but they tend to have the following in common:

>> They bring people together who have similar lived experiences so they can support one another.

>> They're delivered in a place (either physical or virtual) where the peers feel comfortable and can be themselves.

>> They enable all peer experiences and input to be treated equally. No one peer is seen to be more qualified or to have more expertise than another.

>> They involve the peers both providing and receiving advice and support.

Peer support can be delivered in different ways: in a group setting where a number of peers meet face to face; online; or on a one-on-one basis, where two peers give support to each other face to face, by telephone, or online.

The focus of the peer support sessions can vary enormously and is usually dictated by the peers themselves. If you get involved, you might focus on particular topics, or you might do activities together, such as walking, gardening, playing games, or creating something.

TIP

Peer support involvement can provide you with a number of benefits and can be particularly helpful in reducing your feelings of loneliness. By sharing your lived experiences with each other, you will gain a sense of commonality and feel a sense of empathy toward each other. By regularly meeting with a peer or peers, you'll have the confidence to open up about what you're feeling and experiencing and gain ready-made opportunities for conversations that have the potential to lead to more meaningful relationships.

Through sharing your life experiences with others, you can help others and gain a greater sense of belonging and self-worth, which itself will improve your sense of well-being and improve your relationship with yourself.

Your peers are likely to feel lonely too and are experiencing similar issues and challenges. This can reassure you that you're not alone in how you're feeling, which itself will help you feel more positive about options for social contact in the future.

After a while, and almost certainly when the formal peer support sessions come to an end, you'll find opportunities for meeting peers outside of the peer support sessions. Before you know it, it will be like meeting old friends or acquaintances.

Some peer support initiatives offer training to peers. If yours does, it will encourage you to value your strengths, give you the skills and resources to improve your life, build your self-esteem and confidence, and reduce the amount of time you feel lonely.

TIP

Here are some suggestions to help you find the right peer support initiative:

>> **Identify some key characteristics about yourself to help decide which kind of peer support initiative you should join.** You could have a health condition; be a caregiver; have a particular protected characteristic, such as being disabled; a migrant; or LGBTQIA+. Or you might be seeking support as an athlete, setting up a business for the first time, or seeking to gain a promotion at work.

>> **Look into different peer support initiatives covering all types of experiences.** You can search for these online, in your local community or neighborhood, through your healthcare services, through your employer, or through your educational institution.

>> **Discover means of accessing peer support.** You can access peer support through your health practitioner, a local charity or voluntary sector organizations, online, through your employer, or through student services. If in doubt, ask your local library or community center if they know about peer support initiatives running near you.

Peer support can really help you combat your feelings of loneliness, as you can see by reading about Livy's experience.

Livy is a 44-year-old mother of two girls. She has spent most of her career working in universities teaching, but she recently set up a business based on meditation, yoga, and mindfulness in pregnancy. Livy had a lot of work colleagues she used to socialize with after hours, but since setting up her business, she had little free time and started to feel quite isolated and lonely. The only social contact she had was with her customers. Livy joined a peer support group for new female business start-ups. Through it, she regularly met with five other women who were in a similar position. The peer support group ran for 12 weeks and gave her confidence and skills to run her business, while enabling her to have meaningful relationships with her peers. The women continued to meet socially when the peer support group came to an end, and now Livy has an active social life and friends that she can go to for advice and support about her business.

Befriending

If you're feeling lonely and are particularly keen to help others but also gain a one-on-one friendship, befriending might just be the thing for you. This isn't available everywhere, but is very common in the UK and some other countries, and is a practice that I hope will grow in other countries.

You may be wondering how becoming a befriender differs from making friends. Befriending is simply a relationship between a volunteer and someone who needs support. That person might be a service user of a voluntary or statutory agency, which usually initiates the service, matches the participants and volunteers, and monitors the process.

TIP

Consider becoming a befriender if you're lonely and are interested in other people, are reliable and a good listener, understand the need for confidentiality, are able to offer a caring and understanding presence, and can commit to volunteering a couple of hours each week on a regular basis.

Befriending offers a more informal and less structured way to support other people than peer support and is more typically run on a one-on-one basis, whereas peer support is more often done in groups. Some charities which support older people have well-established befriending schemes where older people who are lonely and isolated are matched with volunteers in their community. The volunteer befrienders meet the older person regularly face to face, by telephone, or online. The pair may meet up for a cup of tea and a chat, or the befriender might accompany the participant somewhere, such as to a café, library, or medical appointment.

Befriending services such as these have the dual benefit of reducing loneliness in both the participant in need of support and the befriender themselves. Befriending projects aren't just for older people. They exist for children and young people, families, and people with different physical and mental health conditions.

The impact of befriending can be positive and significant for both parties. If you're lonely and become a befriender, you can expect to

>> **Gain a new direction in life** because it can open up a range of activities and skills that you haven't thought of or tried before.

>> **Learn new skills in communication** to help you with your role. Most organizations running a befriending service provide training and support to help you in your role.

>> **Improve your self-esteem and sense of self-worth** by knowing you're making a positive difference in someone's life.

>> **Increase your chances of gaining meaningful relationships** through regular conversations and shared activities.

>> **Gain confidence to go out and meet new people** and ultimately feel less isolated and lonely.

REAL WORLD EXAMPLE

Lucy, a 19-year-old elite athlete, quit education to focus full time on her sport. When she does get to see her friends, they want to go out drinking and partying, activities she can't do because of her intensive training schedule.

Lucy joined a befriending scheme and was matched with an older person, Janice, from her neighborhood. Janice is lonely and homebound. Lucy now really looks forward to her weekly meetings with Janice, and both have become less lonely. Since becoming a befriender, Lucy's mental health and well-being have also improved, as has her athletic performance because she's feeling more socially connected and has the weekly meetings to take her mind of her sport. Lucy has also learned some key skills from Janice, such as baking cakes and sewing.

Chapter **15**

Finding Meaningful Places

P laces and spaces that are meaningful to you can have an important role in helping you feel connected and less lonely. I've said elsewhere in this book that feeling lonely is a natural part of life, serving as a trigger to connect. Another natural part of being human is attaching meaning to places, which then makes them significant to you.

When you visit or spend time in these places, you can feel connected to your surroundings and feel less lonely. You're usually comfortable and at home in these places and feel as though you can be yourself. Spending time in these places can connect you to other like-minded people with whom you can form social bonds. But importantly, because of the significance of these places to you, you can feel connected even if you're alone.

The kinds of places that are capable of creating meaning vary depending on who you are. They can include open spaces, such as parks, lakes, mountains, beaches, playgrounds, and riverside walks. They can include buildings, such as places of worship, employment, or education. And they can include sporting and leisure venues, such as stadiums and athletic tracks.

In this chapter I discuss the role that places have in creating meaning for you. I first provide an explanation of what a sense of belonging to place means and looks like. I then offer some examples of some of the key places you can gain a sense of belonging to and how visiting them can help you feel less lonely and more connected. Finally, I show you how to identify the places that might be helpful for you to connect with so that you make the most of your connection with them and fend off any loneliness that might emerge.

What It Means to Belong to a Place

By developing a personal attachment to a place, you can acquire a sense of belonging, a sense of place, or an attachment. Visiting or spending time there can then offer you a sense of purpose and meaning. You can find that being alone there doesn't make you feel lonely but enables you to enjoy solitude.

You can discover that you feel more comfortable and accepting of yourself in these places. And, if you do want to make social connections with other people, these are the locations you're likely to achieve most success and connect with like-minded people who accept you for who you are. Here I primarily explore the sense of belonging that's created through places of worship, sporting and leisure activities, and open spaces. You can find more detail on connections to neighborhoods and communities in Chapter 5 and to workplaces in Chapter 6.

REMEMBER

To experience a sense of belonging, it's likely you'll feel one or more of the following when you're in that place:

>> A sense of ease

>> Ability to be yourself

>> Familiarity

>> Connectedness

>> Affiliation

>> Acceptance

>> Commonality

>> Satisfaction

>> A sense of identity

>> Commitment

>> A bond

>> Emotional attachment

Different places will evoke these feelings for different people. A place that evokes these sensations for one person may well have the opposite impact on someone else.

Some key concepts are used to understand a sense of belonging to place. These include sense of belonging, sense of place, and place attachment. These concepts are debated and discussed by academics from different backgrounds and can be complex. A simple summary of these key terms and how they have meaning for you is provided here.

Sense of belonging

A *sense of belonging* is a feeling of being happy or comfortable as part of a particular group and having a good relationship with the other members of the group. However, this sense of belonging involves more than just being acquainted with people. It involves feeling accepted and gaining support from others in the group. It's a strong connection with social groups, physical places, and experiences. It occurs when you can be yourself in a particular setting.

Sense of place

A *sense of place* refers to how you perceive and experience a place or environment. It's the emotive bonds and attachments you develop or experience in particular locations and environments. It's about the interrelationships between you and your physical, natural, and social environment. These environments or locations can include homes, neighborhoods, cities, countries, rivers, forests, lakes, buildings, and structures. A sense of place is often used to discuss the characteristics that make a place special or unique or capable of fostering a sense of attachment and belonging.

Place attachment

Place attachment can be described as an affective bond between people and places. It refers to the feelings you develop over time and experience in specific places. The extent to which you gain place attachment is influenced by your personal experiences there, its characteristics, and the extent to which it can be meaningful enough to enable place attachment to occur. You're more likely to form an attachment somewhere if it meets both your functional and your emotional needs. If your emotional needs are met by the place, it can support your self-identity and self-esteem. Homes and neighborhoods are often places where people form place attachment. But this can be applied elsewhere too.

Identifying with a Specific Place

Everyone identifies with and feels a sense of belonging to different places and spaces. This section offers more detail on the types of places you can feel a sense of belonging to. You'll read some specific real life examples of people who have fended off loneliness because of their sense of belonging to a particular place.

Places of worship

REMEMBER

If you follow a religion or belief, a place of worship can be a place of belonging for you. This includes, but is not limited to, churches, synagogues, Hindu and Buddhist temples, mosques, and Islamic centers. The sense of belonging or attachment you can feel usually extends beyond the physical building and is associated with the wider cultural system that operates in the building. This includes the structures and processes, social norms and behaviors, beliefs, and value systems of the religion or belief.

Your individual sense of belonging, or attachment, to a place of worship can be strengthened by collective endeavors and activities through the congregational focus, which can involve group singing or collective prayers. The architectural design of the place of worship, both externally and internally, is specific to each religion or belief and fosters a sense of familiarity and connection among those who attend for worship. Praying or singing together in unison reinforces the sense of togetherness and commitment.

The religious socialization process, which differs in each place of worship and by religion or belief, reinforces the sense of belonging or attachment to the place. This is done through rituals such as prayer, artifacts such as symbols, sculptures, murals, and paintings. It's also reaffirmed through stories and texts that are presented as sacred scripture, images, storytelling, and singing.

Sporting venues

Recreational, leisure, and sports activities are intrinsically linked to physical places. And the venues in which these activities are undertaken offer another kind of place that's capable of stimulating a sense of belonging. Such venues can include football, soccer, baseball, cricket, and rugby stadiums; athletic tracks; swimming pools; and gyms. Both spectators and participants can form a sense of belonging to these places.

Sporting venues for spectators

Many sports, including soccer, football, rugby, cricket, and baseball, are known as *representational sports*. They represent specific localities, communities, and their associated histories. Almost all soccer clubs in England, for example, are named after places and are traditionally embedded in the community of that place. Frequenting such sporting venues on a regular basis can offer a sense of belonging and attachment to place, which is capable of enabling you to feel connected to a place but also to a community. Both of these connections can help you feel less lonely.

REMEMBER

Sporting venues facilitate a sense of belonging in a number of ways. A good way of explaining this is through the example of an English soccer team and stadium:

>> **The physical building:** The building, in this case the stadium, is a spiritual home for fans, in much the same way that a place of worship is a spiritual home for its religious followers. The construction, colors, and displayed symbols foster an individual sense of belonging and identity besides a collective one. Stadium color schemes, including exterior walls, roofs, seats, and barriers, align with the team's shirt colors, and the team's emblem is often displayed around the venue, reinforcing both individual and collective identity to the place.

>> **The team colors:** You're likely to display your team's colors as a sign of affinity to the team and place by wearing jerseys or other items of clothing such as scarves, hats, hoodies, or coats that exhibit the team colors and emblems. This further reinforces your connection to the place and to fellow fans.

>> **Familiar faces:** The opportunity to purchase a season ticket that admits you to all the games each season means that you're likely to be located near the same people each game, so you not only see familiar faces but share experiences. Even if you attend only a handful of games each season, you'll likely select the same general area to sit or stand, which will expose you to a consistent group of people.

>> **Routines and rituals:** The structure of any pre-game entertainment, half-time, and post-game activity, both in and around the stadium, means that rituals and routines are formed by fans, which adds to the sense of familiarity and connectedness.

>> **A sense of pride:** As a fan, you gain a sense of pride in the place, you celebrate the achievements and successes of the team as though they're your own, and you're able to share those moments with fellow fans.

>> **Social bonding:** A sporting event is a place you can easily attend on your own without feeling alone. In fact, it generates togetherness even if you don't know the people around you. The only thing that matters is that you're on the same side. Conversations strike up about the team's chances and, although there can also be disagreements and arguments, the common bond of the team overrides everything else.

>> **Collective endeavors:** Collective singing, chanting, and clapping in efforts to play a role in the team's sporting success facilitate a sense of togetherness.

I'm a big fan of my local soccer team, Sheffield Wednesday. I attend all games home and away, and going to Hillsborough, the club's stadium, feels like home. I probably feel more at home there than at my house. It's one of the few places in the world I can feel truly connected and experience a strong sense of identity. I can go alone but never feel alone. If I want to chat with people, whether I've seen them before or not, I can easily strike up a conversation. When I'm supporting my team, it doesn't matter how different I am or feel from those around me. I feel a strong sense of identity and connection.

Attachment to place as a sports participant

Forming a sense of belonging to place doesn't just develop if you're a sports fan. It also develops if you're a sports participant. This applies to recreational sports participants as much as it does to those engaging at an elite level. A sense of belonging can apply to all sports, whether it's a team sport or an individual one, and whether it's undertaken indoors or outdoors, in a formal setting or a more informal one.

TIP

As a sports participant, you can gain an attachment and sense of belonging to the place you carry out the sport for three main reasons:

>> **Dependance:** You're likely to be dependent on the sporting venue to carry out your desired sporting activities. Without the venue, which may have particular features or conditions, you're unlikely to be able to undertake the activity that has meaning to you. For example, if you're a swimmer, you require access to a swimming pool. If you're a long jumper, you require an athletics track with long jump facilities.

>> **Place identity:** The place you carry out the sporting activity is likely to create an emotional and symbolic meaning for you, which then reinforces your connection to it. The sense of identity you have with places you participate in your desired sport might vary according to where you regularly visit or the success you've experienced there. For example, my daughter, an athlete, feels a sense of belonging to athletics tracks where she trains regularly or where she has performed particularly well and achieved a milestone in terms of her performance.

>> **Social connections:** The sense of connection that you achieve by frequenting a particular place for sporting activities can also connect you to other people who share that sense of belonging. Walking, hiking, or running along a trail can stimulate a sense of belonging for you and connect you to others who might be using the trail for a variety of sporting or leisure pursuits. In fact, some trail users have mentioned forming a sense of belonging and identity to the trail (see the "Open spaces" section later).

JOINING A GYM

A gym is another example of somewhere people can attend as a participant and form a sense of belonging to place. Because most gyms require membership, by joining the gym you're instantly gaining access to a community of people who engage in a place and enjoy the sense of belonging it provides. Most gym members attend the same gym chain, in the same location, and gain a sense of familiarity to the place. Even if they attend a gym in a different location, it's usually part of the same chain, so the layout is similar. Different branches have the same décor, symbols, and logos that the member can identify with. A gym typically has three areas: a cardio area, a free weights area, and a studio where regular classes take place. The equipment is similar no matter which gym you're in.

It's easy to attend a gym alone. You can attend a class or follow a specific training program that's set for you, and because of the individualized and specific purpose of your attendance, you don't feel as though you need to know anyone else there. However, most people who join a gym do so for a specific reason, often with a goal in mind. The goal could be losing weight, gaining strength, building muscles, or gaining fitness. Because gym attenders share similar goals and target aspirations, they can feel a part of a community. This can also foster a supportive environment where everyone is working towards a common objective: to improve their fitness levels, albeit for different reasons.

People often go to a gym on the same day and time each week, or they might attend certain classes that are held there on a regular basis. This means you often see the same people who might end up becoming your friends. Thus, you can connect with and gain a sense of belonging to the gym but also to other people.

Open spaces

You can develop a sense of belonging to open spaces. Connecting to nature, whether it be through a favorite walk, park, lake, beach, hill, forest, or mountain, can create a sense of meaning, purpose, and connection. And this connection to place can be sufficient to ward off any feelings of loneliness, at least while you're there. You'll know when you're in such a space as it will have a special meaning to you and you'll feel a sense of connectedness and a meaningful relationship with it. You might feel at one with nature or at peace with yourself in the space.

REMEMBER

As I discuss in Chapter 5, spending time in green spaces or indeed blue spaces (around water such as lakes, the sea, rivers, or canals) can improve your sense of well-being, happiness, and quality of life. It can also reduce any negative feelings and emotions you're experiencing, such as depression, tiredness, and loneliness.

Layne is a 58-year-old married woman who has four adult daughters. She has a strong sense of belonging to the mountains. When she spends time there, she feels a strong sense of connection. She first noticed this when she was in her 20s on a skiing vacation. Later in life she started walking in the mountains, and since then she has regularly returned to them.

Layne describes herself as quite nervous and anxious, but once she puts her backpack on and sets off walking in the mountains, she suddenly feels at ease, as though she's at home. When she's in the mountains, her confidence grows, and she can do things that she can't do anywhere else and things that other people might not be able to do. She describes reaching the summit of a mountain as a strong feeling of being where she's meant to be. Somehow the mountains have a pull that feels stronger and stronger for her over time. Once she's at the top of a mountain, she's content, at peace, and at home. Regardless of whether she sees another person on the mountain, she feels a strong sense of belonging that prevents her from feeling lonely. She also describes the way the mountains can connect her to other like-minded people.

She told me of one occasion when she couldn't find the summit, and neither could a boy and his father. The three of them worked together to locate it. She described navigating a tricky and challenging route for the last section of the mountain and the trust that the three of them had for each other even though they'd never met before this. She also spoke about the chance meetings and encounters she had with others, the sharing of advice and knowledge about the mountain or route, and the discussions she often had later on in the pub at the mountain base.

SPENDING TIME ON LOCAL HIKING OR BIKING TRAILS

The TransPennine is a trail that passes close to where I live. A man named Paul, around 80 years old, lives alone and walks the trail every day. He engages in this physical exercise to give himself something meaningful to do, to get out of the house, and to keep fit and healthy. He enjoys a sense of belonging to the trail. At the other end of the spectrum, my daughter, a full-time athlete, runs on the trail regularly for her easy and long runs. She feels a sense of belonging to the trail because it symbolizes a stable and steady part of her life; no matter what's around her, this place is always there. Running along it is part of her daily routine that helps her avoid the chaos. She says everyone needs somewhere to go where you can switch off from the pressures around you and connect with your surroundings.

Paul and my daughter often pass each other on the trail. They first connected when Paul asked my daughter about her training. They then started waving to each other as they passed, and now they high-five each other. Their ages have a gap of 60 years, and they have different purposes for being on the trail. But the trail brings both a sense of belonging and reinforces their identity with the trail and with themselves. What's more, their connection to the trail has brought them in contact with each other and created a social connection and bond.

Enjoying a Sense of Belonging

The feeling of belonging to a place can be expressed in a whole range of ways. It emerges when you're in a particular place and you feel at ease, at peace with yourself, or at home. These places inevitably vary for everyone, depending on personal circumstances, tastes, and preferences. Places of belonging can vary in size and scale too. They can include your bedroom, home, or garden; a community, neighborhood, or city; a country; an open space; a place of work, education, or leisure; and many, many other places.

REMEMBER

When you're in these places, you can feel a different sense of being with your surroundings and yourself and possibly with other people who are there. Everyone can enjoy a sense of belonging to place. But sometimes you may need a little assistance identifying one. Sometimes the places you feel a connection to are far away or inaccessible. In these cases, you can find ways to visit virtually, or you may need to seek out additional places of belonging. The next section has an exercise to help you identify the places that have meaning to you.

Mapping your meaningful places

TIP

Assess the extent to which you have a sense of belonging to a specific place so that you can identify where it might be a good idea to spend more time. Identify a range of places you've been, where you feel you may have a sense of belonging. It doesn't matter where they are, or how big or small they are. They could range from an office at work to a beach or a country. On a scale of 1 to 5, assess which of the following feelings are evoked by the place. 1 means you strongly disagree, and 5 means you strongly agree.

Name of place: . . . .

To what extent does the place make you feel

at ease [_____]

safe [_____]

able to be yourself [_____]

a sense of familiarity [_____]

connected [_____]

an affiliation [_____]

accepted [_____]

a sense of commonality [_____]

a sense of satisfaction [_____]

a sense of identity [_____]

a sense of loyalty or commitment [_____]

an emotional bond or attachment [_____]

TOTAL Score _____

Once you've done this exercise for a place, add up the scores and insert the total at the end. Then repeat the exercise again for a few more places. The higher the total score, the greater the sense of belonging you're likely to have to that place and the more likely that spending time there will assist you in feeling more connected and less lonely. A score of 40 or more indicates that you're likely to have a sense of belonging to the place. Once you've identified the specific places you have a greater sense of belonging to, visit them on a regular basis, and notice how you feel before you go, when you're there, and when you return. If you find that you feel a greater sense of belonging and connectedness when you're in the place, it's worth making regular trips there.

TIP

If you're not quite sure where you have a sense of belonging to or even what the different options might be, turn to the next section, which provides some examples. Once you've read that through, return to this exercise.

You might feel a strong sense of belonging to a place that's far away or that you're unable to get to, perhaps because you're homebound or have a health condition. If this is the case, it's worth exploring whether you can visit virtually (see Chapter 7). If a virtual visit isn't possible, you can get some photographs or pictures of the location and create a collage to display in your home. Looking at this regularly might just be enough to make you feel a sense of connection.

Sometimes if you can't visit a place that feels significant to you, you can feel worse. If this is the case for you, put that place to one side for now and focus on other locations. You can also identify some other spots that are closer by, that you can get to, or where a virtual visit is possible. If you return to that special place in the future, you might feel more comfortable seeing images of it or visiting it virtually.

Testing the waters

TIP

Many places can induce a sense of belonging, but this will vary from person to person. What evokes a sense of belonging for one person might have the complete opposite effect for someone else. I provide some different options in this section of places you might feel a sense of belonging. If you're not sure how you feel in these places, visit them and assess how you feel when you're there by using the exercise in the previous section.

>> **Open spaces:** This includes anywhere in nature. It could be a green space such as a garden, a park, a woodland, a hill, a trail, a mountain, or a forest. Or it might be a blue space, such as a waterway, a canal, a river, a lake, or a sea.

>> **A sporting or leisure venue:** This can include both indoor and outdoor locations. It might be indoor buildings and constructions such as stadiums, sports halls, swimming pools, ice rinks, or climbing walls or outdoor places such as athletics tracks, trails, mountains, car racing tracks, skate parks, playing fields, or caves. You might enjoy a sense of belonging in these places if you visit as a spectator, a participant, or both.

>> **Places of worship:** These are structures or spaces that are specifically designed for people to practice or demonstrate their religious affiliation. They vary according to the particular religion or belief and can include churches, synagogues, temples, and mosques. They can also include natural or topo-graphical features that are considered holy in some religions. An example of this is the Ganges River, which is considered sacred in Hinduism, or the Sanctuary of Lourdes, which is a Catholic shrine and spiritual healing place.

>> **Neighborhood:** This refers to a specific geographic area where people live. A neighborhood is usually defined geographically by physical boundaries such as streets, buildings, and landmarks. A neighborhood can vary in both size and population density. It could have a small number of houses dispersed in a rural hamlet or be a densely populated suburb of a city. You may have a sense of belonging to the neighborhood you currently live in, to one you've resided in previously, or to one you've visited.

>> **Home:** Home can mean different things to different people. The simplest definition of home is the place where you live or reside. But home can be anywhere you feel safe, comfortable, and connected and thus, experience a sense of belonging. You might feel a sense of belonging only to a particular part of your home, such as your bedroom, the kitchen, or the garden. Or you might not feel a sense of belonging to your current home, but to one you previously resided in, where your parents or grandparents lived, or where you've visited for a vacation. I spent around ten years returning to the same couple's home in Austria for my annual skiing vacation. I still feel a strong sense of belonging there.

>> **Educational institutions:** Have you heard the saying that school days are the best days of your life? For some people this holds true. Whatever your age, whether you're currently a child attending school or a middle-aged person looking back fondly on your school days, the school you attend can give you a sense of belonging. The same sense of belonging can also be evoked by a college you attend now or one you attended years ago.

>> **Place of work:** You may also have a sense of belonging to a place of work. It could be a current place of work or a previous one. It's most likely to be somewhere you personally have worked, but it could also be where someone you know works. When I was growing up, my father was a politician and worked in the town hall. Consequently, I spent a lot of time there. I felt a very strong sense of belonging to the town hall at that time. I discuss more about workplaces in Chapter 6.

Chapter **16**

Building Resilience to Loneliness

I f you follow the suggestions and tips throughout this book, any transient lone-liness you're experiencing will feel less daunting and disappear much quicker. You'll also be more prepared and better able to deal with chronic loneliness if it does emerge.

Loneliness is often associated with a stigma both by the people who feel lonely and by those around them. Because of this, people can be reluctant to admit to being lonely both to themselves and to others. This can prevent people who feel lonely from talking about it and seeking help. And those who don't feel lonely might be fearful of talking about it with those who do. Some are more likely to be affected by this stigmatization than others. Younger people can feel particularly embarrassed about being lonely and thus more inclined to disguise it.

This stigmatization of loneliness is problematic because it can lead to feelings of shame and can place the blame of loneliness on the individual. However, this isn't accurate. If anything, this book has demonstrated that loneliness is a complex issue that's determined by a whole range of individual and societal factors that interact with external triggers and events and that are often beyond our control. Everyone can play a part in eliminating the stigma of loneliness and normalizing it so that it becomes easier to discuss, manage, and beat.

In this chapter I give you the tools you need to be more resilient to the stigma of loneliness. I then provide a step-by-step guide to becoming more resilient to loneliness during those key life transitions that are part of the human experience. Lastly, I offer some final advice on how you can be "loneliness-ready."

Squashing the Stigma of Loneliness

Stigma relating to loneliness can include both actual and perceived social stigma, as well as self-stigma.

>> **Actual social stigma** refers to negative attitudes or beliefs that are directed towards an individual or group — in this case, those who are lonely. Social stigma can lead to people who are lonely being stereotyped and suffering discrimination.

>> **Perceived social stigma** refers to an assumption or expectation that loneliness is viewed as a stigmatized condition by others in society. This can lead people who are lonely to fear being judged in a negative way or rejected by others.

>> **Self stigma** occurs when the stigma is internalized and you start to hold a negative belief or view about yourself and your loneliness. It can lead to feelings of shame, and people will invariably feel it imperative to conceal their loneliness from others.

REMEMBER

Stigma, in all its guises, is a socially constructed phenomenon. This means that it's not an objective reality but has simply been socially created as part of human interaction in society. Everyone can play a part in changing the stigma by talking about loneliness more and raising awareness of it. If you have doubts about the extent to which it's possible to achieve this, just think about the way in which attitudes toward members of the LGBTQIA+ community have changed in recent years.

Spreading the word

The more that loneliness is normalized and talked about, the better. Verbalizing loneliness can break the taboo and change the way it's perceived. Both those who are feeling lonely and those who aren't should talk about loneliness. Importantly, so should anyone who plays a part in shaping cultures and environments that influence whether people feel lonely and to what degree. This includes employers, town planners, educational leaders, teachers and lecturers, health professionals, shop workers, neighbors — indeed, everyone!

TIP

Here are some tips to get you talking about loneliness — whoever you are, whether you're feeling lonely or not, and whatever role you have in society.

Having open conversations about loneliness

At home, at work, at school, in your community, and everywhere else that's appropriate, discuss loneliness in an open and honest way. Don't feel as though you need to shy away from the topic because it might be an upsetting and stigmatized issue. Talking about loneliness will enable those who feel lonely to articulate how they feel and to ask for the help they need. Everyone can do their bit here, but it's particularly important for professionals such as health and social care professionals, teachers, and volunteers to discuss loneliness and normalize it as an issue.

Discussing loneliness in the third person

Initially, when broaching the topic for the first time, it can be helpful to talk about loneliness in the third person. For example, if someone asks you about loneliness and you don't want to admit that you feel lonely, you can talk about your experiences as though they relate to someone else. Likewise, if you're a service provider, it can be helpful to ask people if they know anyone who's been lonely, how it made them feel, and if they know why they were lonely. That way people don't have to admit feeling loneliness themselves if they don't want to. This doesn't mean you should shy away from admitting that you're lonely, but talking about other people's experiences first can ease your way into the discussions.

Using sensitive and inclusive terminology

Although it's important to bring loneliness into everyday vocabulary, it's also important to frame the discussions in a sensitive and inclusive way. Take care to use appropriate language when discussing loneliness, and particularly when developing interventions, loneliness services, and associated marketing materials. When discussing loneliness for the first time, it can be helpful to use alternative language and frame discussions in a more positive way. For example, you might ask someone if they have sufficient companionship, if they ever feel as though they'd like more friends, or if they'd like to feel a greater sense of connection and belonging. If you're helping others open up, you can articulate your experiences of loneliness first; that way they're more likely to feel comfortable discussing their own experiences. Also, remember that certain words and phrases have different meanings in different cultures.

Being nonjudgmental

When opening up about loneliness and listening to experiences of others, avoid being judgmental both in terms of the language you use and in your body language and gestures. Everyone experiences loneliness at times and responds to it in different ways. There's no right or wrong way to deal with loneliness.

Avoiding assumptions

You might make assumptions about what other people do and don't want to talk about based on our own perceptions and stereotypes. A few years ago I was working with a local Non-governmental organization (NGO) that asked people in the local area about their loneliness. I carefully designed some questions to explore the issue, but some of the staff were reluctant to ask the questions because they assumed people wouldn't want to talk about the topic. The reality was that they didn't mind discussing loneliness, and many actually wanted to discuss it.

Contacting helplines

It can be difficult to talk to people you know about your loneliness. You might be embarrassed, you might feel they won't understand, or you might not want to bother friends and family. In these cases, you can call one of the many dedicated loneliness helplines and explain how you feel. The more you talk about your loneliness, the better. These helplines are usually anonymous and give you an opportunity to discuss your loneliness openly without fear of judgment. You're likely to feel a lot better once you've had that initial conversation. Indeed, callers to helplines report that after the call they feel less lonely, more confident, safe, and that someone cares about them. You can get advice on what support is available, and you might find that having opened up about loneliness once, you're more ready to discuss it with others. See the Appendix for some suggestions.

Raising awareness

To help people talk about and normalize loneliness, a number of campaigns are geared specifically to raising awareness about the issue. The campaigns seek to change the narrative around loneliness and normalize it so that lonely feelings can be legitimized without any blame being attached. Many of the campaigns are helpful if you're feeling lonely because they can connect you with other lonely people and services that can support you. If you're not lonely right now, you can play your part by getting involved and showing support. With everyone working together to raise awareness, the stigma of loneliness can be reduced. People will be able to discuss it freely and openly and feel comfortable asking for support and help when needed.

You can find some of the main loneliness awareness campaigns across the globe in the Appendix.

Preparing for Life Transitions

Although loneliness can strike at any time and hit when you least expect it, sometimes you can anticipate that you might feel lonely. Periods when you're more susceptible and at risk of loneliness tend to arise when you encounter a life transition, such as losing a loved one, becoming or ceasing to become a caregiver, moving, changing jobs, or starting a new school.

I provide more details about these and other life transitions and how you can deal with the loneliness that can emerge then in Part 3, in Chapters 8, 9, 10, 11, and 12. That isn't to say that you'll necessarily feel lonely during these periods or that you should worry in advance that you might be lonely. But if you do have advance knowledge that a transition point is looming on the horizon, you can take some time to plan ahead. That way you'll be more resilient to loneliness if it does strike. The more armored you are, the better!

TIP

The following sections have suggestions for building your resilience to loneliness. You'll find these particularly useful for dealing with any loneliness that might emerge during life transition points. When you adopt these strategies, you limit the transient loneliness you might feel during these times of change so that your loneliness doesn't become chronic. Chronic loneliness can lead to both physical and mental health conditions (see Chapters 9 and 10).

Embracing change

REMEMBER

If you know that a life transition point is looming, spend some time preparing for it emotionally and trying to embrace the change. If it's a change that was thrust upon you or one you didn't want, such as a layoff, health condition, separation, or divorce, it can be a little more challenging to embrace, but by doing so you'll come out of the transition stronger than ever. By embracing change, you become more resilient and better equipped to deal not only with this particular change, but with any challenges that life throws at you. Focus on utilizing the change as an opportunity to make new connections and undertake new meaningful activities.

TIP

One way to embrace change is to encourage yourself to acknowledge that change is happening. Instead of focusing on the negatives, explore the positives of the change too. Make a list of all the positive aspects, even if you can think of only one. The voice in your head might try to ignore these rational written positive statements and keep reminding you of the negatives. Change is hard, and the temptation to resist it is easy. If this happens, recognize the voice and reassure yourself that everything will be okay. Remain open-minded and embrace the new life ahead of you, whatever that entails.

Planning for change

REMEMBER

As soon as you're aware that a change is about to occur or has occurred and that it might trigger transient loneliness, get your planning head in gear. Don't just sit there with your head in your hands. Take control of the situation and plan for a transition so that you can create the best possible outcome for yourself.

TIP

Grab a pen and paper, open your laptop to a word processing application, or go to the notes pages on your smart phone and write down your answers to the following questions:

1. What issues might you face following this change?

2. Do any of these have the potential to make you feel lonely?

3. How can you respond positively to the change?

4. What techniques or strategies have you used before that you can apply to this situation?

5. What actions can you take to avoid loneliness, and in which order should you take them?

Once you've done this exercise, write down a plan of action you'll take, the order in which you'll undertake it, and why you think it's important. Then give yourself some deadlines for implementing each of the action points because that will help ensure that you achieve them.

Establishing goals

REMEMBER

The planning process that I mentioned before will help you manage the change. But once you have a plan in process for dealing with this life transition point, it's helpful to establish some goals for the future. It doesn't matter how challenging or insurmountable the life change is. You can always do or achieve something that will bring you some comfort and joy and reduce your feelings of loneliness.

A colleague whom I was very fortunate to work with a few years ago was working for Age UK when he was diagnosed with Motor Neurone Disease. Phil's ability to undertake everyday life activities was severely affected. His ability to talk and walk soon deteriorated, but he set and achieved massive goals. He achieved two Guinness World Records and wrote two books. Even when his movements were reduced to blinking, he undertook blinkathons, raising money and awareness for charity in the process.

TIP

Go for a short walk in the open air, preferably in a green space. As soon as you return, write down at least one goal you'll aim to achieve. It doesn't matter how big or how small your goal is or how restricted your goal might be at the moment. Just write the goal on a small card and place it somewhere in the house where you'll see it regularly, such as on the fridge, on the bathroom mirror, or on the inside of the external door so you can see it each time you leave the house. If you want, you can place multiple cards around the house in prominent positions. The goal you set is up to you. It can be anything you want.

Remaining optimistic

REMEMBER

When you face challenges, it can be easy to become pessimistic and to view life changes negatively. Even when you choose the change yourself, such as deciding to get a new job or going away to study, you can feel apprehensive about the change and experience loneliness. Embarking upon a major life transition can feel lonely, but if you prepare as I've mentioned previously and set out with a determined optimistic outlook, you're much more likely to get through any periods of loneliness unscathed. Optimism is a mindset you can develop that enables you to understand and focus on the positive aspects of situations.

Remaining optimistic requires you to engage in positive thinking. This doesn't mean that you're ignoring the issue. It means that you accept the change, acknowledge that you might feel lonely, and understand that the loneliness and any other challenge is only temporary and that you have the skills and abilities to overcome the challenges you face.

TIP

You can engage in positive thinking in a number of ways. One technique you can try is keeping a gratitude journal or diary. Get a book or diary and write in it every day the things you're grateful for. It's often a good idea to do this before you go to bed. The things you express gratitude for can be large or small, simple or complex. They might include things like being grateful for a nice view out your bedroom window, a sunny day, a walk in the park, or a phone call or a text from a friend or loved one. Recognizing the things you're grateful for on a regular basis can help you focus on the positive aspects of your life, regardless of the changes occurring around you. This will help you develop a more optimistic perspective if transient loneliness strikes and make you more resilient to its impact.

Acknowledging your skills and abilities

REMEMBER

It's common to suffer a crisis in confidence from time to time. Some suffer with that more often than others. At times of transition, it can be easy to focus on the difficulties and challenges without acknowledging that you have the skills and abilities to deal with and overcome them. Having confidence in your own ability to meet new people, form new relationships, connect to new work colleagues or fellow students, and find meaningful activities to carry out can play an important part in your resilience to loneliness.

TIP

If you're finding that your life change is making you feel lonely or you anticipate that it might and you find yourself worrying that you don't have the skills or abilities to overcome the loneliness, acknowledge how you're feeling and then take action. Listen to any negative thoughts in your head. As soon as you hear them, replace them with positive thoughts, such as, "I can do this," "I'm a great friend," or "I'm good at my job." For example, if you're a young person who has left home for the first time to go to college and you're worried that you won't be able to make any new friends and will feel lonely, tell yourself that you *can* make friends. Think of times you've made friends in the past and tell yourself that if you've done it before, you can do it again. If you're really struggling with your confidence and believe you don't have the skills to overcome loneliness, turn to Chapter 13, which has a whole range of techniques and therapies you can explore.

Developing new skills

Resilience skills can take time to develop, but once you've mastered them, they'll be useful not only if you experience loneliness, but for any challenges that life throws at you. Follow the suggestions I've provided in this section, and keep working at your skill base. No matter how much you know or how many skills you have, my motto is that you can always learn more. Don't become discouraged if you've had difficulties with some skills or aspects of life. The resilience approach varies from person to person. Some skills will be easier than others. But everyone can learn to be resilient, and resilience doesn't involve any specific set of behaviors or actions.

TIP

Build on your existing strengths, and remind yourself continuously of them. If you have certain skills you feel less confident in or are struggling to come to grips with, identify them and focus on developing these skills in the coming weeks and months. These might be skills you can gain by attending a class or group. You can also search for tips online, such as through YouTube. Further, you can ask people you know, or you can get help through support groups either face to face or online. By developing your range of skills, you'll be better prepared to cope if and when loneliness emerges.

Finding a sense of purpose

Throughout this book I've discussed the important role that having a sense of purpose and engaging in meaningful activities plays in your feelings of loneliness. To ensure that you're resilient to changes that can trigger loneliness, having a sense of purpose, or activities that you engage in, can be a big help. For some, having a sense of purpose comes almost naturally. They might be committed to a particular cause, such as climate change, equality, or social justice. At turbulent times this sense of purpose gives their life meaning, and they can return to it to keep them busy and connect them to other people. However, for others a sense of purpose doesn't feature so easily or prominently in their lives. They may need to work on it.

TIP

If you have a clearly defined sense of purpose, focus your attention on meaningful activities associated with maintaining and achieving it when you're going through a transition. This will ensure continuity among the other changes that are occurring and keep loneliness at bay. If you can't easily identify a sense of purpose, sit in a quiet room and have a brainstorming session. Write down or type onto an electronic device anything you find especially important. It could be creating art, making music, helping people in your community, promoting a specific political view, playing a sport, electronic gaming, eating healthily, following a vegetarian or vegan diet, or following a spiritual or religious practice. Once you've identified a list of potentials, select one and think about how you can get more involved in progressing it. Having such a sense of purpose will help you better deal with loneliness if it emerges.

Developing a strong social network

Developing a strong social network of family and friends you can confide in can be helpful when you encounter these life transition points. You don't necessarily need to have a massive group of people you can call on, but it can help to have a few people you have a meaningful relationship with. Having caring, supportive people around you can act as a kind of protective factor during times of change and uncertainty.

TIP

Map out your social network by carrying out the activity in Chapter 14. This will help you identify friends, family members, and work colleagues whom you can call on for certain types of advice and support. You can call on different people for different things; no one person will necessarily offer you everything you need. If, after completing the activity in Chapter 14, you feel that your social network needs strengthening, try some of the tips and suggestions later in that chapter, which will help you create and maintain a wider social network. Even if you're not currently lonely, it's worth spending time developing your social network and investing some time and energy into nurturing it so that if loneliness strikes, you can quickly eliminate it.

Accepting and nurturing yourself

Elsewhere in this book I discuss the role that your self-perception has on feelings of loneliness. I explain that a positive self-perception and acceptance of who you are can combat your feelings of loneliness. It's worth practicing the art of accepting and nurturing yourself when you're not necessarily feeling lonely so that if loneliness does strike, particularly at a time of transition or change, you can have that inner confidence to protect you from the more damaging consequences of loneliness.

TIP

Make nurturing yourself and practicing self-compassion a regular habit. It's fine to help others, but don't neglect your own needs. Make sure that you eat well, get enough sleep, engage in regular exercise, and carry out activities you enjoy. These important acts of self-compassion will help you be better able to deal with any major changes in your life. If you find that accepting yourself or feeling comfortable with yourself and your identity are particular issues you need to address, turn to Chapter 13, which has a whole range of techniques and strategies you can try. Many can be done on your own, but some require support from a qualified therapist. The important takeaway is that if you can address these issues of self-acceptance and self-compassion on a regular basis, if and when you face a life transition point you can be more resilient to any loneliness that might emerge.

Finding a sense of belonging

In Chapter 15 I discuss the role that having a sense of belonging to place can play in your experience of loneliness and in your ability to beat loneliness. Developing a strong sense of belonging to places and spaces in your community, neighborhood, or city can certainly act as another protective layer in your armor against loneliness. It can be particularly helpful if you encounter a life transition loneliness trigger.

TIP

You can develop a sense of belonging to places and spaces ranging from your workplace, place of worship, or favorite sporting stadium to a local park, beach, mountain, trail, or riverside walk. During times of transition, it can be helpful to spend time in the places and spaces where you have a sense of belonging. They can steer your feelings of loneliness away.

Being Loneliness-Ready

A recurring theme throughout this book is that loneliness is a natural part of being human. Although it's an unpleasant feeling, it's nothing to worry about in the short term. It's simply a trigger to seek more social connections. However, if and when loneliness strikes, it's good to be prepared. I identify four main ways you can make yourself loneliness-ready. Implement each of these to ensure that you can mediate any adverse implications of loneliness and get rid of your feelings as quickly as they emerge.

Changing the narrative

When something bad happens, the temptation is to go over and over it in your mind. It's easy to see the past with rose-tinted glasses, imagining it was better and happier than it really was. And when you think about the future, you might imagine it to be negative, dark, and gloomy. When something happens in your life to make you feel lonely, you contemplate the hurt and discomfort. At times it can feel like you're stuck on a hamster wheel you're unable to get off of. Unpleasant thoughts can whirl around and around in your head. Although this process is a natural part of feeling lonely, it can prevent you from moving on, and your loneliness can spiral out of control.

TIP

If you're feeling lonely and everything around you seems negative and gloomy, the first thing to do is change the narrative. One way to do this is to write down your feelings about your loneliness continuously for 20 minutes. Express in writing your deepest thoughts and feelings about feeling lonely. Repeat this exercise for four or five consecutive days. By doing this you're forced to confront your fears, which can trigger you to view your feelings with a new perspective. Once you've done this, for the next three or four weeks, on a daily basis, write down up to five positive things about the situation you currently find yourself in. Read the positive things out loud before you go to sleep each night and again when you wake up. If you can, keep this practice going all your life, when you're lonely and when you're not. The more you practice writing and repeating positive messages, the more resilient you'll become to loneliness. It will also have a positive impact on other aspects of your life. To supplement this, search for positive quotes you like, and write down or print a few of them to stick around the house. You might put them inside cabinets when you open doors, in the bathroom, or on your bedside table. When you come across these positive quotes, repeat them to yourself or say them out loud.

Facing your fears

Writing down and repeating the positive side of loneliness is one thing, but overcoming your current loneliness requires you to take action. Taking action can feel scary and require courage, and you may not feel like you have much courage at the moment. For example, if you've recently separated from your partner, you might be feeling lonely. You might think that going on a date will help, but that can feel scary. The phrase "Feel the fear and do it anyway" is required here.

TIP

Whether it's fear of meeting new people, dating, joining a new group, or going somewhere on your own, "feeling the fear and doing it anyway" helps you change the negative associations you have with a particular stimulus. If you want to attend a local book group at your library but are worried about entering the building alone, feel the fear and do it anyway. The more you go to the book club, the more you'll realize that nothing bad is going to happen to you, and you'll have greater courage to keep attending.

Practicing self-compassion

Practicing self-care and self-compassion is something you should do on a regular basis. It can be particularly helpful if you feel overwhelmed by thoughts of feeling lonely or the distress, anxiety, and depression that might accompany it.

TIP

To practice self-compassion, first recognize how you feel. Notice what you're feeling and say to yourself, "I notice that I'm feeling particularly lonely today." Don't make any judgments on why or how you feel like this. Next, remember that you're not alone in your feelings. Everyone experiences loneliness. Tell yourself, "I'm not alone; this is part of life. Everyone feels lonely from time to time. I just need to find other people or places to connect to." Once you've done this, focus on being kind to yourself. Put your hands on your heart and say, "I accept myself as I am."

Living in the present moment

Quite often the painful or unpleasant thoughts about loneliness relate to either the past or the future. You might regret and dwell on things that made you feel lonely or decisions that resulted in loneliness, or you might worry about what might happen in the future. For example, you might worry about what will happen if you go somewhere on your own, meet new people, or try a new activity. You may start creating negative future scenarios, such as these:

>> What will I do if I get there and they all look at me?

>> What if I don't have anything in common with them?

>> What if I don't know what to say?

The best way to deal with these unpleasant thoughts is to remain in the present moment. When you do that, you usually feel much better.

TIP

One way to be in the present moment is to practice mindfulness. This brings you into the present moment and helps you deal with any negative emotions. To do that you can try doing a short meditation exercise once a day. Try scheduling a time that you'll do this each day, and stick to it. The more you practice mindfulness, the more effective it is. Start by sitting in a warm room. Make yourself comfortable. Focus first on mindful breathing. Breathe in through your nostrils for a count of five and out through your mouth for a count of eight. Bring your attention to your breathing. Notice how your stomach rises and falls. If your mind wanders away from your breathing, bring your attention back to your breathing. For more information on mediation and mindfulness, see Chapter 13.

5

The Part of Tens

Chapter **17**

Ten Tips to Break Out of Loneliness

L oneliness is a natural part of being human. However, because it creates a series of negative feelings that are generally unpleasant, it's an unwanted emotion that people try to avoid.

If loneliness becomes *chronic* — that is, if you are feeling lonely often or always, and if it's been like this for months or years — it can also lead to a range of both physical and mental health conditions. It's logical, then, to want to avoid loneliness, and when it does surface, to try to dispel it as soon as possible. Taking action to prevent loneliness from emerging, and if it does appear, stopping it from hanging around for too long, generally revolves around developing meaningful relationships with other people, with places and spaces, and with yourself.

You can break out of loneliness by working on one or each of these three angles. Attacking it from all three sides is recommended if your loneliness is particularly severe, is affecting your health and well-being, or has been around for some time.

Recognizing and Accepting Loneliness

REMEMBER

None one wants to feel lonely, but acknowledging loneliness when it does emerge, and understanding its purpose, is the first step to beating it. When you feel lonely, just remember that it's a trigger reminding you to make more connections. It's the same as feeling hungry or thirsty; both are unpleasant, but unless there are severe food shortages or you're in the desert without water supplies, you just recognize it as a sign to get food or drink.

TIP

View loneliness the same way. Recognize that you feel lonely, remind yourself that it's a signal to make more meaningful connections, and make a plan to develop those connections. The connections can be with other people, with places that give you a sense of belonging, and with yourself.

Preparing for Life's Transition Points

REMEMBER

Undergoing a change or transition point can trigger loneliness. Transition points can include starting school, moving away to college, becoming a parent, watching your children leave home, becoming a caregiver, ceasing to become a caregiver, starting a new job, retiring, losing someone, and more. It's impossible to eliminate these life transition points and the temporary loneliness that can accompany them. But you can be prepared for the transitions if and when they occur, recognize that any loneliness is likely to be temporary, and equip yourself with skills and knowledge to make positive connections to yourself, to other people, and to places that have meaning to you during these times.

TIP

If you notice that one of these life transition events is on the horizon, prepare for the change and put measures in places to tackle any loneliness that might emerge. If a change is suddenly thrust upon you, start planning a way to deal with it as soon as you can. You can achieve this by developing resilience skills that enable you to fend off loneliness, ensuring that it remains a temporary experience and doesn't become chronic. This involves accepting and embracing the change and creating a plan for it that encompasses creating relationships with others, feeling positive about yourself, and connecting to places where you feel a sense of belonging.

Building Your Social Network

REMEMBER

When you feel lonely, you might say to yourself, "If only I had someone to talk to" or "If only I had someone to go out with." However, developing a social network of friends and family that you have a meaningful relationship with requires some effort. It takes work to build a relationship in the first place, and once developed it continues to change. People enter and leave your life over time, so you need to respond to those changes and adapt your social network accordingly. This comes more naturally to some than others. Some find it easy to make social connections, and some don't. Likewise, some need only a small number of close friends and family to feel good, whereas others need a lot of people around them.

Regardless of whether social connections are easy or challenging for you, make a concerted effort to build meaningful relationships with both family and friends. Try not to rely on just one person to fulfill all your social and relationship needs. Even if you're not lonely at the moment, it's a good idea to take stock of your social network and assess whether it needs expanding. Do this periodically, and make adjustments when required.

Once you identify the need to expand your network of meaningful relationships, you can take various steps: Reconnect with people from the past, connect with your neighbors, take advantage of chance encounters with people, and initiate conversations with them. The chance encounters can be with passersby in the street, people at the bus stop, fellow shoppers, those on the train, or people you run into at a café, at work, or at school. Not everyone you meet will be able to connect in a meaningful relationship, so focus your efforts on meeting like-minded people who share your values or interests.

TIP

Try joining social media groups or dating and friendship apps. Attend groups and activities, or frequent places where like-minded people might be.

Connecting to Others through Work

Because people spend such a large portion of their daily lives at work, opportunities for meaningful relationships can emerge there. Using the workplace as a mechanism for developing social connections is a good strategy. Having meaningful relationships with coworkers also helps you avoid workplace loneliness.

Lone working is commonplace for numerous jobs, and since the Covid-19 pandemic, remote working has become much more widespread. Many are working remotely. However, regardless of your working environment, you can deploy techniques to make social connections through your employment.

You can connect with coworkers in various ways. Don't wait for your line manager, employer, or other coworkers to make the first move. If you're working remotely, suggest and initiate regular real-time communication or invite coworkers to lunch, coffee, or drinks. If you work for a large employer, it might have a peer support group, or organized lunchtime sporting or leisure activities, you can join.

Engaging in Meaningful Activities

Getting involved in activities that have meaning to you and that you enjoy is a good way to distract you from your feelings of loneliness, get you out of the house, and meet other like-minded people with whom you might form a meaningful relationship. Such activities can include anything of interest to you, such as DIY, yoga or meditation, dancing, singing, playing a musical instrument, creating with arts and crafts, or knitting. The list is endless.

You might start by returning to a hobby you indulged in for a while or taking up a new hobby you've always wanted to try. Engaging in a hobby alone can alleviate loneliness, but group-based activities are beneficial because they can connect you with other like-minded people in the process. Joining a local group in your neighborhood connects you to your neighbors, and joining one through your place of employment or study connects you to your peers. Watch for posters and advertisements of groups that appeal to you.

Visiting Familiar Places

Spending time in places and spaces that feel familiar to you, where you feel a sense of belonging, can help you tackle your feelings of loneliness in three main ways. First, you can often spend time in these places alone but not feel lonely. The sense of connection you feel means that you can enjoy solitude. Second, familiar places can help you connect to yourself in a more positive way. If you feel comfortable in your surroundings, you're more likely to experience a sense of well-being, feel happy, and be comfortable being you. Third, familiar places can connect you to others who enjoy spending time in similar localities.

Identify the places and spaces where you have a sense of belonging. Assess how you feel when you're there. If you feel comfortable and at home, start visiting those places on a regular basis. The places could range from a local park, to a beach, mountain, forest, or sporting venue. While you're enjoying spending time there in solitude, also take the opportunity to capitalize on chance encounters with others you might eventually form a meaningful relationship with.

Immersing Yourself in Green Spaces

Visiting and spending time in green spaces is known to enhance your well-being, whether you're currently lonely or not. If you're lonely, spending time among the green can reduce your feelings of loneliness. If you're not lonely, green spaces can act as a protection against your future loneliness. If you live in a large city or a built-up urban area, enjoying green spaces doesn't necessarily mean a lengthy trip to the countryside; it can include communal gardens and parks, trails, canal paths, sports fields, or even streets with lots of trees. If you're homebound, looking out onto a tree-lined street or green space can help, as can a few strategically placed houseplants.

TIP

Identify green spaces where you live or work, and spend 20 minutes a day there to ensure that you maximize the benefit it can have on your well-being. If you have a dog, walk somewhere with plenty of green space, which both of you can enjoy. If your time is limited, take a slightly different walking route to work, school, or the shops that involves some green space. Even just walking around your garden can help. And use every opportunity in these green spaces to engage in fleeting encounters with passersby. You never know where such chance encounters can take you.

Getting Active

Physical exercise is a great way to help you feel less lonely. It makes you feel better about yourself and improves your health and well-being. The exercise setting can give you a sense of belonging. It can also act as a vehicle to connect you with other people. The positive thing about exercise is that you can do it alone, but you're often in a group setting, which means you can strike up conversations with other people. In fact, sometimes group settings force you to have a conversation. In the gym, for instance, you may need to ask a fellow gym goer if they're still using a piece of equipment.

TIP

All exercise is beneficial, and most exercise options offer opportunities to engage in chance encounters with others. To maximize your opportunities for engaging in meaningful encounters with others, select group classes. Or if attending alone, make a habit of going to the same venue, on the same day of the week, at the same time. Doing so increases your chances of seeing familiar faces, which will help foster a social connection. Select your favorite form of exercise, and start undertaking it on a regular basis. The options are endless.

Helping Others

Helping others can be a good way to engage in a purposeful activity, connect with others, and feel good about yourself. It gets you out of the house and gives you an opportunity to learn a new skill. It has all the traits of an activity that can reduce your feelings of loneliness.

There are various ways you can help others. Maybe it's offering to tend a neighbor's garden, or shop for an older resident's basic necessities. Or maybe you want to engage in more formal volunteer opportunities like offering your services to a local charity, becoming involved in fundraising or through corporate volunteering opportunities at work. The most important factor in volunteering is engaging in something that's important to you, has meaning to you, and fuels your passion. That way you'll be carrying out a meaningful activity, feel more positive about yourself, and have more chances of meeting like-minded people you can connect with.

Getting Therapeutic Support

Sometimes it's helpful to turn to others to ask for support. If you feel lonely often and your feelings of loneliness have been going on for a few months, it can be beneficial to seek counseling or therapy. This can be particularly useful if you're experiencing chronic loneliness because your loneliness can be accompanied by other symptoms such as depression and anxiety, and you can start to experience a heightened sense of social threat. This can lead you to isolating yourself for fear of rejection, or it might mean that you fear trying to connect to people because you believe they have a negative perception of you. The result can be a downward spiral of loneliness that can lead to further health conditions.

TIP

Various therapies are available if you feel lonely. You can undertake some of them using self-help guides. Others require a qualified therapist. Check out Chapter 13, which details various therapeutic options available, and select one that most suits your requirements.

WARNING

If you decide to get a therapist, ensure that they're qualified for undertaking the technique and have positive reviews and recommendations from others. If in doubt, contact your doctor or medical adviser.

Chapter 18

Eleven Suggestions for Young People

People often assume that loneliness is experienced primarily by older people, but that's not entirely correct. Older people are more susceptible than some other age groups to loneliness, but young adults, particularly those aged 18 to 25, are more likely to feel lonely than any other age group. So, if you're a young person and feel lonely, you're definitely not alone. In fact, loneliness is one of the main things that young people worry about. Loneliness can be particularly difficult as a young person because you're expected to have an active social life, with lots of friends to see, places to visit, and parties to attend. Whilst this might be the situation for some, it's certainly not the case for all young people. Many can be isolated and feel lonely.

You might feel lonely as a young person for a whole range of reasons. You may feel that you have fewer friends and a less active social life than other young people you know or see on social media. You may have moved away from home for the first time to start college, and might miss your family and friends back home. Maybe you started your first proper job and find it a bit overwhelming because you don't know anyone, aren't sure what to say, and are still figuring out how to behave. Perhaps you've just recently moved in with a partner, had your first child, and are encountering lifestyle changes that are triggering feelings of loneliness. Or you might be grappling with issues related to your sexuality, sexual orientation, or gender identity that are leading you to question your relationship with other people and with yourself. Whatever your reason for loneliness, note that it's a natural part of life that's usually only temporary. Loneliness is unpleasant, but you can do something about it by making more social connections.

Prioritizing Face-to-Face Contact

In contemporary society, many contacts with other people occur electronically via text messages on smart phones, through social media messenger services, by email, and through video chats. Virtual contact has been on the rise for a number of years but escalated somewhat with the Covid-19 pandemic. Maybe you're taking college classes online, working remotely, or gaming with friends but by yourself and from the comfort of your own bedroom.

Electronic contact is helpful to keep you connected, especially if you're young, but it's also important to include some face-to-face contact in your everyday life. Face-to-face contact enables you to develop and maintain meaningful relationships with people, and it's these high-quality relationships that can prevent or reduce your loneliness.

TIP

Make an effort to suggest and partake in face-to-face contact when possible. If you're in college and classes are available online as well as in person, select the latter. Likewise, if you have an option to work onsite or at home, ensure that you select the former. That way you can get to know your coworkers better.

Face-to-face contact may require more time, travel, and expense, but the additional benefits you get from it are worth it. Discussions often take place after and alongside formal online lectures and meetings, and you'll miss those if you're not there in person. These informal chats can lead to social outings, such as trips to grab a coffee or go out for drinks.

Attending educational and workplace settings also facilitates the development of a sense of belonging to place, which can alleviate feelings of loneliness. And remember that you can gain health and well-being benefits enroute. Walking involves physical activity, which improves your well-being, and both walking and traveling on public transport offer opportunities for chance encounters with people, which can lead to conversations and meaningful connections.

Joining a Sports Group

REMEMBER

If you're an athletic type, you can benefit from joining a sports group. A sports group can help you keep fit, improve your physical activity levels, and release endorphins that make you feel happier and give you a greater sense of well-being. Whether you're joining a team sport, a group activity, or participating in an individual sport, you can attend alone and not feel left out. Because everyone there is focusing on their sport, you have an opportunity to meet like-minded people and talk to them about something you already have in common.

TIP

You can join a sports group in your local community, through a local sports or community center, through your college or university, or through work. Colleges often have a whole variety of groups and societies you can join. They're an excellent way of making connections with other like-minded people, and they provide meaningful, enjoyable activities to participate in.

Gaming Interactively

Although face-to-face contact can be a preferred medium for facilitating meaningful relationships, virtual and interactive gaming can be beneficial ways to meet new people or to maintain regular contact with others you live a distance from. Interactive gaming can be particularly helpful if you've moved away to college and want a way to remain connected with your old friends back home or with those who have gone to a different place. Gaming can also distract you from any lonely feelings you have. It can create a sense of purpose as you aim to achieve a specific mission or objective, and celebrate your success. And because it has a competitive element too, it facilitates a sense of achievement that can improve your relationship with yourself.

Whether you're a serious gamer or a novice, think about using gaming as a way not only to beat your opponent(s) but to maintain and strengthen existing relationships and expand your social network. If you usually game alone, try getting involved in interactive gaming. Use the opportunity to discuss gaming and other topics through the game communication channels. There are a range of games to suit all tastes and preferences. They're not all about killing your opponent, although you can do that too!

Connecting with Technology

If you can't meet face-to-face, text messages, voice messages, video calls, and phone calls are a useful way of keeping connected with friends and family. Connecting electronically in this way can ensure that you don't lose people from your social network. Don't forget that connecting with older friends and family members electronically can also be effective. Some may require your assistance to use the technology, but this in itself can form a useful point of connection between you.

TIP

To make these electronic connections meaningful, try introducing deeper conversations in your texts or messages. Sharing emotions, personal experiences, and ideas can give more weight to your conversations and can increase your chances of creating or sustaining a meaningful relationship.

Using Social Media Cautiously

If you feel lonely, social media can be an excellent medium to use. It can connect you virtually to people all over the world and keep you up-to-date on those in your social network: what they eat, where they go on vacation, if they visit the doctor, what time they go to bed, if they've slept at night, and a whole range of other things. You can find all this out without talking to them directly or having any face-to-face interaction. However, the negative side of social media usage is that young people can gain unrealistic perceptions of others who appear, through their posts, to have happy and active social lives and many social connections. Comparing your situation to your peers in this way can then exacerbate your loneliness. Social media usage also detracts from face-to-face contact, which is important to foster and sustain meaningful relationships and fight against loneliness.

TIP

Use social media, but use it cautiously. Limit the daily time you spend on social media to 30 minutes, and avoid comparing yourself to others if you can. After all, people only post on social media what they want you to see and read. Use social media in a positive way to reach out to a range of social contacts. It can connect you to people you no longer see, face-to-face, on a regular basis, such as old school buddies. The interest groups on many social media platforms can bring you in contact with like-minded people.

Connecting Through Apps

Making friends is a sure way to combat feelings of loneliness. Although young people today arguably spend more time alone than they did in the past, it's easier now than ever before to make instantaneous social connections. Friendship apps are becoming increasingly popular ways to develop platonic relationships and widen your social network.

TIP

One way to find new like-minded people to connect with, who are matched to your interests and preferences, is through friendship apps. Search through the growing number of friendship apps on the market, and select an app that's appropriate for you. You can find apps designed for all types of personalities, identities, and interests.

Listening to Music

Music is a good distraction because it can disguise the quietness that often accompanies loneliness. It can boost your mood, give you a sense of well-being, and make you feel less lonely. Listening to music you love can help you enjoy solitude.

Listen to your favorite tunes or preferred radio station to get an instant boost to your mood. This can be particularly helpful if loneliness is making you feel anxious and depressed, and you've started to isolate yourself from others. Listening to music can give you the energy and motivation to start engaging in social contact again.

WARNING

Select your music carefully. Some music and lyrics can trigger feelings of loneliness, which can actually make you feel worse.

Getting a Part-Time Job

If you're still in eductaion and are feeling lonely, consider getting a part-time job. Participating in paid employment can enable you to carry out meaningful activities and bring you in contact with other people. It can also earn you some money that you can spend on buying the perfect outfit for your active social life!

TIP

Pay a visit to your college career center and explore the current job vacancies. Alternatively, look at ads in the local paper or pop into your local shops, bars, and restaurants with your resume and ask if they're hiring. Once you've settled into your new role, make a concerted effort to get to know your coworkers and join in any after-hours social gatherings.

Becoming a Befriender

It's easy to assume that you need to make connections with people of your own age to avoid becoming lonely or to reduce your feelings of loneliness. But intergenerational connections can also provide meaningful relationships that can fend off loneliness. If you're a young person, try offering your services as a befriender to make intergenerational connections. A *befriender* is someone who volunteers to support another person by offering friendship and support.

TIP

Look for befriending opportunities in your local community. One option is to become a befriender for an older person. You can meet up with them on a regular basis for a cup of coffee or tea or accompany them to the store, library, or a doctor's appointment. You'll benefit by helping someone else, which will in turn give you a sense of purpose and boost your self-esteem. This person can become someone whose company you truly enjoy.

Letting People In

Because it's often assumed that young people aren't lonely, it can be difficult to admit to yourself and to others that you're feeling lonely. However, talking about your feelings and opening up about how loneliness is affecting your life is an important rung on the ladder. Sometimes expressing your feelings and emotions is sufficient to make you feel better. By talking to others, you'll undoubtedly realize that loneliness is quite common. Others who have experienced loneliness will be able to share their experience and offer you some sound advice.

TIP

Open up about how you're feeling to someone you feel comfortable talking to and can trust. This might be a parent, older sibling, grandparent, professor, lecturer, doctor, or counselor. If you prefer to remain anonymous, you can contact various helplines.

Spending Time Where You Belong

Spending time in places and spaces where you feel a sense of belonging can help you feel less lonely. When you're there, you feel comfortable with yourself, regardless of whether other people are present to connect with you.

TIP

Identify the places and spaces where you feel a sense of belonging and visit them regularly — in person if possible, but virtually if not. Places that derive a sense of belonging to you could be a town or city, or a place in nature such as a park or beach. But other places and spaces can also give you a sense of belonging such as your school, your workplace, your bedroom, a club, a bar, a community venue, or a space such as a skate park, sporting venue, sports field, or festival site.

Chapter 19

Ten Pointers for Men

All types and ages of men feel lonely from time to time, whether they're high-flying executives, successful sportsmen, rockstars, young men who are still in college, older men who are retired, heterosexual men, or gay men. The statistics show that men aren't as lonely as women, but that statistic isn't necessarily clear cut. Loneliness among men is largely hidden. Men don't like to admit even to themselves that they feel lonely. And they definitely don't like to talk about it.

One of the reasons for loneliness among men is that they find it particularly challenging to develop and maintain meaningful relationships with other men. They often find it difficult to express their feelings, demonstrate affection, and show any sign of vulnerability, especially to other men. Society socializes men to believe that these traits are incompatible with the image of what a man should be: strong, powerful, independent, and emotionally detached. Confiding in another man can be seen as a sign of weakness, and some men fear that it would damage their reputation.

Even if men acknowledge and accept that they feel lonely, they're less likely than women to reach out for support. With this in mind, here are some top tips for you if you're a man who feels lonely.

Showing Your Sporting Prowess

Playing sports or doing any kind of physical activity can reduce your feelings of loneliness. Being physically active improves your well-being, gives you a sense of purpose, acts as a distraction from your emotions, and is likely to bring you in contact with others. The good thing about engaging in sports is that you can attend alone. Many people do, and it's easy to strike up a conversation with others while you're there. Before long you'll find yourself chatting away to fellow sports participants and being invited for a well-deserved drink after your physical exertion.

TIP

Select the sport or physical activity you enjoy the most and make a pact with your-self to participate. Getting involved in any sport you enjoy will help you feel good. Maybe it's gentle exercise like going for a walk in the open air or peddling around the neighborhood on your bike. Regardless of your ability, joining a park run on a Saturday morning is a great place to get some exercise and meet other people. These occur in many countries, and you can walk, jog, run, bring your dog, or push kids in a stroller. Another good option is to join a gym. You can often join with a day membership if you don't want to commit to a monthly fee. Try golf or a team sport like football. There are many options for older men too, such as pick-leball, or walking football.

Becoming a Sports Spectator

If you're not the physically active type and prefer to watch others get sweaty, spectator sports are another great way to help you feel more connected. Attending sporting events enables you to switch your thoughts from loneliness to cheering on your team or sporting hero. It's easy to attend a sporting event on your own because once you get there, everyone is engrossed in watching the sport. At the same time, you can find yourself engaging in conversations about the quality of the performance or the result with people you've never met before. If you support your team regularly, you might find yourself gaining a sense of identity and belonging to the club, team, or sporting venue, which can alleviate feelings of loneliness. Team sports that are locality based are perhaps the best way to gain a sense of belonging.

TIP

Identify which sport you enjoy watching the most and support your local team. If you're not sure what you'd enjoy, try out a range of different sports and clubs to see what works. Wear the club colors so you feel a greater sense of connection to fellow fans and the club. Engross yourself in the performance of the team, and when opportunities allow, strike up a conversation with a fellow fan about the team's performance. If this helps, return another day, and make sure you get a ticket for a similar part of the stadium so that you're likely to encounter the same group of spectators. Within no time you'll be the best of buddies.

Offering your Expertise and Skills

Volunteering is a good way to share your skills and expertise with others while helping you feel more connected. It enables you to spend time out of the house engaging in meaningful activities while helping others, making a difference, and meeting new people in the process.

TIP

To get the most benefit from volunteering opportunities, find an activity or task that you care about, and do it on a regular basis. Many options are available. You could get involved in a local grassroots sports team, join the board of a local community organization, or take advantage of corporate volunteering opportunities through your employer.

Connecting Through Work

As an adult, you spend most of your time at work, so it's an ideal venue to develop meaningful relationships. Building these connections during the workday can help with workplace loneliness. Also, by getting to know your work colleagues better, you can form friendships outside of work.

TIP

Make the most of your social connections at work. Suggest getting together with your colleagues for lunch or drinks, or organize an online chat and coffee break. If you're asked to meet up socially, jump at the chance to get to know your coworkers in a nonwork context. If you're employed by a large company, join any work-based groups and associations to find like-minded people.

Setting Yourself a Challenge

Setting yourself a goal or a challenge can be just the trick to distract you from your loneliness. You can enjoy the greater self-esteem and confidence that reaching your goal brings, which can improve the way you perceive yourself. If your challenge is for a charity, you can enjoy the feeling of supporting a good cause at the same time.

Select a challenge, prepare a plan, and set a timescale for achieving this challenge. Options can include running a marathon, rock climbing, ziplining, bungee jumping, skydiving, or something equally challenging, like abstaining from alcohol or sugar for a month.

Going Outdoors

Most of your time is probably spent at home or at work, and it can feel monotonous and lonely frequenting the same spaces and places even if you're with other people. Getting outdoors, particularly to green spaces, can be a great antidote. It can connect you to nature, improve your sense of well-being, and be a good way to engage in chance encounters with other people.

TIP

Set yourself a target of leaving the house or workplace on a daily basis. Identify an outdoor place that you enjoy being in, and spend time there. This could be anything from a local playing field to a riverbank or forest. If you have a dog, combine your daily dog walk with a visit to a green space you enjoy and feel a sense of belonging to. Connecting to outdoor places that have meaning to you can diminish your feelings of loneliness, at least while you're there.

Gaming

Interactive electronic gaming can enable you to connect to other people you may or may not know while competing against or with them in a gaming experience. It's a great way to harness your competitive spirit, have some lighthearted fun, meet and interact with other people, and escape your loneliness for a while.

TIP

Select your preferred way to engage in gaming, whether it's a game console, tablet, laptop, or smart phone. Once you've done that, choose from the array of games on the market. You might want to select a sports-based game such as football, golf, or skiing; an action-packed game where you're required to kill your opposition before they eliminate you; or a strategy or more sedate puzzle game. Select multiplayer platforms so you can connect with others, and use any community forums to have conversations beyond the gaming experience.

Building and Creating

Many men enjoy building and making things. Use your construction and problem-solving skills for creative purposes to divert your mind from feeling lonely. Your completed creation can give you a sense of purpose and fulfillment.

TIP

If you're already a keen DIY participant, instead of engaging in the activity alone, why not join one of the many groups that bring men together to connect and create?

Talking to Other Men

Whoever you are, if you feel lonely, it's important to open up to others. Loneliness isn't always easy to talk about. You might feel that if you're lonely, you're a failure and it's your own fault. These feelings can feel particularly strong for men, but they're not true. Many men don't like to talk about their feelings or admit that they need help, but opening up about your emotions is important. It's okay to talk. Just telling somebody that you feel lonely can be enough to set you on the path to recognizing and accepting your feelings and taking action to deal with them.

TIP

Identify somebody you feel you can trust, and tell them how you feel. It could be a friend, a family member, or a work colleague. If you don't feel quite ready for that kind of discussion with people you know, it might be easier to talk to strangers in similar positions. You can do this anonymously through helplines, or you can join a support group specifically targeted at men. If you want a less organized forum for opening up, pop into your local bar, where it's quite easy to strike up a conversation with other men. You might start by chatting about the price of beer, but if you keep returning regularly, you'll strike up conversations about an assortment of issues. No doubt you'll find that other men are feeling lonely too.

Accessing Social Prescribing

Social prescribing is growing in popularity in many countries. It is used by a range of health care professionals, including doctors. They can provide a nonmedical referral for you so that you can access services provided in the community, often by voluntary organizations. You can also refer yourself to this kind of support. The services cover a range of issues and are targeted at different groups, including men who feel lonely.

TIP

If you feel lonely and it's starting to affect your physical or your mental health and you're not quite sure what kind of support you need, schedule an appointment with your doctor or medical practitioner and ask them to refer you to a local service. If social prescribing is available where you live you could be referred to a range of loneliness services. This could include physical exercise classes, gardening or DIY activities, or even respite care for a loved one. Engaging in such activities will give you a sense of purpose, a meaningful activity to engage in, and opportunities to meet other people who are dealing with similar issues.

IN THIS CHAPTER

» **Exploring alternatives to human company**

» **Looking at intergenerational connections**

» **Using your life skills**

» **Going places**

Chapter **20**

Ten Tactics for Later Life

lthough loneliness can hit you at any time during your life, as you get older you can be particularly vulnerable to it. This doesn't mean you'll necessarily feel lonely as you get older. In fact, some older people are more connected than ever before, enjoying active social lives. However, if you're 65 and over and find yourself feeling lonely, you're certainly not the only one encountering such feelings.

Loneliness can strike in later life for all kinds of reasons. It's a time when a variety of life transitions start to occur that can disrupt your social networks, your lifestyle, and your health. As you age, your social circle of family and friends can start to diminish as peers pass away and children grow up and move away. Retirement from work can give you more spare time than you're used to. Your spouse can become ill and need you to care for them, which can limit the time and energy you have for social connections. You may be diagnosed with health conditions that can adversely affect your ability to socialize and go out. All this can sound quite grim, but it doesn't need to. Numerous mechanisms of support are available for older people who feel lonely — there are probably more options than there ever have been.

Finding a Surrogate Relationship

A quick and immediate way to halt your feelings of loneliness is to find a substitute to human interaction. This can be a useful strategy to deploy while you're working your way through the other tips that will widen your social connections to both other people and to places. Immediate replacements can include the TV, radio, and music. Not only do they provide an alternative pseudo-social connection, but they offer a mechanism to disguise the silence and distract from any unpleasant feelings that loneliness creates.

Switch on the TV or radio to watch your favorite show or listen to some music. Select TV programs such as soap operas or dramas that can enable you to gain a fictional bond with the characters onscreen, or listen to a radio show that's hosted by a presenter whose virtual company you enjoy. If you want to go one step further, participate in radio phone-ins and quizzes where you can talk directly to the presenter and others. If you feel lonely because you miss spending time in a particular place, identify TV or radio shows that are based in, or centered on, those locations to revive or maintain your sense of belonging.

WARNING

Use surrogate relationships such as those provided through TV and radio as a temporary measure only. They shouldn't replace human interaction on a long-term or a permanent basis.

Getting a Four-Legged Friend

Actually, your pet doesn't have to have four legs. It could have no legs, fins, or wings! Having a pet can supply companionship, offer purposeful and meaningful activities to undertake on a daily basis as you care for your pet, and form a focal point of discussion that can connect you to other people. What's more, owning a pet can be easier post-retirement because you have more time on your hands.

TIP

If you feel that you have the time, commitment, and appropriate living space, welcome a pet into your home. It could be a dog, a cat, a bird, or a fish. A dog is an obvious choice because it can act as a companion and bring you in contact with fellow dog walkers. This can trigger chance encounters and possibilities for the development of meaningful relationships. However, don't write off other options. Hen keeping, for example, can be a particularly helpful strategy to beat loneliness.

Taking Up or Resuming a Hobby

Engaging in a hobby or a meaningful activity can serve as a good antidote to loneliness. It can distract you from your lonely feelings, give you a sense of purpose, idle away a few hours, and bring you in contact with other people.

TIP

Identify a hobby you've enjoyed in the past or a new hobby you've always wanted to do but never had time for, and take the plunge. If you're able to get out of your home, try a hobby you can do elsewhere, ideally in a group environment, so that you can maximize your opportunities of meeting other people. Hobbies that take you outdoors or enable you to engage in physical activity are particularly beneficial because they improve your health and well-being too. If you struggle on your feet or are particularly frail, be sure to look out for chair-based exercise classes. If you're homebound, select an activity you can do at home alone but might also allow you to connect to other people virtually, such as learning a foreign language, singing in an online group, or participating in a virtual choir.

Chatting by Phone and Video

A good way to keep connected to friends and family is to have regular conversations by phone through FaceTime or online through a video call. Video calls are a great way to keep connected to loved ones. Live calls, too, are an excellent way to keep connected to people who live a distance away from you. Hearing the voices of loved ones is perhaps as important in combatting your feelings of loneliness as the content of the conversations. Sometimes just hearing someone's voice or seeing their face is sufficient to improve your mood.

WARNING

Seeing or talking to someone who's a distance away can sometimes make you feel worse, but if you ensure that you have regular contact with the person, those temporary feelings of sadness are likely to be replaced by ones of contentment.

Identify the people within your social network — friends and family members — with whom you can have a phone or video chat and arrange a regular slot when you can talk. That way you'll have something to look forward to, and they'll be able to build the call into their busy schedule.

Intergenerational Bonding

There's often an assumption that if you're older and feeling lonely, you should connect with other older people. However, it's just as valuable, if not more so, to engage in meaningful relationships with younger people. Having conversations with, eating with, or carrying out meaningful activities with people of different ages is hugely beneficial. It can keep you in touch with behaviors and attitudes of the younger generation, enable an exchange of skills and advice, foster positive attitudes relating to age, and diminish age-based stereotypes.

TIP

The easiest and simplest way to engage in intergenerational activities is to have regular contact with your grandchildren, if you have any. If they live close by, arrange to spend time with them, taking turns selecting activities to do together. If they don't live nearby, make your grandkids feel important by asking their advice on how they can connect with you remotely or help with other IT-related tasks that you find challenging. Take them to the movies, to the local park, or bowling. If you don't have younger people you can connect with, consider becoming involved in one of the many intergenerational projects that are offered by local loneliness support services in your community. If you live alone and want some younger companionship as well as a bit of help around the house and with tasks such as shopping, consider renting a room in your house to a younger person or student through an initiative such as Homeshare International, or explore other forms of intergenerational living.

Accessing Support Groups

Numerous support groups are available for older people who are feeling lonely. Voluntary organizations in your local community often run them. They offer a range of services, and accessing their support can enable you to connect with like-minded people, often of a similar age. They also provide opportunities for engaging in group-based meaningful activities as well as advice and individualized services to meet your needs.

TIP

Identify the local services in your area that might be beneficial to you. Look for ones that target older people, people who feel lonely, or people who want to enhance their social connections. The local library or an internet search can help you identify the best services to approach. If you're struggling to find appropriate services, ask your doctor or medical practitioner if they can refer you to a service through social prescribing or another mechanism.

Getting a Befriender

A befriender is someone who volunteers to offer a relationship to another person needing support. Befrienders are available, in some countries, to older people or to those who have specific health conditions. Befriending services are usually provided by voluntary sector service providers who train the befrienders, ensure that they're checked for safeguarding purposes, match befrienders to those in need of support, and monitor the relationship. Joining a befriending service is a great way to form a meaningful relationship quickly. Befrienders can be helpful while you're working on other strategies to develop meaningful relationships with people, and are especially good for people who are homebound because they can visit you at home.

TIP

Depending on where you live, you may be able to access befriending in your local community. Ask about befriender services in your local community support groups or in your local library, or do an internet search. If you have grandkids, draw on their skills to help you find a suitable service; that way you can foster some inter-generational bonding at the same time. Befriending may be available through a social prescribing referral from your doctor, so be sure to ask.

Offering Your Services

As you age, it's easy to overlook that you have a lifetime of knowledge, skills, and expertise that can be helpful to others. Offering your skills to local charities can be a good way to keep your mind active, get you out of the house, fill your time, dis-tract you from feeling lonely, and meet other people — both fellow volunteers and the people you're helping.

TIP

Select a charity whose cause resonates with you or whose values align with yours. That way you'll be more likely to meet like-minded people and feel a stronger sense of purpose and fulfillment. Look for volunteering opportunities where you can use your existing skills. Alternatively, if you'd like to widen your horizons, identify opportunities that enable you to develop new skills. Choose a charity that you can identify with, and you'll find yourself meeting new people, learning new skills, and helping others.

Learning a New Skill

You're never too old to learn, and it's never too late to pick up a new skill. Chal-lenging yourself to learn a new skill can give you a sense of purpose and a sense of achievement, both of which can improve your well-being and help you feel less lonely. This is often reinforced by the social connections you make during the skill-acquiring process. You can form friendships and meaningful bonds with fel-low participants and tutors alike.

TIP

Identify a skill you don't have that you think you should, one that will be practi-cally useful, or perhaps one you don't necessarily need but you've always wanted to develop but didn't have time for before. Join a class or course either in person or online. Watch for ads in the local shops or libraries, or do a search online. Enjoy the challenge of learning the new skill and meeting new people along the way.

Visiting Meaningful Places

Spending time in places that have meaning to you can be a great antidote to loneliness, especially if you don't have family and friends around to connect with. The bond you form to places can create a sense of belonging that keeps you from feeling lonely even if you're there alone. In fact, spending time in these places can actually be enjoyable and stimulate positive feelings of solitude.

TIP

Identify places and spaces where you feel good, where you connect to the place and to yourself. If you're able to, visit these places regularly, and particularly when you feel lonely. If they're too far away or you can't physically get there, visit virtually through the use of technology. Ask younger family members to help if you're unsure of your IT skills, or seek support from a local charity that supports older people. If you're not sure which places you feel a connection to, try visiting various places to find out. They could range from a local park bench or a riverside walk to a beach or a city or country.

Appendix

Further Resources

The following pages are an alphabetical guide to some of the key organizations, initiatives, and services that you might find helpful if you're experiencing loneliness or you're supporting someone who is. This guide has useful resources and support across many of the topics I've covered in the book.

Alcohol and Drug Misuse

Al-Anon (https://al-anon.org/): Find support for family members or friends of those with drinking problems. Alateen is part of Al-Anon and offers help for teens affected by someone else's alcoholism.

Alcoholics Anonymous (https://www.aa.org/): Visit the website to find local service for anyone who has a desire to stop drinking, regardless of race, gender, sexual orientation, religion, income, or profession. AA supports you with all aspects of alcohol addiction, including loneliness.

Alcohol.org: Call 866-203-2825 to discuss your addiction treatment options. You'll find a range of support, including peer groups, help for those living with alcohol addiction, and help for those wanting to assist a loved one with addition problems.

National Substance Abuse and Addiction Hotline (https://drughelpline.org/): Contact them at 1-844-289-0879 or via their website for free help.

SMART Recovery (https://meetings.smartrecovery.org/): This organization assists young people and adults who have alcohol or other addictions through group therapy. Recovery meetings are free, self-empowering, mutual support gatherings focused on addictive behaviors. Trained volunteers organize and facilitate the meetings.

Substance Abuse and Mental Health Services Administration (SAMHSA) (https://www.samhsa.gov/): For the suicide or crisis line, call or text 988. For the national helpline, call 1-800-662-HELP (4357). The disaster distress helpline is 800-985-5990. SAMHSA offers a range of programs and support, including for loneliness, alcohol abuse, and drug use or misuse. The toll-free number is available 24 hours a day, 7 days a week, 365 days a year. All calls are completely confidential and private and can be made without fear of getting in trouble with the law. The website has useful resources if you or someone you know is living with alcohol or drug misuse.

Bereavement

Compassionate Friends (https://www.compassionatefriends.org/): This offers support for families who have experienced the death of a child. You can find online support, private Facebook groups, resource packs, and local assistance.

Mental Health America (https://www.mhanational.org/bereavement-and-grief): This site offers specific guidance on bereavement and grief.

Cancer

America Cancer Society (https://www.cancer.org/): Call the helpline at 800-227-2345. You can find information, day-to-day help, and emotional support, including transportation and accommodation for treatment and a network of survivors.

Cancer Support Community (https://www.cancersupportcommunity.org/). If you have cancer or are a caregiver to someone with has it, you can find support here. Assistance for all ages and all cancer types includes access to an online community, provision of advice from experts, and a number of programs run locally, such as support groups, yoga classes, and educational workshops.

Caregiving

Caregiver Action Network (https://www.caregiveraction.org/resources/agencies-and-organizations). This site has useful advices and resources for caregivers, including a Caregiver Help Desk which offers free support to family caregivers across the country.

NAC – National Alliance for Caregivers (https://www.caregiving.org/). Focuses on translating the lived experience of caregivers into policy and innovation. Has a hub that showcases the stories of caregivers from across the USA. You can read their stories and submit your own.

Children and Young People

Childline International (https://childhelplineinternational.org/): This website has details of ChildLine numbers across the globe, including in certain US states, for specific topics of interest.

Mental Health America (https://www.mhanational.org/youth/young-adults): You'll find some specific support — including peer support — for young adults suffering from mental health issues.

NAMI (National Alliance on Mental Illness) (https://www.nami.org/Your-Journey/Kids-Teens-and-Young-Adults/Young-Adults): Call the helpline at 800-950-6264 or text "Helpline" to 62640. NAMI offers specific resources and information for young adults who have mental health issues.

Counseling and Therapy

Mental Health America (MHA) (https://www.mhanational.org/therapy): Visit this website for information on types of therapy.

Psychology Today (https://www.psychologytoday.com/us/therapists): Visit this website to find a therapist across the United States.

Crime and Safety

Crimestoppers USA (https://www.crimestoppersusa.org/): Call 800-222-TIPS. This is the national Crime Stoppers organization that spans the United States to create a network of local programs that work together to prevent and solve crimes in communities and schools across the nation.

National Neighborhood Watch (https://www.nnw.org/): Visit this website for information on how to join or start a watch group in your area.

Dementia

Alzheimer's Association (https://www.alz.org/): Their 24/7 helpline, 800-272-3900, is available around the clock, 365 days a year. Through this free service, specialists and master's-level clinicians offer confidential support and information to people living with dementia, their caregivers, their families, and the public.

Dementia Friendly America (DFA) (https://www.dfamerica.org/): DFA is a national network of communities, organizations, and individuals seeking to ensure that communities across the US are equipped to support people living with dementia and their caregivers. You can find information on where the dementia-friendly communities are and a useful toolkit on how to set up a new one on the DFA website.

Dementia Society of America (DSA) (https://www.dementiasociety.org/): Telephone 1-800-DEMENTIA (1-800-336-3684); Federal ID:46-3401769. DSA is the nation's leading volunteer-driven dementia awareness organization. It provides a hotline, many online resources, and an easy-to-use, web-based locator that can help families and individuals find valuable support near them.

Domestic Abuse

National Domestic Violence Hotline (https://www.thehotline.org/): Call 800-799-SAFE (7233). Text "START" to 88788, or text STOP to opt out. It offers a 24/7 hotline and online resources, including information on how to plan for safety yourself, help others who are being abused, and access information on other services that might be useful. **If you're in immediate danger, call 911.**

Eating Disorders

F.E.A.S.T (https://www.feast-ed.org/): This has global support and an education community of and for parents of those with eating disorders. Several online resources are offered.

National Eating Disorders Association (NEDA) (https://www.nationaleating disorders.org/about-us/): NEDA is the largest nonprofit organization dedicated to supporting individuals and families affected by eating disorders.

Various helplines are available. For the ANAD helpline, call 888-375-7767. For the National Alliance for Eating Disorders helpline, phone 866-662-1235. And for the Diabulimia helpline, reach out to 425-985-3635. You'll find a number of services and support groups.

Friendship Apps

Bloom Community (https://bloomcommunity.com/): This is an app for everyone 18+ who shares a similar set of community values and is looking for connection. It helps people connect, play, and belong.

Bumble BFF (https://bumble.com/bff): This site helps you find friends or dates online.

Hey! VINA (https://www.heyvina.com/): This is a great way for women to find friendships with other women.

Meetup (https://www.meetup.com/): Meet people through common interests in your area.

Peanut (https://www.peanut-app.io/): This is a safe space for women who want to meet and find support about fertility, pregnancy, motherhood, and menopause.

TalkLife (https://www.talklife.com/: TalkLife is a global peer support community that connects you to those dealing with the same stuff as you so that you don't feel alone.

Youper (https://www.youper.ai/): Youper offers an empathetic and clinically validated chatbot for mental health care that uses Cognitive Behavioral Therapy (CBT).

Yubo (https://www.yubo.live/): The focus here is on young people. Instantly connect to people all over the world based on your interests. You can jump into a livestream and discover something new or play a game and show off your skills.

HIV

AIDS United (https://aidsunited.org/): Here you'll find information and advice for individuals and support for organizations working with people living with HIV.

Poz Community Forum (https://forums.poz.com/): This is one of the largest and longest-running discussion boards for people living with HIV in the United States. You'll find insights and advice about HIV testing, treatment, care, and prevention. It also has a separate dating site.

THRIVE SS (https://thrivess.org/): This is a free service designed for Black gay men who have HIV. The organization's programs include social events, such as brunches and potlucks, workshops for men over 50, and support groups for young Black men. The site also has online blogs, peer support events, and live-streamed webinars for those unable to attend in-person events.

The Well Project (https://www.thewellproject.org/): This is a nonprofit organization dedicated to the needs of women and girls living with HIV. The organization aims to increase health literacy and peer-to-peer support through free community boards, forums, and other features to registered members.

Marital Issues

American Association for Marriage and Family Therapy (https://www.aamft.org/): This website has a section on marital distress and offers advice on what to do and who to talk to. It also has a useful list of resources and therapists.

Mental Health Support

Mental Health America (MHA) (https://www.mhanational.org/): Reach MHA at 703-684-7722 or 800-969-6642. MHA is the nation's leading national nonprofit dedicated to the promotion of mental health, well-being, and illness prevention. It offers public education, research, advocacy and public policy, and direct services for you to benefit from.

National Loneliness Responses

Coalition to End Social Isolation and Loneliness (https://www.endsocial isolation.org/): Its mission is to increase public awareness of social isolation and loneliness and advance approaches that improve social connectedness for all Americans.

Far from Alone (https://farfromalone.com/): This campaign aims to increase the public's awareness of the importance of human connections to address loneliness.

Surgeon General Advisory (https://www.hhs.gov/sites/default/files/ surgeon-general-social-connection-advisory.pdf): The advisory, "Our Epidemic of Loneliness and Isolation: The U.S. Surgeon General's Advisory on the Healing Effects of Social Connection and Isolation," offers advice on how to build more connected lives and a more connected society and community.

Obesity

American Obesity Foundation (https://americanobesityfdn.org/): This foundation aims to prevent obesity and obesity-related diseases, particularly among children and adolescents who are most at risk for poor health. The site has a number of community initiatives, such as Childhood Obesity and Type-2 Diabetes Prevention Program, Houses of Faith Health-Is-Wealth Program, Pets-N-Owners Stay-Fit Initiative, Nile-America and Healthy Kitchens Initiative, and Mother-Infant Obesity Prevention Workshop.

Obesity Action Coalition (OAC) (https://www.obesityaction.org/): The OAC helps individuals along their journey toward better health through education, advocacy, awareness, and support. The site offers community discussion forms, links to obesity health care providers, a video platform to share your stories, and engaging online educational and awareness-raising tools.

Parkrun

Parkrun (https://www.parkrun.us/) is a free, community event where you can walk, jog, run, volunteer, or spectate. The events for adults are 5k and take place every Saturday morning. Events for juniors ages 4 to 14 and their families are 2k and take place every Sunday morning. They're a great way to feel part of a community, opt outdoors, and meet new people.

There are runs emerging all the time all over the world. They formed in the US in 2012 at Livonia, Michigan. Recent events have taken place in Clermont, Florida and Durham, North Carolina.

Sexual Orientation

LGBT National Help Center (https://lgbthotline.org/): Call the LGBT national hotline at 888-843-4564. You'll find free and confidential peer support, information, and local resources through national hotlines and online programs. The site has peer support and weekly youth chatrooms. You can also find a number of local services by going to https://www.lgbtnearme.org/.

Skin Conditions

The American Academy of Dermatology (https://www.aad.org/): You can reach this professional organization of dermatologists at 866-503-SKIN (7546). The website offers patient information on dermatology topics, publications, and assistance in finding a dermatologist.

The National Psoriasis Foundation (https://www.psoriasis.org/): Reach their helpline at 800-723-9166, ext. 480. Advocates for patients with psoriasis are available for education and research support. The website includes information about treatment, research updates, and a physician directory. The foundation has produced a toolkit for children who have psoriasis.

Social Prescribing

Social prescribing is a nonmedical referral that a range of health and social professionals use. For more information on social prescribing, go to https://social prescribingusa.com/.

Suicidal Thoughts

Suicide and Crisis Lifeline: If you're in crisis, call or text 988 (Spanish-speaking services and for Deaf & Hard of Hearing) or text "HOME" to the crisis line at 741-741 (Spanish-speaking services).

Urinary Incontinence

Toilet-Finding Apps: If you're going out, use a toilet-finding app to determine the best and closest toilets in your area. Following are some of the apps.

>> **Bathroom Scout**: Check out Bathroom Scout at https://bathroom-scout.en.softonic.com/android?utm_source=bing&utm_medium=paid&utm_campaign=bing_itunes_sb&utm_source=bing&utm_medium=paid&utm_campaign=bing_itunes_sb&msclkid=c60bcd9688d3124479bba8ee0126d22b.

>> **Flush**: You can find this app at https://play.google.com/store/apps/details?id=toilet.samruston.com.toilet&hl=en_US&gl=US.

>> **National Association for Incontinence**: Look no further than https://nafc.org/ for bladder and bowel incontinence support. You'll find advice and help with products and services.

>> **SitOrSquat**: Go to https://appadvice.com/app/sitorsquat-restroom-finder/511855507.

Loneliness Awareness Campaigns

World Health Organization (WHO) Commission on Social Connection (2024–2026) (https://www.who.int/groups/commission-on-social-connection) is a global commission that aims to see loneliness and its opposite — social connection — recognized and resourced as a global public health priority. The Commission, which at the time of writing had just been formed, will propose a global agenda on social connection, working with high-level commissioners from across the globe to stimulate action and the upscaling of effective solutions.

The Campaign to End Loneliness (https://www.campaigntoendloneliness.org/) in the UK has a vision that everyone can live a life free from chronic loneliness. Be More Us and #LetsTalkLoneliness were specific campaigns that sought to change the narrative around loneliness. Be More Us was a digital campaign run that encouraged people to connect with others. The #LetsTalkLoneliness campaign used the line, "All of us can experience loneliness at some point in our lives. It's time we started talking about it." It was an attempt to encourage people to share stories of loneliness to normalize the experience.

Loneliness Awareness Week (https://www.lonelinessawarenessweek.org/) is a week each year in June that's dedicated to raising awareness of loneliness. It aims to create supportive communities by encouraging people to have conversations with family, friends, or work colleagues about loneliness. The idea is that by talking about loneliness, people can support themselves and others. The week helps people connect, have conversations, and raise awareness about loneliness. It was launched in 2017 and started in the UK, but it has been growing and spreading internationally since its inception.

Coalition to End Social isolation & Loneliness, (https://www.endsocial isolation.org/) a US-based initiative, has a mission that includes increasing public awareness of social isolation and loneliness and advance approaches that improve social connectedness for all Americans. The coalition has been actively involved in promoting loneliness awareness week, aligned with the week in June that was initiated in the UK.

Far from Alone, (https://farfromalone.com/) a US-based campaign, aims to increase the public's awareness of the importance of human connections to address loneliness. It also partners with stakeholders who advocate for policy change that aims to create greater opportunities for social connectedness.

Ending Loneliness Together (https://endingloneliness.com.au/) is Australia's main organization that has been responsible for awareness-raising campaigns. Its mission is, in fact, "Raising public awareness and inspiring action." In August 2023 the organization initiated Australia's first national loneliness awareness week. It aimed to shine a spotlight on the millions of Australians who are lonely by sharing real stories about loneliness.

The GenWell Project (https://alliance2030.ca/members/the-genwell-project/) is a global movement that was launched in Canada in 2016 and aims to raise awareness about the importance of face-to-face social connection. It activates specific weekends a year that are designed to inspire people to reach out and connect with family, friends, neighbors, or colleagues. Throughout the rest of the year, information is shared through social media to inspire people to connect with others.

You can also find information at Twitter.com/GenWellProject.

Index

evolutionary perspective of loneliness, 13

exercise. *See* physical activity and exercise

Eye Movement Desensitization and Reprocessing (EMDR), 228–230

F

facing your fears, 285–286

Far from Alone campaign, 323, 326

F.E.A.S.T, 321

"feeling lonely in a crowd," 11–12

feelings, sharing. *See also* communication

  emotional loneliness and, 76–77

  health conditions and disabilities, 151

  men, 309

  parents, 68

  young adults, 302

finances, 34–35

Flush app, 325

focused meditation, 233

Fribo, 132

"friends of" groups, 256

friendship apps

  health conditions and disabilities, 153

  resources, 321–322

  young adults, 301

G

gaming

  men, 308

  overview, 131–132

  young adults, 299

gender and loneliness, 26–28

GenWell Project, 326

global disasters, 40–41

grassroots sports club, 256

green spaces, 92, 97–99

grief, 138–139. *See also* bereavement

guilt, caregiving and, 34

gyms, 269

H

Happify app, 124

healing techniques

Emotional Freedom Technique

  evaluating whether it's right for needs, 237

  overview, 234–235

  pressure points, 236

  steps for, 235–236

  hypnosis, 239

  meditation

    focused meditation, 233

    getting comfortable with, 233–234

    loving-kindness meditation, 232

    mantra meditation, 233

    mindfulness meditation, 232

    movement meditation, 233

    progressive relaxation, 233

    spiritual meditation, 233

    transcendental meditation, 233

    visualization meditation, 233

  overview, 231

  self-hypnosis, 237–240

health conditions and disabilities, 29–32

  acceptance, 153

  befrienders, 154

  bucket list, 152

  counseling and therapy, 151

  dating apps, 153

  employment, 153–154

  engaging in meaningful activities, 152

  exercise, 151–152

  friendship apps, 153

  influence on levels of loneliness, 17

  inhibiting disorders

    skin conditions, 160–162

    urinary incontinence, 163–165

  intellectual/developmental disabilities, 157–158

  journaling, 152

  maintaining contact with family and friends, 150

  online coffee lounges, 153

  openness and honesty, 151

  overview, 149–150

  peer support, 154

  physical immobility, 155–156

  sensory impairment, 158–160

  serious illnesses

    cancer, 167

    HIV, 167–169

About the Author

Andrea Wigfield is a professor of applied social and policy research and the director of the Centre for Loneliness Studies at Sheffield Hallam University in England. A leading expert on loneliness and social isolation whose work is regularly discussed on radio shows and in the press, she specializes in understanding why people feel lonely and what kinds of interventions and services can prevent and reduce it. She advises government, local authorities, voluntary sector organizations and charities, and large multinational companies how to tackle loneliness. Andrea combines academic research with real-world evidence-based studies that inform policy and practice. As much as possible, she aims to involve people with lived experience in her research.

With a BA Hons in urban studies and a PhD in economic geography, Andrea has been leading social science research for 25 years. She has worked for a number of universities in the UK and was the cofounder and director of a private sector research company, the Policy Evaluation Group. She has been awarded research funding of more than £3 million and has published over 50 books, chapters, articles, and reports and worked on approximately 90 externally funded research projects.

Andrea was fortunate to have been introduced to Sheffield Wednesday Football Club by her father when she was a young child. As a result, she has been immersed into a close-knit community of fellow fans who share a common bond, passion, and sense of belonging that help her feel connected even if she feels lonely in other aspects of her life. When she's not traveling around the country to watch her beloved football team, she enjoys dancing like no one is watching at Orchestral Manoeuvres in the Dark concerts; visiting a small coastal town in north Wales, Llandudno; skiing in Austria; and spending time with her husband, Royce, children Kione, Shen, and Che, and dog, Musa. When she's not doing all of that, you can find her timing reps at an athletic track or standing in a muddy cross-country field.

Dedication

To all the people who have kindly denoted time to participate in the many research projects I've carried out, and to the fellow researchers who have worked with me to understand loneliness.

Author's Acknowledgments

My sincere thanks and appreciation go to everyone who had a role in bringing this book to life. It has been a great opportunity to fuse many years of work together. Numerous people played a role in this book, but I want to recognize a few specific ones.

To Tracey Boggier, whose foresight and vision created the concept for the book. To the rest of the team at Wiley, for their support, encouragement, and input throughout. In particular, thanks to Georgette Beatty, Tracy Brown Hamilton, and Karen Davis. A special thank-you to my colleague at Sheffield Hallam University, associate professor Antonia Ypsilanti, for reviewing the technical aspects of the book.

To many of my colleagues at the Centre for Loneliness Studies and beyond who advised me on certain aspects of the book and read and commented on specific sections. Particular thanks go to Jan Gurung, Anna Topakas, Liam Wrigley, Jo Britton, and Laura Makey. Your insights have been invaluable.

To my family who support me on a daily basis and have discussed various aspects of the book with me during its creation. To my husband, Royce; son, Kione; and daughters, Che and Shen.

To my Wednesday family for being a source of distraction every Saturday afternoon. To my brother, Simon, for driving me around the country, and to my dad, Alan, without whom I wouldn't have had the confidence or aspiration to pursue an academic career. Finally, to my grandma; although she's no longer with us, she always believed in me.

Publisher's Acknowledgments

Acquisitions Editor: Tracy Bogier
Development Editor: Tracy Brown Hamilton
Copy Editor: Gill Editorial Services
Technical Editor: Antonia Ypsilanti
Managing Editor: Sofia Malik

Production Editor: Pradesh Kumar
Cover Image: © valio84sl/Getty Images

Leverage the power

Dummies is the global leader in the reference category and one of the most trusted and highly regarded brands in the world. No longer just focused on books, customers now have access to the dummies content they need in the format they want. Together we'll craft a solution that engages your customers, stands out from the competition, and helps you meet your goals.

Advertising & Sponsorships

Connect with an engaged audience on a powerful multimedia site, and position your message alongside expert how-to content. Dummies.com is a one-stop shop for free, online information and know-how curated by a team of experts.

- Targeted ads
- Video
- Email Marketing

- Microsites
- Sweepstakes sponsorship

20 MILLION PAGE VIEWS EVERY SINGLE MONTH

15 MILLION UNIQUE VISITORS PER MONTH

43% OF ALL VISITORS ACCESS THE SITE VIA THEIR MOBILE DEVICES

700,000 NEWSLETTER SUBSCRIPTIONS TO THE INBOXES OF *300,000* UNIQUE INDIVIDUALS EVERY WEEK

# of dummies

Custom Publishing

Reach a global audience in any language by creating a solution that will differentiate you from competitors, amplify your message, and encourage customers to make a buying decision.

- Apps
- Books
- eBooks
- Video
- Audio
- Webinars

Brand Licensing & Content

Leverage the strength of the world's most popular reference brand to reach new audiences and channels of distribution.

For more information, visit dummies.com/biz

PERSONAL ENRICHMENT

Staying Sharp
9781119187790
USA $26.00
CAN $31.99
UK £19.99

Facebook
9781119179030
USA $21.99
CAN $25.99
UK £16.99

Guitar
9781119293354
USA $24.99
CAN $29.99
UK £17.99

Investing
9781119293347
USA $22.99
CAN $27.99
UK £16.99

Beekeeping
9781119310068
USA $22.99
CAN $27.99
UK £16.99

Digital Photography
9781119235606
USA $24.99
CAN $29.99
UK £17.99

Meditation
9781119251163
USA $24.99
CAN $29.99
UK £17.99

Pregnancy
9781119235491
USA $26.99
CAN $31.99
UK £19.99

Samsung Galaxy S7
9781119279952
USA $24.99
CAN $29.99
UK £17.99

iPhone
9781119283133
USA $24.99
CAN $29.99
UK £17.99

Crocheting
9781119287117
USA $24.99
CAN $29.99
UK £16.99

Nutrition
9781119130246
USA $22.99
CAN $27.99
UK £16.99

PROFESSIONAL DEVELOPMENT

Windows 10
9781119311041
USA $24.99
CAN $29.99
UK £17.99

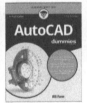

AutoCAD
9781119255796
USA $39.99
CAN $47.99
UK £27.99

Excel 2016
9781119293439
USA $26.99
CAN $31.99
UK £19.99

QuickBooks 2017
9781119281467
USA $26.99
CAN $31.99
UK £19.99

macOS Sierra
9781119280651
USA $29.99
CAN $35.99
UK £21.99

LinkedIn
9781119251132
USA $24.99
CAN $29.99
UK £17.99

Windows 10
9781119310563
USA $34.00
CAN $41.99
UK £24.99

SharePoint 2016
9781119181705
USA $29.99
CAN $35.99
UK £21.99

Fundamental Analysis
9781119263593
USA $26.99
CAN $31.99
UK £19.99

Networking
9781119257769
USA $29.99
CAN $35.99
UK £21.99

Office 2016
9781119293477
USA $26.99
CAN $31.99
UK £19.99

Office 365
9781119265313
USA $24.99
CAN $29.99
UK £17.99

Salesforce.com
9781119239314
USA $29.99
CAN $35.99
UK £21.99

Coding
9781119293323
USA $29.99
CAN $35.99
UK £21.99

dummies.com

dummies
A Wiley Brand